Library of
Davidson College

Joycean Occasions

Joycean Occasions

Essays from the Milwaukee James Joyce Conference

EDITED BY
Janet E. Dunleavy,
Melvin J. Friedman,
and Michael Patrick Gillespie

Newark: University of Delaware Press
London and Toronto: Associated University Presses

© 1991 by Associated University Presses, Inc.

All rights reserved. Authorization to photocopy items for internal or personal use, or the internal or personal use of specific clients, is granted by the copyright owner, provided that a base fee of $10.00, plus eight cents per page, per copy is paid directly to the Copyright Clearance Center, 27 Congress Street, Salem, Massachusetts 01970.
[0-87413-402-1/91 $10.00 + 8¢ pp, pc.]

Associated University Presses
440 Forsgate Drive
Cranbury, NJ 08512

Associated University Presses
25 Sicilian Avenue
London WC1A 2QH, England

Associated University Presses
P.O. Box 39, Clarkson Pstl. Stn.
Mississauga, Ontario,
L5J 3X9 Canada

The paper used in this publication meets the requirements
of the American National Standard for Permanence of Paper
for Printed Library Materials Z39.48-1984.

Library of Congress Cataloging-in-Publication Data

James Joyce Conference (1987 : Milwaukee, Wis.)
  Joycean occasions : essays from the Milwaukee James Joyce
Conference / edited by Janet E. Dunleavy, Melvin J. Friedman, and
Michael Patrick Gillespie.
    p. cm.
  Includes bibliographical references (p.
  ISBN 0-87413-402-1 (alk. paper)
  1. Joyce, James, 1882–1941—Criticism and interpretation-
-Congresses.   I. Dunleavy, Janet Egleson.   II. Friedman, Melvin J.
III. Gillespie, Michael Patrick.   IV. Title.
PR6019.09Z63385   1991
823'.912—dc20   89-40758
                                                             CIP

PRINTED IN THE UNITED STATES OF AMERICA

For the Reverend Robert Boyle, S.J.,
and Florence Walzl,
two eminent Joyceans

Contents

Introduction	9
Acknowledgments	12
1. Reading in *Ulysses* PATRICK A. MCCARTHY	15
2. The Name of Bloom DANIEL P. GUNN	33
3. Joyce's New Womanly Man: Sexual Signatures of Androgynous Transformation in *Ulysses* SUZETTE HENKE	46
4. Comic Narration ZACK BOWEN	59
5. Murphy, Shem, Morpheus, and Murphies: Eumaeus Meets the *Wake* SUSAN BRIENZA	80
6. Apostrophes: Framing *Finnegans Wake* SHARI BENSTOCK	95
7. "The bawk of bats" in Joyce's Belfry: The Flitter-mouse in the Feminine VINCENT J. CHENG	125
8. James Joyce: The Olfactory Factor BERNARD BENSTOCK	138
9. Wilde . . . Joyce . . . O'Brien . . . Stoppard: Modernism and Postmodernism in "Travesties" RICHARD CORBALLIS	157
10. Joycean Provections FRITZ SENN	171
11. "The Veripatetic Imago" SIDNEY FESHBACH	195

12. Davin's Boots: Joyce, Yeats, and Irish History
    MARY REYNOLDS   218

Notes on the Contributors   235

Index   239

Introduction

On alternate years from 1967 to 1979, scholars and devotees from around the world gathered in various European cities—Dublin, Paris, Zürich—in the middle of June to discuss the work of the Irish writer James Joyce. The process has continued through the 1980s—with a slight shift in the schedule in 1982 to accommodate plans for a celebration of the centennial year in his native city—in Dublin, Frankfurt, Copenhagen, and Venice. Although these gatherings have rarely gone unnoticed, the response has been mixed at best. Whenever the symposia occurred, one could generally count on reading a somewhat bemused account of the proceedings in the local press—of the same sort as descriptions of MLA conventions that American papers delight in printing. These stories, which play up the quaintness of academic endeavor, are always quick to seize on the eccentricities that one might find at any such gathering; the spirit of the conference is invariably lost in the process of journalistic caricature. In fact, only after their organizers began to publish volumes of selected proceedings could it be said that reliable accounts emerged.

The first symposium took place in Dublin in 1967. With each subsequent gathering there was a marked increase in attendance and a noticeable increase in the variety and complexity of the topics under consideration. One can relate this growth and maturing to the expanded interest in the work of Joyce, who is now the most studied writer of the century. The present critical climate, which is nurtured on pluralism rather than on a single epistemology or approach, is congenial, it would seem, to Joycean endeavors. The best critical minds seem to be drawn to Joyce and are frequent attenders of conferences held in his honor.

Through the 1980s, in deliberate imitation of their European counterparts, a series of gatherings have been held across the United States in years when no international symposia were planned. These meetings were not intended to be competitive. Rather, they evolved directly from the enthusiasm generated by the European sessions. Indeed, the controlling concept behind the North American conferences has been the desire to sustain the goodwill and inquiring spirit of the European models. Over the past decade the notion of alternating American and international gatherings has taken on a virtually institutionalized character.

Just as the formal design has gradually fallen into place, so the attendance has taken on its own characteristics. While the organizers of the first meeting in Provincetown (1980) probably viewed it as basically an American conference, the national identity quickly expanded. Scholars from Ireland, Switzerland, and Germany attended the Albuquerque sessions (1981); an even more noticeably international segment of the Joyce community was present at the second Provincetown gathering (1983). By the time the Philadelphia symposium was held in 1985, representation had its distinctly European side. Given the new state of affairs, Joyceans no longer wonder whether such a meeting will take place or what form it will assume, but rather where it will occur, who will attend, and how long it will last.

Despite elements of predictability, participants will agree that each gathering of the faithful retains unique characteristics. The impetus for organizing the 1987 Milwaukee conference, for example, came not only from the urgency to explore issues in Joyce criticism and to offer symposiasts an agreeable midwestern setting, but also from the wish to honor the work of two eminent Joyce scholars: the Reverend Robert Boyle, S.J., and Florence Walzl. The design of the meeting followed the accustomed format: presentations by major speakers, sessions devoted to shorter papers, and panel discussions. The topics chosen by individual speakers and panelists recalled both central concerns of the scholars honored and issues dominating contemporary Joyce study. A rapid survey of the program produces the following representative sampling: Joyce and Catholicism; Joyce, Aquinas, and Aristotle; *Dubliners;* Joyce in the classroom; Joyce and Beckett; discursive economies in *Finnegans Wake;* an aesthetics of mystery: Joyce and his words. Additionally, a number of ongoing topics were reconsidered to reflect concerns at previous American meetings and to respond to current issues being debated within the Joyce community: the Gabler edition of *Ulysses;* Joyce politicos: racism, sexism, theory; Joyce/women/women's writing; de/reconstructing Joyce; a reader's response to Joyce; images of the Lacanian gaze in *Ulysses.*

As in all conferences of this kind, the most stimulating exchanges were often unplanned, with some of the most productive even occurring outside the structure of the program. In addition to the give-and-take of the discussion periods, some of the high points of the meeting were dramatizations of selections from *Dubliners* by the Irish Fest Players, a concert of Joycean songs performed by Donna Janusko, and the world première of Margaret Rogers's *A Babble of Earwigs,* a chorale composed especially for presentation in Milwaukee.

In the end, however, the conference will be remembered for the high quality of the papers delivered. The twelve essays that follow are revised versions of some of the best of these offerings. Four are concerned with *Ulysses,* three others largely with *Finnegans Wake.* The remaining five place Joyce in a variety of intriguing contexts. The majority are the work of established Joyceans who already have written distinguished studies about the Irish writer. There is a noticeable international flavor to the gathering, with the presence of Fritz Senn from Zürich and Richard Corballis from Christchurch, New Zealand. The University of Miami, which has recently become the center for Joyce studies in this country, is more than adequately represented. Zack Bowen, Shari and Bernard Benstock, and Patrick A. McCarthy not only have made Joyce central to the Miami graduate curriculum but have initiated an annual conference that brings Joyceans to tropical Coral Gables during the coldest part of the year.

The editors of *Joycean Occasions* feel that the final form of these twelve papers extends rather than recapitulates the ideas first offered in Milwaukee in 1987, reflecting, as well as any written record can, the enthusiasm, wit, and insight of all who participated in the conference.

Many readers will be aware of the recent debate that has taken place at conferences and in the pages of scholarly journals over the primacy that should be accorded various editions of *Ulysses.* Most of the essays appearing in this volume were written when that debate was at its height. The editors, despite strong views regarding the efficacy of particular editions, felt that the contributors should have the freedom to use the versions of *Ulysses* that they felt best served their arguments. Further, the diversity of contributors led the editors to choose not to regularize the citational format.

Acknowledgments

The editors gratefully acknowledge the range of assistance that has enabled this volume to move toward completion. The original conference providing a venue for the presentation of the essays collected here was made possible in part through funds provided by the Andrew Mellon Foundation and the College of Arts and Sciences of Marquette University. The James Joyce Foundation and Prof. Morris Beja of Ohio State University offered useful advice and assistance at various stages of this project. The Rev. Thaddeus J. Burch, S.J., through the Faculty Development Fund of Marquette University, provided timely and continuing support. Professors John Boly and Albert Rivero of Marquette University offered useful criticism on the constitution of this volume. Lisa Rivero, of the University of Wisconsin-Milwaukee, prepared a detailed and comprehensive index. Finally, we should like to thank Deans Jessica Wirth, William F. Halloran, and George Keulks, of the University of Wisconsin-Milwaukee, for their continuing support of research.

Joycean Occasions

1
Reading in *Ulysses*

PATRICK A. McCARTHY

In his influential essay "*Ulysses*, Order and Myth" (1923), T. S. Eliot defended Joyce's novel against charges of formlessness and incomprehensibility by contending that Joyce used a mythological parallel as "a way of controlling, of ordering, of giving a shape and a significance to the immense panorama of futility and anarchy which is contemporary history."[1] Eliot thereby shifted the allegation of chaos and futility from the book to the world, arguing that *Ulysses* made sense even if post-World War European civilization did not. Other reviewers were considerably less charitable; readers were often warned that they would be morally or aesthetically offended by *Ulysses* or that the book would prove either boring or impenetrable. Holbrook Jackson's review, despite its admission that *Ulysses* "is not indecent," is typical of many responses in its concern with the problems of Joyce's readers, who are required "to spend a full day" with Leopold Bloom and come to "detest him heartily." The reader, Jackson says, will be affronted by the style, through which he can become "bored, drowsed, bewildered." Even worse is "the arrangement of the book," which omits "the conventions of organised prose which have grown with our race"; from this, Jackson concludes that "Mr. Joyce evidently believes in making it difficult for his readers—but perhaps he wants to scare them away." In any event, "the reader is continually losing his way and having to retrace his steps."[2]

The focus on Joyce's readers has not diminished over the years, although in general it has shifted from complaints like Jackson's to considerations of the reading strategies that the book demands. In 1945 Joseph Frank assessed the book's method as one requiring an unusually active reader: "the reader is forced to read *Ulysses* in exactly the same manner as he reads modern poetry—continually fitting fragments together and keeping allusions in mind until, by reflexive reference, he can link them to their complements."[3] Thus the reader becomes Joyce's collaborator in discovering the meaning and order that underlie the book's apparently chaotic shape. During the past decade or two, the influence of reader-oriented criticism has helped to keep attention focused on Joyce's readers. Marilyn French, for instance, has identified the reader of *Ulysses* as the epic hero of the book, adding that "the journey taken in *Ulysses* is the book itself, and only the reader traverses it entirely."[4] Likewise, Brook Thomas has commented perceptively on the role of the reader in *Ulysses,* comparing it to the way Molly Bloom reads books and letters and contending that Leopold Bloom's attempts to educate his wife are analogous to Joyce's efforts on behalf of his ignorant but potentially educable reader.[5]

Although Thomas is certainly correct in associating Molly's reading habits with our own, the character most often seen reading in *Ulysses* is not Molly. Nor is it Stephen Dedalus, despite his impressive array of literary references and his recollection of having read "two pages apiece of seven books every night" during his stay in Paris (3.136).[6] More often, our model of the reading experience is Leopold Bloom, who begins his day by reading the partly obliterated text of the legend inside his "Plasto's high grade ha" (4.69–70) and continues reading a variety of materials throughout the day and well into the night. It is true that Molly is an avid reader of soft-core pornography (although she objects to *Moll Flanders* because it has a "Molly" in it [18.657–59]), but her reading is generally uncritical and lacking in self-consciousness; of the novel genre she might well say what she says about the love letter, that "true or no it fills up your whole day" (18.737–38).[7] Bloom, on the other hand, believes that books can improve us in various ways. Thus, while drinking cocoa with Stephen, Bloom "reflected on the pleasures derived from literature of instruction rather than of amusement as he himself had applied to the works of William Shakespeare more than once for the solution of difficult problems in imaginary or real life" (17.384–87).

It is unlikely that many readers of *Ulysses* will find it profitable to use Joyce's book precisely as Bloom has used Shakespeare's. Yet we can learn a great deal about ourselves by reading fiction, as Joyce implied when he told Grant Richards that his intention in writing *Dubliners* was to advance "civilisation in Ireland" by giving the Irish people "one good look at themselves in [his] nicely polished looking-glass."[8] Indeed, while the title of *Dubliners* is normally taken to be simply a reference to the characters in the stories, identified in terms of the urban environment that entraps them, the book's name might also refer to the people whom Joyce imagined as the primary readers of the collection, the Dubliners who should see their own situations mirrored in the volume's fifteen stories. Those Dubliners might also see reflections of their experience as readers when they watch the characters read, or attempt to read, various texts that focus with suspicious frequency either on death or on escapism.

If *Dubliners* is a "nicely polished looking-glass" wherein we might catch glimpses of ourselves as readers and otherwise, *Ulysses* more closely resembles the "cracked lookingglass" that Stephen holds in his hand in the first chapter (1.146). Hugh Kenner has called *Ulysses* "a Berlitz classroom between covers," and Wolfgang Iser has commented that the "repertoire of [*Ulysses*] both reflects and reveals the rules that govern its own communication."9 Watching Bloom read, we see a somewhat distorted version of our own readings, one that makes us more aware of the strategies and assumptions involved in reading. As we proceed, we see how Bloom's reading reflects his situation and his character, and we learn both from his strengths and from his limitations as a reader. If at the end of *Ulysses* we read better than Bloom does, this is partly because we can watch him reading, while he cannot watch us.

One of the differences between Molly's reading and Bloom's is that while Molly prefers to regard her reading material as essentially distinct from herself and to object to books like *Moll Flanders* that appear to blur the line between text and reader, Bloom almost inevitably discovers some relationship between himself and the text at hand. An obvious example is contained in Bloom's reading of the "throwaway" that he receives from a "sombre Y.M.C.A. young man" in the Lestrygonians chapter:

> Heart to heart talks.
> Bloo. . . . Me? No.
> Blood of the Lamb.
> His slow feet walked him riverward, reading. Are you saved? All are washed in the blood of the lamb. God wants blood victim. Birth, hymen, martyr, war, foundation of a building, sacrifice, kidney burntoffering, druids' altars. Elijah is coming. Dr John Alexander Dowie restorer of the church in Zion is coming.
> Is coming! Is coming! Is coming!
> All heartily welcome. (8.7–16)

This passage consists of a single line of narration—"His slow feet walked him riverward, reading"—and several of interior monologue; Bloom's thoughts, in turn, comprise both the text Bloom is reading and his commentary on it. Bloom's momentary assumption that the word beginning *Bloo* is his own name might seem strange, but the various texts he encounters have a habit of referring somehow to him and his situation; earlier in the day, for example, Bloom opened his newspaper directly to an advertisement for Plumtree's Potted Meat (5.144–47), a piece of writing that would resonate in his imagination until it would come to seem as if it might well have been written explicitly for him. Similarly, in reading the flyer for Dowie's revival meeting, Bloom is not so far wrong in thinking that it has to do with him: if *Bloo* begins *Blood* rather than *Bloom,* it is still true that the description of the flyer as a "throwaway" connects it to Bloom and that Bloom's thought of the kidney he burned that morning is as much a transformation of his own breakfast into religious terms as it is a commentary on the themes of the Dowie flyer.

In Wandering Rocks, Bloom will open the novel *Sweets of Sin* at random and will discover therein a passage that might almost have evolved directly out of his own marital situation. Kenner has noted that Bloom is inadvertently practicing *sortes Virgilianae,* or Virgilian lots, since he begins reading "where his finger opened" (10.607).[10] The *sortes* technique is actually the most common way Bloom reads, at least on 16 June 1904, judged by Bloom's readings of such documents as the newspaper, the throwaway, and *Sweets of Sin.* The procedure and its origins are described in Sidney's *Defense of Poesy*:

> Among the Romans a poet was called *vates,* which is as much as a "diviner," "foreseer," or "prophet," as by his conjoined words *vaticinium* and *vaticinari* is manifest. So heavenly a title did that excellent people bestow upon this heart-ravishing knowledge. And so far were they carried into the admiration thereof that they thought in the chanceable hitting upon any of such verses, great fore-tokens of their following fortunes were placed. Whereupon grew the word of Virgilian lots, when by sudden opening [of *The Aeneid*] they lighted upon some verse of his (as is reported by many), whereof the histories of the Emperors' lives are full.[11]

The tradition Sidney is describing dates back at least to the first century after Virgil's death. Later Saint Augustine reported being told by a child's voice to take up a Bible and read; the book fell open to Romans 13:13, an attack on lust that Augustine read as a providential allusion to his own sinfulness. Petrarch, in turn, randomly opened Augustine's *Confessions* during his ascent of Mont Ventoux and discovered that it seemed to refer directly to his own situation. Similar occurrences may be found in English literature: in *Robinson Crusoe,* for example, where a chance opening of the Bible to Psalms 50 contributes to Crusoe's repentance; in Tennyson's "Enoch Arden," where Annie uses the technique to find out whether Enoch is dead (but misinterprets the text, assuming that "Under the palm-tree" is a metaphor for heaven rather than a literal description of her husband's location); and in Malcolm Lowry's *Under the Volcano*, whose protagonist, Geoffrey Firmin, practices what he calls "sortes Shakespeareanae."[12]

In these acts of reading and interpretation, then, Bloom is taking part in a tradition with a respectable pedigree, albeit one at odds with his generally scientific and rational approach to life. It is interesting that when he looks randomly at a text he finds some personal significance, but that when he tries to regularize the process, he has less success. Thus the voice that catechizes itself in the Ithaca chapter reports that Bloom has had only qualified success in solving problems by consulting Shakespeare: "In spite of careful and repeated reading of certain classical passages, aided by a glossary, he had derived imperfect conviction from the text, the answers not bearing in all points" (17.389–91). Readers of *Ulysses* (and, even more, of *Finnegans Wake*) know pretty much how Bloom felt.

Bloom's inability to discover clear and certain meanings in Shakespeare suggests one of his many connections with Stephen, who develops an elaborate theory about *Hamlet*, but when asked "Do you believe your own theory?" immediately answers "No" (9.1065–67). Stephen develops his theory not merely as a demonstration that *Hamlet* is based on Shakespeare's alleged cuckolding but as an attempt to define his own relation to the play; his statement that he does not believe his theory is both a refusal to expand this personal interpretation to the realm of objective fact and an admission that any reading based on selected passages is bound to be found lacking, "the answers not bearing in all points." Even so, Stephen is correct in asserting that all readings—of the book and the world—are inevitably personal readings: "We walk through ourselves, meeting robbers, ghosts, giants, old men, young men, wives, widows, brothers-in-love. But always meeting ourselves" (9.1044–46). This process through which we discover ourselves (imperfectly) in a book is neatly reversed in the Circe chapter, when Stephen and Bloom look into a mirror and see "*The face of William Shakespeare, beardless . . . rigid in facial paralysis, crowned by the reflection of the reindeer antlered hatrack in the hall*" (15.3821–24). Note that if Bloom's readings of, and reflections on, Shakespeare produce imperfect answers, the literal reflection of Stephen and Bloom produces an imperfect Shakespeare, for every creative act involves an element of distortion just as every act of interpretation is, in the terminology of another Bloom, a "misreading."

A good example of Leopold Bloom's misreading appears fairly early in *Ulysses*, when Molly asks him to interpret a puzzling passage in the book she has just read, *Ruby: the Pride of the Ring*. Molly's problem involves a word that (as we discover later [8.112]) she pronounces "met him pike hoses." The original passage is important enough to quote at length:

> —Met him what? he asked.
> —Here, she said. What does that mean?
>   He leaned downward and read near her polished thumbnail.
> —Metempsychosis?
> —Yes. Who's he when he's at home?
> —Metempsychosis, he said, frowning. It's Greek: from the Greek. That means the transmigration of souls.
> —O, rocks! she said. Tell us in plain words.
>   He smiled, glancing askance at her mocking eyes. The same young eyes. The first night after the charades. Dolphin's Barn. He turned over the smudged pages. *Ruby: the Pride of the Ring*. Hello. Illustration. Fierce Italian with carriagewhip. Must be Ruby pride of the on the floor naked. Sheet kindly lent. *The monster Maffei desisted and flung his victim from him with an oath*. Cruelty behind it all. Doped animals. Trapeze at Hengler's. Had to look the other way. Mob gaping. Break your neck and we'll break our sides. Families of them. Bone them young so they metamspychosis. That we live after death. Our souls. That a man's soul after he dies, Dignam's soul. . . .
> —Did you finish it? he asked.
> —Yes, she said. There's nothing smutty in it. Is she in love with the first fellow all the time?
> —Never read it. Do you want another?
> —Yes. Get another of Paul de Kock's. Nice name he has.
>   She poured more tea into her cup, watching it flow sideways.
>   Must get that Capel street library book renewed or they'll write to Kearney, my guarantor. Reincarnation: that's the word. (4.336–61)

Throughout this passage two sorts of things are going on. First, and more obviously, we are being introduced to, or reminded of, major themes of the book. *Metempsychosis* is not only a word that occurs in Molly's book (and, appropriately enough, a word "from the Greek") but a major theme in *Ulysses,* where Bloom is, in Kenner's terms, a "wily wandering Greek [hero] . . . reincarnated as a wandering homebody Jew."[13] This theme of reincarnation, return, or renewal generally spills over into Bloom's thoughts, which is probably why he unexpectedly thinks of a library book whose loan needs to be renewed. The idea of renewal is also implied in the way the passage returns us to motifs that have been introduced earlier in the book. For example, we are reminded of Bloom's interest in cruelty, an interest evident earlier in the morning in Bloom's thoughts about his cat:

"Cruel. Her nature. Curious mice never squeal. Seem to like it" (4.27–28). The sadomasochistic theme reappears in Bloom's thoughts about the servant girl next door, so that by the time we watch Bloom reading *Ruby* we are prepared for his interest in the "Fierce Italian with carriagewhip" standing over the naked girl; the connection between violence and comedy ("Break your neck and we'll break our sides") is more unexpected but no less perceptive an observation.

Our introduction to such themes as metempsychosis and sadomasochism so dominates this passage that it risks overshadowing the second, related, job of the passage, which is to demonstrate how Bloom reads. Bloom's reading is filled with personal associations that he believes help him to understand the text, as when he thinks of the difference between the way he responded to the trapeze artists at Hengler's circus (by looking away) and the way the rest of the crowd responded (by gaping). Until just a few years ago, it was possible to believe that Bloom was doing a good job of impromptu criticism of *Ruby*, but Mary Power's discovery of Amye Reade's *Ruby. A Novel. Founded on the Life of a Circus Girl* (1889) introduces a new element in the equation.[14] Power demonstrates conclusively that Joyce modeled *Ruby: the Pride of the Ring* after *Ruby. A Novel*, but she also notes that there are significant differences between Amye Reade's *Ruby* (1) and the version in *Ulysses* (*Ruby* 2): in addition to changing the subtitle, Joyce alters the name of Signor Enrico to Signor Maffei and adds a key word that does not appear in *Ruby* 1: *metempsychosis*. All of these changes are made by Joyce, not by Bloom, and only a knowledge of the original *Ruby* allows us to enjoy the ironies of *Ruby* 2: the subtitle *Pride of the Ring*, for instance, is ambiguous unless we know that the book is about a circus, while *metempsychosis* introduces an element that, as Power says (121), is relevant to *Ruby* 1 (where it does not appear) but is even more important to *Ulysses*, a book in which it appears solely on the authority of Joyce's emendation of *Ruby*. Note that the word also appears in *Ulysses* directly as a result of Molly Bloom's faith in her husband's powers of interpretation, her respect for his vocabulary and for his knowledge of literature.

Joyce's change of Enrico (Henry) to Maffei is equally significant, for it shifts the text of *Ruby* 2 away from what would be a natural tendency to identify Signor Enrico with Leopold Bloom, alias Henry Flower.[15] The abandonment of Enrico therefore lets Bloom off the hook and allows him to think disparagingly of other people's cruelty. It is interesting that the sentence Bloom reads appears almost exactly as it does in *Ruby* 1, except that the name Maffei has been added;

there would have been no direct reference to Henry if the sentence had been printed without alteration, but as soon as a diligent scholar like Mary Power located the original *Ruby* it would have appeared that the passage referred obliquely to Bloom, that he was in effect reading about himself and censoring a text that associated him with cruelty. The way similar names seem to imply guilt by association is indicated not only in Molly's dislike of *Moll Flanders* but also in the fact that whenever Bloom thinks about the Phoenix Park murders case he is either wrong (5.378–82, 16.1053–54) or uncertain (8.442–43) about the first name of the informer, James Carey, presumably because James Joyce wants to avoid any personal association with an informer.[16]

We can't call "Maffei" a misreading on Bloom's part, but it is a sort of collaborative error by Joyce and Bloom and (until the discovery of Amye Reade's original *Ruby*) a private joke of the author, to boot. Bloom makes a real error—one that remained undiscovered until Power published her find—when he thinks, "Must be Ruby pride of the on the floor naked"; actually, Bloom is looking at the picture of another woman, Victoria Melton.[17] This is the sort of erroneous snap judgment that we all make, one comparable to the assumption made by one of my undergraduate students that *Surprised by Sin* is a pornographic novel, while *Venus in Furs,* which happened to be on the same shelf, is about classical mythology. Likewise, some readers who learn that Bloom has made a mistaken identification of the woman in the picture may well remember that when they first read *Ulysses* they initially assumed, as the real John Eglinton admitted that he did, that the Ulysses of the title was Stephen Dedalus.[18] Having mistaken Victoria Melton for Ruby, Bloom will misidentify another woman later, when he speculates that the woman he sees with George Russell "might be Lizzie Twigg" (8.527); as Zack Bowen has shown, it is more likely that Bloom is looking at Susan Mitchell.[19]

In a letter to Harriet Shaw Weaver, Joyce said that Ezra Pound "understood certain aspects of [*Ulysses*] very quickly" and made "brilliant discoveries and howling blunders."[20] On a lower level, most of us read erratically, like Pound, just as on a still lower level Bloom proves an adequate interpreter of *Ruby* (a book, let it be remembered, that he has not read) but manages to damage his own credibility— with us, not with Molly—by making a howling blunder when he tries to clarify his definition of *metempsychosis*. Immediately after thinking of the word he has been searching for—*reincarnation*—he gives Molly a lucid definition of the term, then muddies the waters by giving an example inspired by the *Bath of the Nymph* picture hanging over the bed:

—Metempsychosis, he said, is what the ancient Greeks called it. They used to believe you could be changed into an animal or a tree, for instance. What they called nymphs, for example. (4.375–77)

Bloom has tried to define metempsychosis but instead has given an example of metamorphosis. Ironically, this erroneous example developed out of Bloom's ruminations on "Naked nymphs: Greece: and for instance all the people that lived then" (4.372–73), thoughts that are relevant to our reading of *Ulysses* because they not only remind us of Bloom's sexual interests and of the book's ubiquitous Hellenic theme, but metempsychotically connect the world of *Ulysses* to ancient Greece and "all the people that lived then." Bloom's error, which he repeats in Nausicaa (13.1118–19), is significant in another way, too, for metamorphosis is a theme already associated with Stephen Dedalus, both through the Ovidian reference in his surname and through his musings on supernatural metamorphosis (the Holy Ghost changing into a bird to impregnate Mary) and protean shape changing. It is only upon rereading that we are likely to discover these parallels, however, at which time Bloom's errors become our portals of discovery.

Elsewhere in Calypso, Bloom takes extended looks at two other texts: Milly's letter and the *Titbits* story, "Matcham's Masterstroke." Milly's letter (4.397–414) sets up a number of significant motifs, including the salutation "Dearest Papli," the phrase "beef to the heels," and the song "Seaside Girls." Aside from this thematic importance, the letter allows us another glimpse at the reading process, which begins a few pages earlier with Bloom's skimming of the letter ("Thanks: new tam: Mr Coghlan: lough Owel picnic: young student: Blazes Boylan's seaside girls" [4.281–82]),[21] continues with the text of this chatty and occasionally ungrammatical letter, and concludes with Bloom's interpretation of the postscript—"Excuse bad writing. Hurry. Piano downstairs. Coming out of her shell" (4.421–22). The postscript itself says merely "Excuse bad writing am in hurry. Byby," but Bloom is surely correct in associating Milly's rush to conclude the letter with the presence of the picnickers congregated downstairs at the piano and in interpreting the letter generally as meaning that Milly is "coming out of her shell." This is a simple text to work on, one for which Bloom's powers of interpretation are sufficient.[22]

In the case of the prize *Titbits* story by Philip Beaufoy, Bloom needs hardly any interpretive ability at all, only the good sense to be able to judge a work like "Matcham's Masterstroke," which he reads while seated in the outhouse:

> It did not move or touch him but it was something quick and neat. Print anything now. Silly season. He read on, seated above his own rising smell. Neat certainly. *Matcham often thinks of the masterstroke by which he won the laughing witch who now.* Begins and ends morally. *Hand in hand.* Smart. He glanced back through what he had read and, while feeling his water flow quietly, he envied kindly Mr Beaufoy who had written it and received payment of three pounds, thirteen and six. (4.511–17)

Bloom has sized up Beaufoy's work as a formula story, executed competently (unlike Bloom's bowel movement, it is "quick and neat"), ending not only morally but positively ("*Hand in hand.*"), but basically trite ("Print anything now. Silly season."): the sort of story, that is, that you would read in the jakes or in the dentist's office rather than in the library. In almost every sense, "Matcham's Masterstroke" is the literary antithesis of *Ulysses:* Beaufoy's brief story begins conventionally and ends happily, Joyce's long novel begins somewhat unconventionally and ends ambiguously; the story Bloom reads is "Neat certainly" and makes few demands on its reader (who picked it up precisely because it was "Something new and easy" [4.501]), while the book we are reading is, in Holbrook Jackson's memorable phrase, "an ungainly, loose-limbed book which falls to pieces as you read it"[23] and at times requires a serious effort on the reader's part just to follow the narrative line. H. G. Wells complained, in his review of *Portrait,* that "Mr. Joyce has a cloacal obsession. He would bring back into the general picture of life aspects which modern drainage and modern decorum have taken out of ordinary intercourse and conversation";[24] yet while *Ulysses* includes scenes that are too strong for H. G. Wells (or, I suppose, Philip Beaufoy), it contains little, if anything, that is predictable and false. Bloom's final use of Beaufoy's story—as toilet paper (4.537)—might well be regarded as an appropriate act of literary criticism; hence, in Circe, when Beaufoy appears to accuse Bloom of plagiarizing and disfiguring his work, Bloom answers the charges by describing the story as "Bad art" (15.814–40).[25] Likewise, Bloom proves an able critic of political rhetoric at the end of the Sirens chapter, when he farts while reading Robert Emmet's last words (11.1284–94).

For Bloom, a practical man, reading is generally a means to an end, whether that end be instruction (as in the case of Shakespeare's works), sexual arousal (as with *Sweets of Sin*), or something else. The use of the *Titbits* page as toilet paper indicates another aspect of Bloom's use of reading materials: their employment as physical objects independent of whatever writing they might contain. Stephen does something similar, of course, when he tears off part of Mr. Deasy's letter to write his poem; the connection is even reinforced, inadvertently, by Myles Crawford's comment on the torn letter: "Who tore it? Was he short taken?" (7.521). Yet Stephen's action is a more traditionally artistic one, akin to that of the medieval scribe who decides to write his own poem in the margin of some less interesting document or the artist who uses another painting as his canvas. Bloom, on the other hand, seems always to be aware of the way the physical existence of the printed or handwritten page opens it up to nonliterary uses. Some of these uses prove failures, as when Bloom throws the crumpled Dowie flyer into the Liffey in an attempt to outwit the sea gulls; others carry unacceptable risks, as Bloom reflects in Ithaca when he thinks about "the insecurity of hiding any secret document behind, beneath or between the pages of a book" (17.1413–14).

A look at the uses to which Bloom puts the flyer for Agendath Netaim illustrates the tendency of reading materials to serve both literary and extraliterary functions, simultaneously existing as collections of words or ideas that impress themselves on the mind and as physical items. Indeed, within the narrative proper, the announcement first serves as wrapping paper in a butcher's shop; Bloom, who picks up the notice to read it, finds a single sheet sufficient, while Dlugacz picks up two sheets to wrap sausages, one sheet being insufficient to prevent leakage. Later, Bloom will find two other uses for the notice: at the end of Lestrygonians he takes it out of his pocket and pretends to read it so as to appear not to notice Boylan, and in Ithaca he takes it out again and burns it. Even when Bloom actually reads the notice, the narration often refers in some way to its physical existence, the one aspect of any text that clearly separates it from other texts. Note, for example, the description of Bloom's first encounter with the flyer:

> He took a page up from the pile of cut sheets: the model farm at Kinnereth on the lakeshore of Tiberias. Can become ideal winter sanatorium. Moses Montefiore. I thought he was. Farmhouse, wall round it, blurred cattle cropping. He held the page from him: interesting: read it nearer, the title, the blurred cropping cattle, the page rustling. A young white heifer. . . . He held the page aslant patiently, bending his senses and his will, his soft subject gaze at rest. The crooked skirt swinging, whack by whack by whack. (4.154–64)

Although the physical existence of the notice, which establishes its spatial dimensions, apparently distinguishes it from the world around it, Bloom's reading blurs that distinction until it can be said of the Agendath Netaim flyer, as Colin MacCabe has said of *Ulysses*, that "it is impossible to isolate the words of the text from the contemporary words surrounding it: the words of the reader. Despite appearances there is no definite limit to a book."[26] Indeed, Bloom's reference to the "young white heifer" seems to describe the "nextdoor girl" rather than one of the blurred cattle in the picture, so that the text Bloom is reading and the one in which he exists form a continuum. The simultaneous emphasis on the physical separateness of the text and on its linguistic continuity with, or dependency on, the larger text, relates virtually all of Bloom's reading materials to *Ulysses* itself, that is, to a book that focuses our attention both on its existence as a physical object, a product of print technology, and on its relationship to the literary, historical, economic, political, and biographical contexts in which it was conceived, written, and printed.

Bloom's tendency to internalize the texts he reads, and thereby to appropriate them for his own uses, is related to his treatment of texts as objects or possessions and reinforced by the fact that, as a typically modern reader, he reads silently. Silent reading, as George Steiner has noted, is a "late historical development," the by-product of a bourgeois civilization that values privacy and individuality.[27] Likewise, Walter Ong has written that "oral communication unites people in groups. Writing and reading are solitary activities that throw the psyche back on itself."[28] Moreover, according to Ong, "the advent of print intensified the inwardness fostered by script. The age of print was immediately marked in Protestant circles by advocacy of private, individual interpretation of the Bible, and in Catholic circles was marked by the growth of frequent private confession of sins, and concomitantly a stress on the examination of conscience."[29] For a highly literate man like Leopold Bloom—a man whose early literary efforts involved anagrams on his name and a poem with an "acrostic upon the abbreviation of his first name" (17.404–16) and who now makes his living through printed advertisements—written or printed language is something that you experience silently and, therefore, alone.

Bloom is not the only silent reader in *Ulysses*, but the other examples are generally people who are also isolated in some way. I have called attention elsewhere to the way Stephen Dedalus reads silently, both in *A Portrait of the Artist as a Young Man* and in *Ulysses*, so I won't repeat that case here.[30] Instead, I would like to call attention to Master Patrick Dignam, who stops in front of "the window of Madame Doyle, courtdress milliner," to read the announcement of the Keogh-Bennett prizefight while two mirrors in the window reflect his image. Master Dignam resembles Stephen and Bloom in being a solitary figure dressed in mourning; he is also one of the rare minor characters whose interior monologues are presented for our inspection. That interior monologue combines with the text of the announcement in Master Dignam's silent reading:

> From the sidemirrors two mourning Masters Dignam gaped silently. Myler Keogh, Dublin's pet lamb, will meet sergeantmajor Bennett, the Portobello bruiser, for a purse of fifty sovereigns. Gob, that'd be a good pucking match to see. Myler Keogh, that's the chap sparring out to him with the green sash. Two bar entrance, soldiers half price. I could easy do a bunk on ma. Master Dignam on his left turned as he turned. That's me in mourning. (10.1132–38)

Master Dignam is less literate than Bloom, less accustomed to skimming texts for their essence; thus he reads whole sentences or phrases from the poster without seeming to transform them in any way. Nonetheless, the act of reading calls upon his powers of interpretation (he decides, on the basis of a green sash, which of the pictured boxers is Irish); it raises a practical consideration (how can he get the money for the fight from his mother?), and it results in a moment of self-awareness as he sees himself in a mirror. Later in the scene, the boy will think of other people reading his father's obituary in the evening newspaper—an obituary that we will eventually see Leopold Bloom read, complete with various printer's errors including the abbreviation of his name to "*L. Boom*" (16.1260).

That Master Dignam, Stephen, and Bloom (or Boom) read differently from most other characters in the book would be easy to demonstrate. Virtually everyone else reads aloud: Bantam Lyons cannot even skim the racing news without murmuring "Ascot. Gold cup. . . . Half a mo. Maximum the second" (5.532–33). Other readings take on the aura of public performances—for example, when the Citizen reads the *Irish Independent*'s list of recent births, deaths, and marriages, emphasizing the large number of non-Irish names (12.219–237). The purely verbal quality of these oral readings contrasts with the tendency of Bloom's readings to focus on the visual aspects of a piece—on the inappropriateness of placing an ad for Plumtree's Potted Meat "Under the obituary notices" (8.744), for example, or the "Crooked botched print" in a copy of Aristotle's *Masterpiece* (10.585). When Bloom reads his letter from Martha Clifford, he notes two typographical errors; when he reads the Dignam obituary, he discovers various printer's errors as well as errors of fact concerning attendance at the funeral. Bloom's professional immersion in, and awareness of, print helps to force his attention on these visual elements of the text. His commercial interests are related to print culture in another way, for print is associated with a double sense of literary proprietorship: the individual reader is the owner of the physical book itself, while the author is the owner of the words contained therein. (Thus Ong notes that the concept of plagiarism does not exist in purely oral cultures, where private ownership of a linguistic event would seem to be at odds with the communal nature of oral performance.)[31]

The confusion over ownership of a book—whose book is it, the author's or the reader's?—is one aspect of the fundamental duality of the author (or reader) and his other self. In practice, the author imagines a reader who, like Baudelaire's *hypocrite lecteur,* is his double, his brother; likewise, the reader creates the author in his own image. The early scene in which Bloom envies "kindly Mr Beaufoy" is a good example of the reader creating an author who reflects himself, while Beaufoy's charge of plagiarism in Circe (15.822) suggests Bloom's uneasy awareness that authors also exist not merely as extensions of ourselves but as distinct individuals whose rights do not end when we purchase their stories.

The connections between reader and writer are crucial to my own understanding of *Ulysses.* Fritz Senn has described the reading of *Ulysses* as an activity requiring continual "righting" of the text. "Readers," according to Senn, "are mediators who shape, or forge, the matter at hand"—people, that is, who are much like authors in their righting/wrighting/writing of the text.[32] Joyce implies the connection in another way at the end of the *Portrait,* in Stephen's diary, where the historical author and the present reader are merged in the figure of Stephen Dedalus, whose silent composition and perusal of his text places him on both sides of the literary confessional. The feat is repeated in *Ulysses,* with a twist, in the scene where Bloom silently writes (and reads) a letter to Martha Clifford, using the pseudonym Henry Flower and disguising his handwriting, but murmurs aloud bits and pieces from an entirely different letter—one he is *not* writing—to conceal his activity from Richie Goulding. Vocal reading is normally a sign of community, a shared experience, and it is a mark of Bloom's isolation from his environment that this rare example of his vocal reading is a carefully constructed fiction. In his silent composition and perusal of the real letter and, indeed, in his largely silent meditations throughout the novel, Bloom is both author and reader;

in his murmuring of a phony letter whose text exists nowhere but in his own breath, Bloom is not so much author or reader as a character in a fiction of his own creation.

I began with a reference to the mirroring effects of literature, and it is to this that I want to return in my conclusion. The mirror, of course, is one of the most common metaphors for art, but it seems to me peculiarly appropriate in relation to the experience of the reader. In a work of literature, presumably, we "see ourselves," which suggests one parallel with the act of looking in a mirror; moreover, while Buck Mulligan speaks to his image in the mirror in Telemachus (1.121)—a feat repeated by Issy in *Finnegans Wake*—looking into a mirror is normally a silent activity, comparable in that respect to the way most of us read. Finally, mirroring always involves some distortion or disorientation; extreme examples may be found in the concave and convex mirrors in Circe that produce variant Blooms—"*lovelorn longlost lugubru Booloohoom*" in the concave mirror, "*jollypoldy the rixdix doldy*" in the convex (15.145–49)—but even the most perfect mirror reverses left and right. Reading words in a mirror, then, is not an activity that we can perform by simple habit, passively; to read a mirrored text—as Bloom must do in reversing the letters on the title of the books that he sees in his mirror (17.1357–1414)—we must read actively, actually creating a new mental perspective for ourselves as we go along.

This, I think, is what Joyce demands that we do and what he shows us occurring in Bloom's readings, both of the book and of the world. Bloom questions himself, backtracks, tries another perspective, judges the logic of whatever he reads. Whereas Homer's Ulysses was the product of an oral culture, one in which all literary values are inevitably communal values, Bloom stands in the midst of the individualistic, modern age: created by a self-exiled author whose persona in an earlier novel had spoken of "forging" a national "conscience" or consciousness—not reflecting or even reviving it, but creating it—Bloom is likewise a loner who internalizes his world, transforms it, judges it. In this transformation, he reflects our own experience as readers of our texts, interpreters of an age in which we continually feel displaced and seek comfort not in traditional knowledge but in our own resources as "competent keyless citizen[s]" (17.1019). If the logic of the Homeric analogy suggests a metempsychotic connection between Ulysses and Leopold Bloom, the logic of the book's representation of reading should give us, as readers, a shock of recognition every time we watch Bloom reading part of the book that we are reading. If this is a further example of metempsychosis, of Bloom somehow being reincarnated in us, so be it.

NOTES

1. T. S. Eliot, "*Ulysses,* Order and Myth," in *James Joyce: The Critical Heritage,* ed. Robert H. Deming (New York: Barnes and Noble, 1970), 1:270.
2. Holbrook Jackson, "Ulysses à la Joyce," in Deming, *Joyce: Critical Heritage* 1:198–200.
3. Joseph Frank, "Spatial Form in Modern Literature," *Sewanee Review* 53 (1945): 234.
4. Marilyn French, *The Book as World: James Joyce's "Ulysses"* (Cambridge: Harvard University Press, 1976), 3–4.
5. Brook Thomas, *James Joyce's "Ulysses": A Book of Many Happy Returns* (Baton Rouge: Louisiana State University Press, 1982), 162–63.
6. James Joyce, *Ulysses,* ed. Hans Walter Gabler (New York: Random House, 1986). Parenthetical citations refer to chapter and line number.
7. Molly's reflection that reading a letter "fills up your whole day" may suggest a link between reading and sexual activity if we associate it with her use of "full up" in "I never in all my life felt anyone had one the size of that to make you feel full up" (18.149–50). Similarly, Bloom's question about Molly's reading—"Did you finish it?" (4.354)—seems to foreshadow Molly's repeated use of *finish* to refer to sexual climax (18.99, 18.156, 18.809).
8. *Letters of James Joyce,* 3 vols.: vol. 1 ed. Stuart Gilbert; vols. 2 and 3 ed. Richard Ellmann (New York: Viking Press, 1966), 1:64.
9. Hugh Kenner, *A Colder Eye: The Modern Irish Writers* (New York: Alfred A. Knopf, 1983), 155; Wolfgang Iser, *The Act of Reading: A Theory of Aesthetic Response* (Baltimore: Johns Hopkins University Press, 1978), 84. Likewise, Louis O. Mink has asserted that *Finnegans Wake* "contains its own interpretation to every discussion of it, prepared and ready to go" (Mink, "Reading *Finnegans Wake,*" *Southern Humanities Review* 9 [Winter 1975]: 1).
10. Hugh Kenner, *"Ulysses"* (London: George Allen and Unwin, 1980), 53.
11. Sir Philip Sidney, *The Defense of Poesy,* ed. Lewis Soens (Lincoln: University of Nebraska Press, 1970), 7.
12. The technique is also mentioned several times in *Finnegans Wake:* "volve the virgil page" (270.25); "SORTES VIRGINIANAE" (281.R2); "open virgilances" (569.16). See James S. Atherton, *The Books at the Wake: A Study of Literary Allusions in James Joyce's "Finnegans Wake"* (1959; reprint, Carbondale: Southern Illinois University Press, 1974), 287–88, and John Bishop, *Joyce's Book of the Dark: "Finnegans Wake"* (Madison: University of Wisconsin Press, 1986), 305, 311.
13. Hugh Kenner, *The Pound Era* (Berkeley: University of California Press, 1971), 380.
14. Mary Power, "The Discovery of *Ruby,*" *James Joyce Quarterly* 18 (Winter 1981): 115–21.
15. Cf. Bernard Benstock, "Reflections on *Ruby,*" *James Joyce Quarterly* 19 (Spring 1982): 340. The name Enrico does not appear in *Ulysses,* but its equivalent may be found when one of the parodies in Cyclops converts Henry Flower into "Senhor Enrique Flor" (12.1288).
16. Patrick A. McCarthy, "James Joyce and the Phoenix Park Murders: A Forum," *Irish Renaissance Annual* 4 (1983): 77, 80.
17. Power, "Discovery of *Ruby,*" 121.
18. John Eglinton, "The Beginnings of Joyce," in *The Portable Irish Reader,* ed. Diarmuid Russell (New York: Viking Press, 1946), 57–58. Eglinton was, however, an

unusually inept reader, for he believed that the passage he misquoted as "at rest, he has travelled" (cf. 17.2320) refers to Stephen (58).

19. Zack Bowen, "Lizzie Twigg: Gone But Not Forgotten," *James Joyce Quarterly* 6 (Summer 1969): 368–70.

20. Joyce, *Letters* 1:249.

21. Bloom typically skims before reading carefully. Thus as he stands in front of the window of the Belfast and Oriental Tea Company, he reads phrases from the tea packets—"choice blend, finest quality, family tea"—while he is occupied in searching for his Henry Flower card hidden inside his hat; then he "read[s] again: choice blend, made of the finest Ceylon brands" (5.17–29). In this instance, however, neither reading is complete, for each one contains words that are missing from the other.

22. Bloom may in fact be a more competent interpreter of this passage than we are, for he seems to understand Milly's reference to "Boylan's (I was on the pop of writing Blazes Boylan's) song about those seaside girls" (4.408–9)—the fact that he does not think this is worth interpreting means that he understands it—while we must guess at its meaning. There are two competing interpretations of Milly's words. Zack Bowen believes that the song was written by another Boylan and that Milly is referring to her momentary confusion of two men with the same last name; Richard Ellmann appears to concur with this judgment. Paul van Caspel, on the other hand, argues that Milly "knows [Boylan] is nicknamed 'Blazes' but has probably been told not to call him that. . . . Milly's remark is prompted either by her reflecting that a nice girl should not use bad language or by her fear of seeming to show disrespect with regard to Boylan." My own preference is for the Bowen-Ellmann hypothesis, but without further evidence I see no way of assuring myself that my reading is identical with Bloom's. See Bowen, *Musical Allusions in the Works of James Joyce: Early Poetry through "Ulysses"* (Albany: State University of New York Press, 1974), 85–86; Ellmann, *Ulysses on the Liffey* (1972; reprint New York: Oxford University Press, 1973), index under "Boylan, Blazes"; and van Caspel, *Bloomers on the Liffey: Eisegetical Readings of Joyce's "Ulysses"* (Baltimore: Johns Hopkins University Press, 1986), 67–68.

23. Jackson, in Deming, *Joyce: Critical Heritage* 1:199.

24. H. G. Wells, "James Joyce," in Deming, *Joyce: Critical Heritage* 1:86.

25. Bloom also says, of Beaufoy, "And he, a bachelor, how . . ." (15.857), implying that as a bachelor, Beaufoy cannot write knowledgeably about women. (Bloom's assumption that Beaufoy is a bachelor is apparently based upon Beaufoy's address, given in *Titbits* as "Playgoers' Club, London" [4.503].) Like his creator, Bloom believes firmly in the value of personal experience as a basis for fiction, as he shows when, immediately after reading Beaufoy's story, he thinks of a scheme to write a story based on what Molly says in the mornings (4.518–23); likewise, just after thinking of Beaufoy's literary success, Bloom wonders what luck he might have "suppose he were to pen something out of the common groove. . . . *My Experiences*, let us say, *in a Cabman's Shelter*" (16.1229–31).

26. Colin MacCabe, *James Joyce and the Revolution of the Word* (New York: Barnes and Noble, 1979), 84.

27. George Steiner, "Literature and Post-History," in his *Language and Silence: Essays on Language, Literature, and the Inhuman* (New York: Atheneum, 1967), 383.

28. Walter J. Ong, *Orality and Literacy: The Technologizing of the Word* (London: Methuen, 1982), 69.

29. Ong, *Orality and Literacy*, 153.

30. Patrick A. McCarthy, "Joyce's Silent Readers," in *New Alliances in Joyce Studies: "When it's Aped to Foul a Delfian,"* ed. Bonnie Kime Scott (Newark: University of Delaware Press, 1988). Other aspects of the present essay are related to those I have dealt with in *"Ulysses* and the Printed Page," in *Joyce's "Ulysses": The Larger Perspective,* ed. Robert D. Newman and Weldon Thornton (Newark: University of Delaware Press, 1987).

31. Ong, *Orality and Literacy,* 131.

32. Fritz Senn, "Righting *Ulysses,"* in *James Joyce: New Perspectives,* ed. Colin MacCabe (Bloomington: Indiana University Press, 1982), 13.

2
The Name of Bloom

DANIEL P. GUNN

1

When I read *Ulysses* for the first time, in the summer of 1981, I took obsessive delight, I remember, in the name "Old Ollebo, M.P." (17.409), Bloom's imperfect anagram of his own name, formulated in his youth and reported during the cocoa drinking in Ithaca. I signed letters to friends that way; I tried to make anagrams of my own name; the syllables floated around my head for weeks—Old Ollebo, crafty Ollebo, M.P.—and I played with them. It is difficult for me, I confess, to imagine Bloom as a boy of ten or eleven, fleshy and human, sitting at a desk on Clanbrassil Street and formulating this anagram. For I imagined it, even when I first read it, as something happening at the level of narrative, a game played not by Bloom but by the book, right there, in my living room. It still strikes me as a lovely piece of self-conscious verbal invention—an instance of pure and gratuitous storytelling play, preceded by three cartoonish preliminary efforts (Elpodbomool, Molldopeloob, Bollopedoom) and framed by two poems that also inscribe Bloom's name: the acrostic five-liner that spells out "Poldy" and an unusual piece of original verse—

> *An ambition to squint*
> *At my verses in print*
> *Makes me hope that for these you'll find room.*
> *If you so condescend*
> *Then please place at the end*
> *The name of yours truly, L. Bloom.*

(17.396–401)

This last line may remind us, as I think it is supposed to, that Bloom has appeared in the *Telegraph* account of Dignam's funeral as "L. Boom" (16.1260)—and of course, as Fritz Senn and Richard Ellmann have pointed out, and everyone, surely, has noticed, this brief burst of

Ithacan high spirits is not the only example we have of the novel playing with Bloom's name.[1] He is, by turns, Leopold, Siopold, Stoom, blue Bloom, on the rye, Bloohoom, Him, even Him, ben Bloom Elijah, greaseabloom, Poldy, Poldycock, Henry Flower, so lonely, blooming, Senhor Enrique Flor, of Flowerville, of Bloom Cottage, of the new Bloomusalem. We have caught the habit of such play, all of us, from Joyce: Hugh Kenner says that *Ulysses* is "Bloomocentric"; David Hayman finds the rhetoric of one part of Sirens "unmistakably Bloomish"; Paul van Caspel has written a book about Bloomers on the Liffey.[2]

As I look back, then, my obsessive reaction to "Old Ollebo, M.P." seems normal, to me—that is, it seems to be the kind of reaction that *Ulysses* fosters in its readers in relation to both the name and the character of Leopold Bloom. Like the wistful monosyllable of his name, Bloom is altogether ordinary, in what passes for real life: a commercial traveler, fussy and diffident, a quiet presence in the street. But *Ulysses* subjects him to so many transformations, apotheoses, and abasements, so many polytropic *turns,* Senn would say, that he becomes, like Odysseus, a mythic presence inside of the narrative in which he appears, and everything that appertains to him takes on the status of a mystery. And so, when the narrative transfigures his name into "Bloomusalem" (15.1544), say, we feel, on one hand, how *ridiculous* this is, this fixation with a completely ordinary man's name, and we laugh, but then some part of us feels assent and exhilaration, too, because in *Ulysses* the name of Bloom is shrouded in legend, like the name of a hero or a god, and no attention to it *can* be excessive.

Unlike Odysseus, Bloom achieves legendary status only by virtue of his presence in a novel; he is dragged into heroism by the violent and undisguisedly artificial activity of narration. As a result, in the second half of *Ulysses,* the narrative's increasing fixation with Bloom and all that pertains to him—his personal effects scattered in two drawers, the books on his bookshelf, his love of rectitude in earliest youth—necessarily exists in an atmosphere of intense self-consciousness. We know that Bloom becomes an object of obsession only as a character in a novel—this one, in fact, the one we are reading—and so every ludicrous and obsessive gesture toward him underscores the heroic character of *Ulysses* as artifact. Each time the narrative compulsively manipulates the syllables of Bloom's name, telling them over and over, as if they were some kind of prayer, it reminds us of its own power to make the name of Bloom into a talisman. By the time we reach Circe and Ithaca, the repeated enunciations of Bloom's name and the mock transfigurations of his person are only threads in some larger fabric of reflexive self-celebration, into which we are all steadily and artfully drawn.³ This is a book that cannot stop thinking about itself. Obsessed with the name of its main character, increasingly obsessed with its own still-unfolding universe, *Ulysses* invites and encourages obsession in its readers.

2

The narrative's urgent self-consciousness manifests itself most noticeably in a tendency toward recapitulation and retrospect in the second half of *Ulysses,* and it is to several of these recapitulations that I wish now to turn.⁴ Of course, there is a general tendency to look backward in the novel, as Bloom remembers what has happened to him during the day and the narrative looks back at its own past—in Circe, most notably. But I am concerned in particular with those backward looks that take several motifs from the novel and transform or redefine them, calling attention to their textual status and molding them compulsively into new structures and sequences. The litany that concludes the messianic scene in Circe is one example of such a recapitulation:

> Kidney of Bloom, pray for us
> Flower of the Bath, pray for us
> Mentor of Menton, pray for us
> Canvasser for the Freeman, pray for us
> Charitable Mason, pray for us
> Wandering Soap, pray for us
> Sweets of Sin, pray for us
> Music without Words, pray for us
> Reprover of the Citizen, pray for us
> Friend of all Frillies, pray for us
> Midwife Most Merciful, pray for us
> Potato Preservative against Plague and Pestilence, pray for us.
> (15.1941–52)

Here are twelve separate ejaculations, composed into a litany, chanted by the Daughters of Erin as the martyred Bloom burns, "mute, shrunken, carbonised" (15.1956). The separate prayers mimic the two-beat rhythm of a litany exactly: a strong first beat, several unaccented and largely mumbled syllables, and then a second strong beat before the murmured countersign: pray for us. Against this firmly established norm, the expansion of "Potato Preservative against Plague and Pestilence" emerges as a kind of arabesque, a moment of verbal play embedded in a playful structure of permutations. This play, by the way, has its counterpart in more orthodox litanies: "Queen of angels," we read in the Litany of Loreto, "Queen of virgins," but then "Queen conceived without original sin."

The object of each separate ejaculation is either Bloom in one of his polytropic guises—canvasser, Mason, friend, mentor, reprover, midwife—or an item or attribute associated with him—his breakfast kidney, his lemon-scented soap, his potato, his book. "Flower of the Bath" may refer to Bloom in his role as Henry Flower, bathing, or to his genitalia, preapprehended as "a languid floating flower" (5.571–2) at the end of Lotus Eaters. One invocation is puzzling: "Music without Words." Is Bloom himself a kind of music? Is this a reference to the music that occasionally floats around his head (tarataratara)? Or is the music at the Ormond bar during Sirens to be imagined as somehow one of his attributes, on a par with his soap or his breakfast? With this one prayer excepted, two processes seem to be at work in the series of invocations. First, there is a catalog of Bloom's protean selves—a series of transformations analogous to the declension of his name, which has already taken place in Circe: "Bloom. Of Bloom. For Bloom. Bloom" (15.677). Second, there is a catalog of his accessories, the secondary relics associated with his person. (Stephen, you may remember, cares about the status of such relics; he wonders whether the divine prepuce would deserve "simple hyperduly" or "the fourth degree of latria," traditionally accorded to toenails, hair, and other "divine excrescences" [17.1205–9].) Together, these processes constitute an anatomy of Bloom, an abbreviated grammar of his possibilities and attributes. This, again, is like a more orthodox litany, wherein the object of veneration is similarly taken apart, seen from all possible angles in an exhaustive way. The litany must have seemed an attractive form to Joyce, along with the many other Roman Catholic forms—the confiteor, for example, or the credo—which generate exhaustive lists and anatomies: "*Confiteor Deo omnipotenti, beatae Mariae semper Virgini, beato Michaeli Archangelo, beato Joanni Baptistae, sanctis Apostolis Petro et Paulo* . . ." This is the natural accumulative rhetoric of *Ulysses,* from Cyclops on.

Aside from the anatomy of Bloom, there are other transformations at work here, too. The whole litany has its source in Nausicaa, where the Litany of Loreto is being recited at a men's temperance retreat in the Church of Mary, Star of the Sea, while Gerty MacDowell sits listening on the rocks with Cissy Caffrey and Edy Boardman. If Circe is "*Ulysses* transposed and rearranged," as Hugh Kenner says,[5] then here are a few small fragments of Nausicaa putting in an appearance, as so many fragments do, fantastically altered by the substitution of

Bloom for the Virgin Mary and the Daughters of Erin for men on a temperance retreat. Moreover, the invocations are arranged not only synchronically, as a collection of Bloom-roles and Bloom-signs, the lexicon of his semantic possibilities, but diachronically, according to the order in which Bloom assumed the guise or brought himself into conspicuous relation with the item—that is, according to the book's *syntax*. In fact, as everyone sees right away, or thinks he sees, each of the twelve invocations corresponds roughly to an episode in *Ulysses*, from the kidney Bloom purchases and consumes in Calypso to the potato he hands over to Zoe in Circe. Each episode has thus been transformed into a short prayer, shrunken and reshaped, and the litany as a whole is a microcosm of the Bloomian portion of the novel, the Odyssean wanderings in small. This structure may make us more comfortable with "Music without Words," since that prayer now fits neatly into the slot assigned for Sirens, but again, as Senn points out, there is a dislocated motif: Bloom may wander in Scylla and Charybdis, but his soap appears only at the episode's portal, the end of Lestrygonians.[6]

Now, it is possible that we are meant to gather some symbolic significance from the rough and tantalizing correspondence between invocation and episode; it is possible that we are looking at some sort of schema, a key, disrupted or not, to submerged pattern in the portion of text represented here, after the model of the Linati or Gilbert charts.[7] But I don't think so. What is at stake here, I think, is the gesture of self-reference itself, rather than any meaning that might be associated with the precise nature of its form. After having built up, in the wanderings, a remarkably dense and multiform substance, a web of incident and thought and transformation, all centering around Bloom, *Ulysses* now celebrates not only Bloom but itself, its own heroic and ridiculous journey from burnt kidney through genital flower to charred potato. The rough episode-by-episode correspondence is there to remind us that we are remembering and anatomizing not so much Bloom's day as the presentation of that day in a work of fiction, which has been organized in unusual fashion into episodes radically discontinuous and discrete, especially toward the end. This self-conscious gesture—the book recapitulating its own episodes, one by one, looking back on them with a certain nostalgia—strikes me as perfectly consonant with the increasingly reflexive and inward tendencies of *Ulysses* in Circe and beyond. Like the other instances of Bloomocentric play, the litany engenders a mixture of laughter and wonder; it is at once a burlesque of the novel and a celebration of it, just as the scene surrounding it depicts what is at once a transfiguration and an immolation of Bloom.

3

How is it that Joyce is able to refer so easily to his own novel in the litany? By this time, because of the increasingly insistent presence of *Ulysses* as novel in the texture of the narrative, the earlier episodes have come to exist in almost a material way—as clay to be molded, as plastic substance, immanent and available. In passages like the litany, we take pleasure in recognizing the contours of the old textual material and in seeing them return, numinous and shimmering. In fact, the rich material presence evoked by the invocations of the litany is analogous to the effect created by instances of verbal repetition in *Ulysses*—for example, by the repeated sentences in Wandering Rocks, where verbal units are given almost material weight and where verbal repetition has an almost incantatory power. When we reread a sentence like "The young woman with slow care detached from her light skirt a clinging twig" (10.440–41) in Wandering Rocks,[8] we respond to it not only as an indication of the elaborately worked out synchronicity of the episode, but also as a sentence in the novel that has reasserted itself obsessively, that has refused to go away. The nearly exact repetition of the verbal structure, its radical separation from the context, its painfully crafted air: all of these aspects mark the sentence as a piece of text, something we have *already read*—and we are unusually conscious of its migration from one part of the episode to another. Something similar happens in Sirens, when we are asked to recall the opening sentence of Calypso: "Pat served, uncovered dishes. Leopold cut liverslices. As said before he ate with relish the inner organs, nutty gizzards, fried cods' roes" (11.519–20). What is most obvious to me in these instances—and in the litany—is the exuberant and high-spirited interest this book displays in its own material reality, as a collection of verbal artifacts, made things, words, sentences, adventures. Anatole France said that Rabelais piled words up like rocks, as a child might, on a beach; by the time we reach Circe, sentences and episodes of *Ulysses* have the same material weight as the Rabelaisian word, and we get to watch the narrative pile them up, playing, one by one, and then take them down and pile them up again.

4

The wanderings of Bloom return in a new guise when Bloom recalls them in silent recapitulation near the end of Ithaca:

What past consecutive causes, before rising preapprehended, of accumulated fatigue did Bloom, before rising, silently recapitulate?

The preparation of breakfast (burnt offering): intestinal congestion and premeditative defecation (holy of holies): the bath (rite of John): the funeral (rite of Samuel): the advertisement of Alexander Keyes (Urim and Thummim): the unsubstantial lunch (rite of Melchisedek): the visit to museum and national library (holy place): the bookhunt along Bedford row, Merchants' Arch, Wellington Quay (Simchath Torah): the music in the Ormond Hotel (Shira Shirim): the altercation with a truculent troglodyte in Bernard Kiernan's premises (holocaust): a blank period of time including a cardrive, a visit to a house of mourning, a leavetaking (wilderness): the eroticism produced by feminine exhibitionism (rite of Onan): the prolonged delivery of Mrs Mina Purefoy (heave offering): the visit to the disorderly house of Mrs Bella Cohen, 82 Tyrone street, lower, and subsequent brawl and chance medley in Beaver street (Armageddon): nocturnal perambulation to and from the cabman's shelter, Butt Bridge (atonement). (17.2042–58)[9]

As we watch Joyce compose this passage in the Garland synopsis, we can see the obsessive accretions that transform a rather straightforward question—"What consecutive causes of fatigue did Bloom, before rising, silently enumerate?"—into something slightly crazed: "What past consecutive causes, before rising preapprehended, of accumulated fatigue did Bloom, before rising, silently recapitulate?" (Even this question is reflexive, coiling back on itself, in the repetition of "before rising" and in the way "recapitulate" responds to "preapprehended.") There are layers of accretion in the list that follows, too. In its earliest version, it consisted of thirteen incidents, twelve of them drawn from episodes in the novel, with Wandering Rocks left out and with an additional entry for the time between Cyclops and Nausicaa. There were no parentheses. The reference to the "bookhunt" was added as an interlineation on the Rosenbach manuscript, and then there were a series of small changes on the placards, including the addition of Bloom's trip to the outhouse and expansions like "with a truculent troglodyte" and "chance medley." Only on the page proofs, with the novel nearly in press, did Joyce add the solemn parenthetical references. At first, the reference to the cabman's shelter was "peace offering"; Joyce changed it to "atonement" in a letter to Darantière in January 1922. As Senn points out, this would make it one of Joyce's final adjustments of the text.[10]

That the number of references and their precise nature changed several times, that there are two entries for Calypso, that the parentheses were added so late, that the text read for so long "peace offering" instead of "atonement"—all of this suggests to me that what is at stake here, as in the litany, is not a schematic coherence among the parenthetical entries, some kind of chart or key to the book's structure that we can read back into the episodes themselves, but rather, first, a loose recollection and listing of principal moments in the narrative, low-grade narrative manipulation itself, and then, second, some additional play in the creation of a new plane of arbitrary and ingenious correspondences. Watching Joyce create this passage, we see the original reflexive references expand and blow up, like cartoon figures—and this is the effect the final version has on a reader, too. The passage is primarily comic and self-conscious: we are running our fingers over the events of the book—and the references simultaneously make these events seem sacred (which, for us, they are, since they are *in this book*) and treat them with something approaching derision. Thus the homely kidney, frying in a pan, subject of Calypso, is first ennobled as part of "the preparation of breakfast" and then transformed into a "burnt offering," something tinged with the aura of ritual. This makes sense; the kidney was, after all, our first introduction to Bloom, back across a vast expanse of language, and we look back on it with fondness. But as something homely and common, even grotesque, as one of Bloom's failings or fetishes, and as a *culinary* failure, too, this burnt kidney also insists on its distance from sacred ritual, and we see an example of the gap between language and substance—or, more precisely, the gap between our twin responses of laughter and wonder. When the narrative forces this gap on our consciousness, as it does both here and in the litany, it refers us unmistakably to its own extraordinary character as a work of fiction, since there would be no such gap without the elaborate and undisguised artifice of *Ulysses*.

There is self-conscious play, too, in the very ingenuity of the ritual associations. With the addition of the parenthetical references, the wanderings of Bloom are not only cited but subjected to a new metamorphosis, and their malleable and artificial character is thereby revealed. Once the principle of the transformation is established, it becomes fun to see how the operation will be performed on each item. My personal favorite is the way Bloom's purchase of *Sweets of Sin,* a new sacred text for Molly, expands into "Simchath Torah," the feast on which the reading of the Torah is recommenced after a completed cycle. There is also something charming about the use of "holy place" as an equivalent for the library and museum, where Bloom tried to investigate certain anatomical holes in the resident statuary.

These ritualizing transformations are consistent with the odd reflexive logic that pervades the final chapters of *Ulysses,* where Joyce regularly subjects both Bloom and the events of his day to operations and permutations, celebrating his power to dispose and encode his material as he likes, even as the material itself expands wildly, threatening the universe. In Ithaca, such changes are most often seen as operations performed by the narrative, like the anagrams of Bloom's name. "Reduce Bloom by cross multiplication of reverses of fortune . . . to a negligible negative irrational unreal quantity" (17.1933–35), orders the questioning voice, and the narrative dutifully transforms Bloom into a hawker, a dun, a bankrupt, a pauper, just as he has earlier been lord mayor, emperor-president, and messiah (15.1354–1854). We are conscious of the same kind of narrative manipulation when Bloom soars into the heavens on his final journey at the end of Ithaca, just before the ritualized list:

Ever he would wander, selfcompelled, to the extreme limit of his cometary orbit, beyond the fixed stars and variable suns and telescopic planets, astronomical waifs and strays, to the extreme boundary of space, passing from land to land, among peoples, amid events. Somewhere imperceptibly he would hear and somehow reluctantly, suncompelled, obey the summons of recall. Whence, disappearing from the constellation of the Northern Crown he would somehow reappear reborn above delta in the constellation of Cassiopeia and after incalculable eons of peregrination return an estranged avenger, a wreaker of justice on malefactors, a dark crusader, a sleeper awakened, with financial resources (by supposition) surpassing those of Rothschild or the silver king. (17.2013–23)

This grand expansion of the wanderings, in which Bloom's presence extends to "the extreme boundaries of space" and through "incalculable eons of peregrination," is a natural culmination of the permutations to which he has been subjected throughout *Ulysses.* Like the list of rituals, which follows as a kind of coda, it is the operation of a self-conscious narrative transforming and expanding its own material.

Seen in this light, the list of rituals is not so much a product of Bloom's memory as of the memory of *Ulysses.* Here, as in the litany, we are referred not to events in Bloom's day but to episodes in the narrative, which are seen as material to be transformed. The reference to Bloom's encounter with the Citizen as a "holocaust," for example, would make little sense if we were thinking just about Bloom's day. After all, only a biscuit tin and a mangy rascal of a dog came flying, and when Bloom thinks back on the scene, he imagines it as more of a triumph than a disaster (13.1215–17). But the consciously distorted treatment of the scene, which the narrative recalls here, described a holocaust indeed, with "a violent atmospheric perturbation of cyclonic character," "seismic waves," "an incandescent object of enormous proportions hurtling through the atmosphere at a terrifying velocity," and the palace of justice "literally a mass of ruins beneath which it is to be feared all the occupants have been buried alive" (12.1867–81). Similarly, the incidents that took place between Cyclops and Nausicaa are described as "a blank period of time" and associated with "wilderness" because, as far as the narrative is concerned, as far as we are concerned, as readers, these events *did* constitute a blank. Bloom was wandering in the wilderness outside of the book, in the desert and ghostly realm of the nonnarratable, when these events took place. These are very nearly the only items on the list that are not preceded by the definite article: "the preparation of breakfast," "the prolonged delivery," but "a blank period of time," "a cardrive," "a leavetaking." The events they refer to remain indeterminate and unspecified; they have not been brought into being as the others have, in the novel.

"Urim and Thummim," the most gnomic of the parallel references, also makes more sense if we think of the motif to which it refers, "the advertisement of Alexander Keyes," not as an event, something Bloom does, but as a piece of text, both in the *Telegraph* and in *Ulysses*. Whether they regard it as a part of the high priest's breastplate or some mysterious piece of equipment, encyclopedias of Jewish history seem agreed that the Urim and Thummim is a kind of bifurcated enigma, a mystery, both from our perspective and the perspective of those who used it as an oracle.[11] The Keyes advertisement is also both bifurcated and enigmatic: it consists of two crossed keys, whose meaning must be divined by readers of both the newspaper and the novel. These latter, with enough perseverance, will find in the oracle not only the bicameral Isle of Man parliament, a symbol meant for the *Telegraph*'s readers, but also an elaborately wrought pattern of keys, lost, usurped, and forgotten in *Ulysses,* and a competent keyless citizen, negotiating the incertitude of the void. The reference, then, makes sense if we see that what is being referred to is the Keyes advertisement as a symbol—as the mock-Urim and Thummim of *Ulysses,* the mysterious key to the text. (Like the other keys, this one leads nowhere.) This would make Urim and Thummim consistent with the other references, all of which remind us of narrative motifs rather than "real" events in Bloom's day. These are items from the text of *Ulysses,* reworked, transformed, and presented for our regard, according to the operational logic of Ithaca.

5

Bloom's budget (17.1455–78) is another example of the narrative looking back nostalgically on its own past. Here is the kidney again, this time seen through a new grid, as a debit: "1 Pork kidney 0–0–3." And here is the newspaper Bloom bought and rolled into a baton, his bath, his contribution to Dignam's family, *Sweets of Sin*, lunch and dinner, the coffee and bun at the cabman's shelter, even the hallucinatory sheep's trotter. I take particular delight in reading the solemn "2 Banbury cakes 0–0–1" and remembering Bloom feeding this bread to the gulls in Lestrygonians, along with the throwaway, Elijah is coming, at "thirtytwo feet per sec" (8.57–58). The narrative has kept this incident alive several times by repeating the language of the throwaway and the speed of falling bodies, by following the throwaway's course down the Liffey during Wandering Rocks, by referring to Bloom as Elijah, and by reminding us of the pun on the name of the winning horse in the Gold Cup. In fact, this theme is given its own private recapitulation when Bloom sees Boylan's torn betting tickets and thinks back over the several coincidental references to "Throwaway" during his day (17.327–41). And so here, as in the litany, a whole string of associations is condensed into a single retrospective gesture: "2 Banbury cakes 0–0–1." In the same way, two terse and lugubrious entries scrupulously represent Bloom's kindness in taking care of the remnant of Stephen's funds: on the debit side, "Loan (Stephen Dedalus) refunded 1–7–0"; then, as a credit, "Loan (Stephen Dedalus) 1–7–0."[12] Because this act of Bloomian charity is not essentially a financial transaction at all, because, as far as the budget is concerned, it comes to nothing, there is a discontinuity in the reference, a gap, just as there is in the use of "Simchath Torah" for the selection of a trash novel or "Mentor of Menton" for the scene in which Bloom advises John Henry Menton of a dint in his hat. Like the other recapitulations, this is a comical metamorphosis of preexistent material, and it demonstrates, more than anything else, a tendency to look back at that material with nostalgia and delight.

To respond with delight to an item as small as "2 Banbury cakes 0–0–1"; to think with exhilaration, Yes, I recognize that, I remember, that was when Bloom fed the gulls and threw away Elijah is coming: these are the marks of obsession, are they not? I don't think this fanatic intensity is a symptom only of the kind of reader who might think of attending a Joyce conference. *Ulysses* invites obsession even in its first- and second-time readers because a consciousness of the iconic status of the novel is incorporated into the fabric of the narrative, made in fact a condition of our reading. Our state is thus made to mirror that of Joyce, who was consumed by *Ulysses* for seven years and more. "Everything Joyce did or thought seemed to move in some way toward his book," writes Richard Ellmann, and we can see examples of this on page after page of the biography, as the world of passing verbal accident, Joyce's ordinary life, turns inward toward *Ulysses*.[13] Or, if we need more evidence, there is the record of brute and exacting labor itself, the Flaubertian intensity with which he worked on the book's language, sentence by sentence, word by word: "Grossbooted draymen rolled barrels dullthudding out of Prince's stores and bumped them up on the brewery float. On the brewery float bumped dullthudding barrels rolled by grossbooted draymen out of Prince's stores" (7.21–24). And there is the final convincing evidence of the way Circe and Ithaca and Penelope ballooned and expanded after the constraints of serial publication were lifted, as if, having made this world, Joyce could not leave it.[14] He could only expand or repeat and transform what he had made, manipulating it self-consciously again and again—"Vinbad the Quailer and Linbad the Yailer and Xinbad the Phthailer" (17.2325–26)—until some combination of exhaustion and the publication deadline intervened.

This final period of intense activity was the period when the recapitulations were written, the point when the book, too, was turning inward on its own past, with a certain longing. Reading over these passages, I have thought several times of the homely sketch of Bloom that Joyce drew while testing a pencil in Myron Nutting's studio, the one with the question marks and the scrawled first line of the *Odyssey*.[15] Could anything be less characteristic of the detached artist, paring his fingernails, than this affectionate and backward-looking sketch, drawn in a stray moment and placed beneath an incantation? *Ulysses* is so astonishingly complex and fraught with detail, so *rich*, finally, that it becomes, once we have read through a chunk of it, a more substantial and real presence than the world or human nature or whatever it is that books are supposed to be about, and we may feel, as readers, compelled to formulate our own anagrams, or to draw our own pictures, on matchbook covers, on stray sheets of paper, in the margin of a conference program while someone reads a dull paper, anywhere we can.

NOTES

1. Fritz Senn, "Book of Many Turns," in *Joyce's Dislocutions*, ed. John Paul Riquelme (Baltimore: Johns Hopkins University Press, 1984), 126–27; Richard Ellmann, *The Consciousness of Joyce* (New York: Oxford University Press, 1977), 13.

2. Hugh Kenner, *"Ulysses"* (London: Allen and Unwin, 1980), 55; David Hayman, *"Ulysses": The Mechanics of Meaning*, rev. ed. (Madison: University of Wisconsin Press, 1982), 113; Paul van Caspel, *Bloomers on the Liffey: Eisegetical Readings of Joyce's "Ulysses"* (Baltimore: Johns Hopkins University Press, 1986).

3. For discussions of *Ulysses* bearing on its character as a self-conscious novel, see Brook Thomas, *James Joyce's "Ulysses": A Book of Many Happy Returns* (Baton Rouge: Louisiana State University Press, 1982); Colin MacCabe, *James Joyce and the Revolution of the Word* (London: Macmillan, 1978); Karen Lawrence, *The Odyssey of Style in "Ulysses"* (Princeton: Princeton University Press, 1981); and John Paul Riquelme, *Teller and Tale in Joyce's Fiction: Oscillating Perspectives* (Baltimore: Johns Hopkins University Press, 1983). See also Robert Alter, *Partial Magic: The Novel as a Self-Conscious Genre* (Berkeley: University of California Press, 1975), 140–44.

4. Fritz Senn has treated several of the recapitulations I discuss here from a different perspective, as examples of the "Principle of the Disrupted Pattern," in "Weaving, unweaving," in *A Starchamber Quiry*, ed. E. Epstein (London: Methuen, 1982), 45–70.

5. Hugh Kenner, "Circe," in *James Joyce's "Ulysses"*, ed. Clive Hart and David Hayman (Berkeley: University of California Press, 1974), 356. "We sense a vast closed field," Kenner continues, "the Western mind, within which, like pieces in a kaleidoscope, motifs are permuted, vivid, bright, transient, for ever." This is a helpful gloss not only on Circe but on all of the self-conscious recapitulations I treat here.

6. Senn, "Weaving, unweaving," 54.

7. Despite its emphasis on disruption, Senn's argument in "Weaving, unweaving" implies that the recapitulations are meant to be instances of "pattern" or "significant order" (46). He begins with the assumption, for example, that each of the prayers in the litany is "characteristic and representative" of the episode from which it is drawn (53).

8. Vladimir Nabokov seems to have singled this sentence out for praise in one of his lectures on *Ulysses*. See *Lectures on Literature*, ed. Fredson Bowers (New York: Harcourt Brace Jovanovich, 1980), 331.

9. Virginia Moseley has discussed the elements of this passage at length in *Joyce and the Bible* (DeKalb: Northern Illinois University Press, 1967), 72–117. See also Senn, "Weaving, unweaving," 57–65.

10. Senn, "Weaving, unweaving," 58.

11. See, for example, *Universal Jewish Encyclopedia*, s.v. "Urim and Thummim." See also Moseley, *Joyce and the Bible*, 82–83; Senn, "Weaving, unweaving," 60–61.

12. Several critics have noted that the budget is inaccurate here, since Bloom has received £1–6–11 from Stephen (15.3613) but rendered back £1–7–0 (17.958). See Patrick Boyle, "Bloomsday: A Sloppy Balance Sheet," *Hibernia* 36 (1 December 1972): 14. This may be an error—Joyce's difficulties with the budget are notorious—or it may be, like the imperfect anagram, an example of the kind of transformational flaw that Senn has taught us to notice.

13. Richard Ellmann, *James Joyce*, rev. ed. (New York: Oxford University Press, 1982), 438.

14. In the afterword to *Ulysses: A Critical and Synoptic Edition* (New York: Garland, 1984), Hans Gabler reports that Ithaca expanded by a third during the final typing and proofreading at the end of 1921 (3:1890). "In the process of re-reading for revision," he writes, "reflections on the complexity of Bloomsday appear to have generated matter both for its modifying expansion in the sections already established and for its final permutations under the perspectives of reverie and catechism."

15. See Ellmann, *James Joyce*, plate 37.

3
Joyce's New Womanly Man
Sexual Signatures of Androgynous Transformation in *Ulysses*

SUZETTE HENKE

Leopold Bloom, James Joyce's "new womanly man," emerges in *Ulysses* as an epic hero who seems to inhabit those fragile spaces on the edge of social discourse usually reserved for women and cultural deviants. Fully cognizant of his otherness, he adopts the roles of different dramatis personae on the stage of Irish life and melds a capacious and porous ego with suffering adolescent girls, famished gulls, women in childbirth, an exhausted but inquisitive clerical worker, a blind piano tuner, and a startling array of characters encountered during his Dublin odyssey of 16 June 1904.

A connoisseur of the joys of polymorphous perversity, Bloom proves to be androgynous not only in temperament and sensitivity, but in libidinal orientation as well. He apparently retrieves the primordial erotic impulses rejected by Freud in *Civilization and Its Discontents*—those primitive olfactory and tactile responses that Granddaddy Sigmund ascribed, somewhat speciously, to the female of the species, in contrast to the supposedly visual and oculocentric sexual economy associated with the male.[1] Bloom manifests an infantile fascination with the products of human excrement, smells the pickings of his toenails, relishes the tang of urine in a fried pork kidney, and is obsessively preoccupied with the excrescences of female menses. The phallus is displaced in his imagination by a fetishistic concern with feces, menstrual blood, urine, and bodily secretions. Throughout *Ulysses*, "Baby Bloom" finds himself tantalized by supposedly feminine pulsions that replicate attachment to the imaginary body of a beneficent phallic mother.

Most of the women in the novel take shape in the text as vivid projections of Leopold Bloom's richly erotic fantasy life. They are inscribed in his imagination as figures of physical need or sadomasochistic impulse, visceral pity or sensuous attraction. Despite the epicene aspects of his sexual proclivities, Bloom tends to assess females in the Dublin landscape as amorous objects stoking playful vignettes of the dreaming mind. His farraginous interior monologue offers a pentimento portrait of Irish society filtered through a tentacled and highly charged erotic consciousness. Women excite or repel him, tease or titillate him; but all of their figurations suggest that in the course of *Ulysses,* Bloom is rewriting the text of turn-of-the-century sex-role enculturation in the discourse of polymorphously perverse desire.

In the persona of Henry Flower, Esq., Bloom conducts a clandestine epistolary affair with Martha Clifford, a lonely and pathetic "working-girl" who pines for release from the prison of dreary secretarial duties. Martha complains of boredom and headaches, longs to consummate this furtive liaison with her would-be lover, and takes curious pleasure in his obscene communications. But like the virtuous Victorian lady that she was raised to be, Martha protests, "I called you naughty boy because I do not like that other world" (*U* 63). Too exhausted and bleary-eyed to correct her typographical error, she inadvertently offers a telling comment on theological chicanery. Martha fails, however, to recognize the contradiction implicit in her quest for the "real meaning of that word" she does not like. She assures Henry: "I have never felt myself so much drawn to a man as you. . . . O how I long to meet you. Henry dear, do not deny my request before my patience are exhausted. Then I will tell you all" (*U* 63–64). Martha tantalizes her suitor with promises of forbidden sexual discourse, but her patience and confidence have, indeed, been misplaced in the very much married man she tries to "seduce." Bloom attributes her amorous desires and physical discomfort to menstrual malady rather than situational angst: "Such a bad headache. Has her roses probably" (*U* 64). In Lotus-Eaters, a chapter of flowers, Martha is far too busy earning her bread to be concerned about the roses denied her—though she does, apparently, take some kind of pleasure from the "thorns" of Bloom's pornographic letters designed to pique erotic curiosity.

In the Nausicaa episode, Bloom responds to Gerty MacDowell's sentimental striptease with a kind of Zola-esque naturalism. Aroused by her tantalizing exhibitionism, he gives the young woman the impression that his strange "dark eyes" are "drinking in her every contour, literally worshipping at her shrine." With a little help from Maria Susanna Cummins's *The Lamplighter,* Gerty romanticizes her suitor, sanitizes his masturbation, and idealizes his worshipful attentions. This Virgin Mary of Sandymount invites the tribute of Bloom's profane ejaculations, reinscribed in adolescent consciousness by that "dream of love, the dictates of her heart that told her he was her all in all, the only man in the world for her for love was the master guide" (U 299).[2]

This "sterling man, a man of inflexible honour to his fingertips" (U 299) evaluates the scene with the same "phenomenological" accuracy one might associate with the comic caricature of Herr Professor Luitpold Blumenduft: "Near her monthlies, I expect, makes them feel ticklish. . . . How many women in Dublin have it today? Martha, she. . . . Anyhow I got the best of that. . . . Thankful for small mercies. Cheap too. Yours for the asking. Because they want it themselves" (U 301). Bloom's matter-of-fact interpretation of his seminal encounter with Gerty is fairly mechanical: "My fireworks. Up like a rocket, down like a stick" (U 304). His response may seem self-serving, if not brutal: "Did me good all the same. . . . For this relief much thanks" (U 305). But his postorgasmic thoughts about Gerty are also imbued with pity and tinged with paternal solicitude. Stunned by her lameness, Bloom thinks: "Poor girl! That's why she's left on the shelf and the others did a sprint" (U 301). He feels grateful to Gerty for reaffirming his manhood and acknowledges that their erotic adventure involved "a kind of language between us" (U 305). Bloom sees in this postpubescent girl a figure of his own "lost" daughter Milly, whom he tenderly recalls in nostalgic reverie. He remembers Milly's fear of being deserted and the terror she experienced at the first "bloody" sign of female maturation: "Her growing pains at night, calling, wakening me. Frightened she was when her nature came on her first. Poor child! Strange moment for the mother too" (U 311). Just as Molly will later think through Stephen to Bloom, so the husband moves from the incident with Gerty to memories of female fragility and his daughter's growing pains, and finally to that ever-present object of amorous desire, Mother Molly.

Bloom's reveries about women seem to circle around reproductive potential, and menstruation and motherhood are high on his list of sex-linked preoccupations. He worships female generative capacities, and all his attention is obliquely focused on the ideal of maternity, which he holds in reverence and psychological awe. Although he can crassly reduce women to figures of oral, genital, and anal absence ("Three holes, all women" [U 234]), he is the only male in the novel to feel genuine pity for "poor Mrs Purefoy" in the throes of a painful accouchement: "Three days imagine groaning on a bed with a vinegared handkerchief round her forehead, her belly swollen out. Phew! Dreadful simply! . . . Kill me that would. . . . Life with hard labour"

(*U* 132). Bloom, as new womanly man, can imagine the pain of parturition in a vivid evocation of the heroic labors of women, and his fantasies later collapse into a dream of masculine motherhood in the Circe episode of *Ulysses*. Apparently, Bloom tends to fear what he most desires: woman as mother and fertile creator, that figure of matriarchal power he tacitly worships in Molly and concretizes in his hallucinated encounter with Bella/Bello, the Circean circus master.

When sex roles are tested on the stage of language, however, as they are in Circe, gender-linked scripts prove absurdly intransigent. Bloom's deepest and most repressed fears are given expressionistic form in dramatic fantasies of erotic compulsion and sexual loathing evinced in Bella Cohen's ten-shilling whorehouse. Power relations, culturally inscribed in Edwardian consciousness, remain surprisingly stable, as phallocentric authority passes from male to female in a sexual drama that articulates, but never criticizes, the psychosexual scripts that dominate 1904 Dublin. Even the new womanly man acting out the "feminine" vulnerability of his epicene nature gives voice to iterations of female helplessness, subservience, and sexual humiliation.

It is only within the heterogeneous representation of Bloom's masculine-feminine, active-passive character that gender identity becomes dynamic and reversible. As Shoshana Felman explains: "Masculinity is not a substance, nor is femininity its empty complement, a *heimlich* womb. . . . Femininity *inhabits* masculinity, inhabits it as otherness, as its own *disruption*. Femininity, in other words, is a pure difference, a signifier, and so is masculinity." In the expressionistic world of Circe, Joyce explores that specular icon of the feminine that inhabits the male imagination. Bella/Bello Cohen, as fetishistic embodiment of the terrifying phallic mother, serves as a screen image for Bloom's projected fantasy of his own somewhat willful and tyrannical spouse. He himself is transformed into a woman and then into a pig through a "substitutive signifying chain which subverts . . . the clear-cut polarity, the symmetrical dual opposition, of male and female, masculine and feminine."[3]

As Daniel Ferrer observes, "Bloom's masochistic phantasy paradoxically takes the form of a kind of breaking-in of Bella/Bello: the masculinization of the dominating woman is quite as important as the pseudo-feminization of the victim. The game is double-edged: on the one hand the woman is eliminated by making her adopt a masculine role; on the other hand, when the make-believe stops, she can be humiliated as a fitting punishment for the cruelty she has just displayed." Woman is portrayed in a dual, archetypal aspect: "now a figure of fun like a music-hall clown . . . now a terrifying bogey. . . .

The counterpart of the masculinization of the mother, and of Woman in general, is not the assumption by the males of a truly feminine position, but the adoption of a mere disguise."[4]

Precisely what is in question in the Circe episode is Leopold Bloom's manhood and the phallic signifier that affirms or denies his rightful status as male/father/husband in Joyce's modern epic. The chapter offers a plurality of signs confirming Bloom's androgynous aspect. He is first male, then female; and, finally, at the "Bip" of a trouser button, he regains his precarious manhood. The primordial sign of Bloom's maleness, his phallus, is first symbolically present, then absent in a game of sexual metamorphosis and phallic writing that entails both cross dressing and genital transformation. Bloom is symbolically castrated by Bello, the imperious semitic circus master who, as priestess of a nonsemitic ritual circumcision, "debags" her timid victim. In Circean fashion, she porcines the obsequious male who admits to being a secret "adorer of the adulterous rump" (U 432). A pagan devotee and worshipper of the voluptuous female body, Bloom admires those aspects of femininity that Molly scorns as impersonal features of animal passivity, the "same two lumps of lard" that fail to confirm personal attractiveness.

Bello, as Circean temptress and erotic priest of a ritual castration and Levitical holocaust, destroys the proof of Bloom's manhood, then reduces him to the signified status of Jewish scapegoat.[5] Bloom's political pretensions are incinerated when his imperial fantasies go up in smoke and he emerges "mute, shrunken, carbonised," a voiceless sacrifice to the futility of political aspiration. "Lynch him! Roast him! He's as bad as Parnell was" (U 492), screams the crowd. Bloom, wearing *"a seamless garment marked I.H.S. stands upright amid phoenix flames"* (U 406). Signs of phallocratic authority prove illusory and ephemeral, as the self-styled demagogue-cum-Christ rises, like a phoenix, from the ashes of ritual burning to reclaim a place in the protean text of Joyce's carnivalesque drama.

The icon of Bloom's manhood is present in the mode of absence as he acts out the sexual metamorphosis imposed by Bello. Paradoxically, when the androgynous signifiers of Bloom's epicene personality—his sympathy, gentleness, vulnerability, and solicitude—are reinscribed on an ostensibly female identity, they are significantly transformed in the context of cultural interpretation. His compassion and gentleness give way to masochistic subservience; his "womanly" sympathies are brutally victimized; and his talent for maternal nurturance is graphically mocked in fantasies of capitalistic parturition. Enacting deeply buried desires for couvade, Bloom declares: "I so want to be a mother," then *"bears eight male yellow and white children . . . handsome, with valuable metallic faces*" (U 403). Although the new womanly man is a recognizably androgynous hero, his most sympathetic qualities take on absurd dramatic resonance when the ground of gender changes from male to female. What is admirable in the emotionally bisexual male becomes a sign of feminine weakness and masochistic vulnerability on the part of a defenseless, quaking "womanly woman" exploited by the "manly man" of Victorian tradition. Bella/Bello has leapt from the pages of Frank Harris and nineteenth-century pornographic texts to perpetrate lascivious acts of phallocratic brutality on the feminized body of an epic hero hypostasized as female. Joyce seems to be suggesting that the cultural laws of gender are constant insofar as they are manifest in contemporary society. The seductive whoremistress acquires all the accoutrements of imperialistic power as soon as she dons male trousers and sprouts a moustache. As ringmaster and phallic mother, Bella/Bello demeans, humiliates, and tortures her obsequious victim. Bloom succumbs to ritual degradation and becomes the ham-holocaust to be slaughtered and skewered, then served up as "fat ham rashers" in a sumptuous, nonkosher cannibalistic feast.

At this point, tropes are reified, and signifiers of sex and gender prove absurdly interchangeable. The "swinish" behavior of lascivious males is mythically hypostasized, first in the Homeric narrative of Circe, the evil temptress, then in a Joycean expressionistic drama that forces Bloom dramatically to play out his most shameful libidinous drives. The text of Joyce's carnival reinforces those fetishistic signs attributed by the unconscious to the dreaded phallic mother, an imperious female who ostensibly offers nurturance but enjoys, at the same time, invidious power to demean, desex, and castrate the defenseless male. The phallic sign of masculine identity, once subverted or repressed, releases a flood of male fantasies depicted by the psyche in female guise. The traditional signs of gender-related power appear inexorable—indelibly inscribed on twentieth-century cultural consciousness, albeit in atavistic form.

In her male incarnation, Bella/Bello becomes aggressive, cruel, and violently sadistic, torturing Bloom to the point of absolute alterity. He is "Other," "*l'Autre*"—first trembling in shame before his masterful captor, then enslaved to her dictates, and finally derided as "maid of all work" in the chaotic Edwardian bordello of Joyce's fictive imagination. As soon as Bloom's gender changes from male to female, his ostensibly "heroic" qualities are deracinated from their masculine context and merge with cultural stereotypes of feminine passivity. The new womanly man is prostituted to the archaic image of powerless "womanly woman," as the "female" aspects of male desire erupt in comic mockery. Compassion degenerates into impotence, androgyny into transvestite humiliation. The dramatic text is uprooted from realistic mimesis, and expressionistic drama explodes in jubilant *écriture*. The narrative erupts in a riot of comic *jouissance,* and Circe fully enunciates the polyphonic novel's "underlying unconscious: sexuality and death. Out of the dialogue . . . the structural dyads of carnival appear: high and low, birth and agony, food and excrement, praise and curses, laughter and tears."[6] The symbolic poles of Joyce's dialogic imagination are those of Bakhtin's carnival: subject/object, male/female, death/birth, excrement/nurture, blood/milk.

In his/her female incarnation, Poldy/Paula manifests all the signs of feminine gender dictated by the ritual inscriptions of sex-role stereotypes. This new womanly man "mothers" the brothel prostitutes by ministering to their erotic demands and consenting to sadomasochistic practices. "O, it's hell itself!" (*U* 435) s/he screams, but nevertheless allows gestures of physical defilement to be perpetrated on his/her female flesh by Bello, Zoe, Florry, and the bordello cook, Mrs. Keogh. Bowing at the feel of Bello, Bloom acknowledges his/her authority as "Master! Mistress! Mantamer!" (*U* 439). Auctioned off to the highest bidder, he undergoes various animal metamorphoses as horse, cow, and chicken: "Fourteen hands high. Touch and examine shis points. Handle hrim. This downy skin, these soft muscles, this tender flesh. If I had only my gold piercer here! And quite easy to milk. Three newlaid gallons a day" (*U* 440). The defenseless Bloom is forced to give milk and lay eggs in agricultural postures that parody his/her mammary obsession and henpecked connubial role.

It is clear from role reversals in Circe that female gender confers parodic marginality. Woman seems to be destined by nature and culture to play the part of *l'Autre,* alienated "Other" in the specular projections of the male sexual imagination. When Bloom is auctioned by Bello in a satirical rendition of the bourgeois marriage market, his feminized genitalia become objects of commercial exchange. Female sexuality—as a gap, a "hole," a Freudian absence—absorbs a plethora of masculine fantasies that fill the "castrated" signature envisaged at the heart of female identity. Bello "*bares his arm and plunges it elbowdeep in Bloom's vulva*" (*U* 440) in mock imitation of sexual penetration and homosexual fisting. The victim's genitals are visibly mutilated as indelible signs of woman's enslavement to the vicissitudes of masculine desire. "That give you a hardon?" (*U* 440) Bello inquires. Then s/he orders: "Let them all come. . . . Bring all your powers of fascination to bear on them. Pander to their Gomorrahan vices" (*U* 441). Bello savagely violates the vaginal "hole" denied the "wholeness" of sexual integrity. Every feminine orifice, it seems, is for sale and on display; every hole can be purchased, raped, or penetrated for the purpose of phallic satisfaction. And a "good" woman, raped, knows, like the disgraced cuckold, what to do: "Die and be damned to you if you have any sense of decency or grace about you" (*U* 443). In this expressionistic battle of the sexes, the sexual power of the transmogrified phallic mother manifests itself as monstrous and obscene. As textual icon of matriarchal authority, the brutal circus master assumes the right to deform and colonize the vulnerable female body. The semiology of gender in Circe inveterately points to feminine alterity, masochism, and symbolic cultural enslavement.

As woman/Jew/victim, the hapless Poldy is reduced to a cipher of racial and sexual oppression signifying nothing to his/her sadistic persecutor. The male/female drama of courtship and conquest unfolds as an age-old atavistic tale of sexual aggression:

> Woman, undoing with sweet pudor her belt of rushrope, offers her all-moist yoni to man's lingam. Short time after man presents woman with pieces of jungle meat. Woman shows joy and covers herself with featherskins. Man loves her yoni fiercely with big lingam, the stiff one. . . . Then giddy woman will run about. Strong man grapses woman's wrist. Woman squeals, bites, spucks. Man, now fierce angry, strikes woman's fat yadgana. (*U* 423–24)

This primitive tableau of meat and mating, of giddy flirtation and animal friction, erupts, pornographically, in sexual violence. Brutality inhabits the underside of romantic courtship, and if the playmate of this behemoth lover dares to arouse his lust, she must suffer the consequences of anger and cupidity.

When Bloom is literally "womanized" by Bella/Bello, he loses his dignity along with the accoutrements of masculine pride. The repressed "feminine" tendencies of this heroic androgyne erupt in a ludic game of erotic madness. The matriarchal figure, usurping the "man's role" that Poldy is hesitant to play, becomes a nightmare fantasy of the stereotypical virago—a phallic mother invested with all the savage rights of patriarchal law. The semiology of gender remains unchanged, as various dramatis personae appear in transvestite or transsexual guises. Even the comedy of language cannot alter the embedded sex roles inscribed in cultural consciousness. Woman, granted phallic power, will persecute her mate with unbridled ferocity; and man, bereft of paternal authority, will sink into sexual debasement.

When sex roles are once again reversed, a feminized Bello plays the saccharine part of a spiritualized nymph who incarnates the Edwardian feminine ideal—an icon of grace and reverence, unsullied by either food or feces. "We immortals," proclaims the nymph, ". . . have not such a place and no hair there either. We are stonecold and pure. We eat electric light" (*U* 449). This self-glorified, asexual image is no more attractive than her opposite narrative number, Bello the sadistic ringmaster. Because sexual violence contaminates both ethereal and aggressive icons, the mirror image of Bloom's virginal seductress is an angry phallic mother intent on castration. The saintly sprite, offended by Bloom's erotic desires, grabs a poniard and threatens castration: she strikes at his loins, then "*flees from him unveiled, her plaster cast cracking, a cloud of stench escaping from the cracks*" (*U* 451). Recognizing the antagonistic Bello emerging from angelic disguise, Bloom recovers his phallic authority and insults the phallocrat before him: "Clean your nailless middle finger first, your bully's cold spunk is dripping from your cockscomb" (*U* 452).

Bloom would appear to be sexually triumphant; but the sign of his manhood is again obscured when he witnesses a dramatic enactment of his wife's recent seduction by that Dublin Don Giovanni, Blazes Boylan. Here the "coronado" (*cornuto*) husband wears a visible signature of his cuckoldry, the antlered "hatrack" of conjugal infamy. He serves as eager flunkey to Molly's suitor, whose penile equipment is ostentatiously on show:

> BOYLAN: . . . You can apply your eye to the keyhole and play with yourself while I just go through her a few times.
> BLOOM: Thank you, sir. I will, sir. May I bring two men chums to witness the deed and take a snapshot? . . . Vaseline, sir? Orangeflower . . . ? Lukewarm water . . . ?
>
> (*U* 462)

Bloom voyeuristically peeps at the scene of ritual conquest and yells locker-room "cheers" through the keyhole, urging his sexual surrogate to prodigious heights of erotic performance:

> BLOOM: (*his eyes wildly dilated, clasps himself*) Show! Hide! Show! Plough her! More! Shoot!
>
> (*U* 462)

The presence/absence of the ithyphallic member signifies both surrogate *jouissance* and conjugal humiliation. But the timorous Bloom, psychologically unmanned by the death of his infant son, Rudy, relives the tragedy of paternal loss in the mode of philandering farce. He mentally panders to the lascivious Boylan, the sex surrogate whose virility signifies the erotic potency absent from Bloom's own sexual relations with his wife. Voyeuristically participating in Molly's infidelity, Bloom reinterprets the signs of conjugal debasement from the privileged perspective of dramatic choreographer. Acting as technical "director" of this traumatic tableau, he symbolically sutures the wound of cuckoldry by dramatizing marital transgression in the mode of comic pantomime. The seriously embattled scenario of *Exiles* is here replayed as commedia dell'arte.

Like a latter-day Richard Rowan, Bloom revises the text of his wife's "betrayal" in a grotesque mental fantasy that resembles French farce, not to mention the voyeuristic fabulations of Victorian pornography. The impetus is a carnivalesque subversion of male prowess and patriarchal authority. By unconsciously colluding in this marital comedy, by obscuring the sign of his manhood and putting phallic powers under erasure, Bloom participates in the drama of cuckoldry not as traditional victim, but as author/actor/director of this "play" of infidelity. Through the dual role of playwright and spectator, he is able to reduce his sexual humiliation to an absurdly comic and specular image. He becomes both author and reader of his own domestic narrative, gaining artistic and psychoanalytic control over emotional trauma by re-creating the dread event in preposterous detail in the dream landscape of a charged erotic imagination. A whimsical projection of deeply embedded guilt, the scenario offers him the gratifications of aesthetic mastery and emotional catharsis. Bloom doffs the culturally inscribed role of irate cuckold to wear the costume of flunky; but, like a dramatist who plays the Fool in a script of his own making, he asserts authorial primacy as godlike "director" of the scene. As playwright and participant, Bloom witnesses his wife's infidelity from the standpoint of God, Shakespeare, and androgynous voyeur. He imitates that picaresque "playwright who wrote the folio of this world and wrote it badly, . . . the lord of things as they are," the "hangman god" who "is doubtless all in all of us, ostler and butcher, and would-be bawd and cuckold too but that in the economy of heaven, foretold by Hamlet, there are no more marriages, glorified man, an androgynous angel, being a wife unto himself" (*U* 175). Playing "bawd and cuckold" onstage, Bloom strives to become in his own imagination a self-sufficient and self-delighting "wife unto himself" in this Joycean drama of playful postcreation.

By the end of Circe, Bloom has been psychologically purged of both guilt and sexual humiliation and feels ready to reassert the inherently feminine dimensions of his androgynous personality. Pursuing the inebriate Stephen, he solicitously takes charge of the young man's affairs and rescues the nascent poet from the grasp of the Dublin watch, those policemen who point to the abuse of patriarchal power and the illegitimate law of the father. At the conclusion of this cathartic comedy, Stephen lies semiconscious and battered at the feet of his ersatz spiritual guardian. But the nature of the relationship between the two men is highly ambiguous. Is Bloom symbolically assuming the Homeric role of "adoptive father" to Stephen . . . as most critics have argued? Or is he subverting the name and law of the father in an act that replicates the movements of "maternal" nurturance and care?

Bloom's psychological reward at the end of Circe is a somewhat sentimentalized evocation of his lost son, the lamblike and erudite Etonian scholar "little Rudy" might have become. Although the text embodies that phallic sign of Bloom's procreative powers, the male child he once engendered, it is significant that the dead son can be resuscitated only in the dreamy, inchoate world of Bloom's nostalgic reveries. The specter evokes an aching fantasy of paternal desire and loss—a final, enigmatic figure of the disappointed father gazing out through the unseeing eyes of a phantasmal, ever-living son.

In Circe, Bloom's polymorphous perversity, his infantile desire for protection/punishment at the hands of a beneficent phallic mother, has imploded in rich, hallucinatory images. The expressionistic drama depicts Bloom's repressed terror and obsessive fascination with the imago of a "manly woman." In Joyce's carnival, sadomasochistic desire explodes in a perversely polymorphous dissemination of sexual signifiers that destroy the univocal, phallocentric drives of masculinity and explore the fantasy of gender reversal embedded in the psyche of a new womanly man. Circe delineates what Hélène Cixous calls "an abundant, maternal, pederastic femininity," a "phantasmatical mingling of men, of males, of messieurs, of monarchs, princes, orphans, flowers, mothers, breasts, . . . around a marvelous 'sun of energy' love, which bombards and disintegrates these ephemeral amorous singularities so that they may recompose themselves in other bodies for new passions."[7]

By the end of the episode, Joyce has restored the implicit bisexuality of the artist/God who manipulates the figures in this carnivalesque drama of uninhibited sexual desire. Bloom and Stephen are united, however, not in Homeric paternity, but through a common masculine fantasy that hinges on the dread of maternal abjection. In the Scylla and Charybdis episode, Stephen, as nascent artist, betrayed his lust for creative mastery by articulating a paradigm of aesthetic parthenogenesis. Like Shakespeare, he would become father and mother to fictitious dream-children and give birth to dramatic progeny in the secondary world of art.

In the final tableau of Circe, Bloom the bereft father is coupled with the memory of a lost son in the presence of an adoptive surrogate whom he guards and protects with tender solicitude. But in some sense, Bloom has, ironically, become more of a *mother* to Stephen than a substitute father.[8] He has symbolically supplanted the terrifying specter of May Dedalus, whose withered hand points a finger of guilt as the ghost-mother counsels repentance and refuses to utter the word of love "known to all men." Stephen apparently finds in Bloom that imaginary maternal surrogate he has been searching for throughout the novel—the absent object of filial desire that informs the young man's poetic theory and resides at the heart of his artistic aspirations. Bloom, now united with Stephen and the long-lost Rudy, successfully displaces his own sadomasochistic obsession by bonding with filial figures who defuse the perversities of guilt-laden fantasy and allow him freely to express the more "effeminate" dimensions of his polymorphous sexuality. It is precisely these "womanly" characteristics, in fact, that have attracted the inscrutable Molly Tweedy, the Oriental prize of Dublin, to Leopold Bloom, a suitor "so foreign from the others" (*U* 311).

NOTES

1. See Jane Gallop, *Feminism and Psychoanalysis* (London: Macmillan, 1982), 27. Gallop cites Michele Montrelay's Freudian critique that the "unbearably intense immediacy of the 'odor di femina' produces anxiety, a state totally threatening to the stability of the psychic economy . . . because it threatens to undo the achievements of repression and sublimation, threatens to return the subject to the powerlessness, intensity and anxiety of an immediate, unmediated connection with the body of the mother" (Ibid.)

2. As Wendy Steiner notes, "Bloom watches Gerty seated on the beach; Gerty watches Bloom watching her. . . . Each creates the other by creating the other's response, inducing him or her to display and to desire. Thus, Gerty, totally engrossed in her role as Bloom's voyeuristic object, imagines herself in the third person and composes Bloom's response to that objectified self. . . . Each character projects a fantasy of the other in the course of this subject-object interplay—Gerty through the fallen romance clichés of ladies' journals, Bloom through the primordial symbolism of femininity and the homely wisdom of his own experience. . . . Gerty and Bloom here demonstrate the problem of intersubjectivity through the model of vision common to painting and romance—the temporary appropriation of another solely by looking" (" 'There Was Meaning in His Look': The Meeting of Pictorial Models in Joyce's 'Nausicaa,' " *University of Hartford Studies in Literature* 16, nos. 2–3 [1984]: 98).

3. Shoshana Felman, "Rereading Femininity," *Yale French Studies*, no. 62: 42, 31. It is not surprising that Joyce chose a brothel as the setting for the Circe episode of *Ulysses,* since, as Michel Foucault points out, the brothel and the mental hospital were two places that escaped the nineteenth-century injunction to silence that surrounded sexual discourse beyond the boundaries of the nuclear family. "If it was truly necessary to make room for illegitimate sexualities, it was reasoned, let them take their infernal mischief elsewhere: to a place where they could be reintegrated, if not in the circuits of production, at least in those of profit. The brothel and the mental hospital would be those places of tolerance: the prostitute, the client, and the pimp, together with the psychiatrist and his hysteric—those 'other Victorians,' as Steven Marcus would say—seem to have surreptitiously transferred the pleasures that are unspoken into the order of things that are counted. Words and gestures, quietly authorized, could be exchanged there at the going rate. Only in those places would untrammeled sex have a right to (safely insularized) forms of reality, and only to clandestine, circumscribed, and coded types of discourse" (*The History of Sexuality,* trans. Robert Hurley [New York: Penguin, 1978], 4.)

4. Daniel Ferrer, "Circe, Regret and Regression," in *Post-Structuralist Joyce,* ed. Derek Attridge and Daniel Ferrer (Cambridge: Cambridge University Press, 1984), 136–37.

5. For an informative discussion of Bloom's role as Levitical holocaust, see Beryl Schlossman, "Love's Bitter Mystery: *Blumenlied,*" in *Joyce's Catholic Comedy of Language* (Madison: University of Wisconsin Press, 1985).

6. Julia Kristeva, *Desire in Language: A Semiotic Approach to Literature and Art* (New York: Columbia University Press, 1980), 78–79.

7. Hélène Cixous, "Sorties," in *New French Feminisms,* ed. Elaine Marks and Isabelle de Courtivron (New York: Schocken Books, 1981), 98.

8. In "A Clown's Inquest into Paternity," Jean-Michel Rabaté suggests that in "Lacanian terms, Stephen is the phallus for Bloom even more than for Molly, the phallus as a signifier of absence; this representation triggers the movement of ellipse back to the mother." For Stephen in Circe, "the dead mother is alive—the living father is dead" (*The Fictional Father,* ed. Robert Con Davis [Amherst: University of Massachusetts Press, 1981], 91, 93).

4
Comic Narration

ZACK BOWEN

During the last part of the seventies and the beginning of the next decade, the Joyce industry turned its most astute observers loose on the problems of the narrative patterns in *Ulysses*. Two books especially, Marilyn French's *The Book as World*[1] and Karen Lawrence's *The Odyssey of Style in "Ulysses"*,[2] were landmark studies offering new insights into structure and meaning through close scrutiny of Joyce's narrative techniques. Other critics such as Adams[3] and Groden[4] have divided the novel into two or three segments based not on plot or characters' acquisition of the knowledge traditionally gained in the novel form but on shifts in the narrative pattern from the "initial style" to a variety of narrative experiments in the later chapters. Joyce is said to have lost interest in writing in his "initial style," which itself includes a variety of narrative innovations, such as portmanteau words, a shifting of perspective to accommodate the focal character of the sequence, and stream of consciousness. He moved in the latter half of the book to a variety of parodies or imitations of styles found in the daily press, in pulp publications, in classical English literature, and in the speech of his contemporaries in turn-of-the-century Dublin.

What most critics who have studied the narrative techniques have failed to treat at any length, perhaps because it is so obvious, is that the change in narrative pattern also signals a change from serious, or at least realistic, to comic intent. The language becomes increasingly parodic. While funny things can be expressed in everyday language, as they are in the early chapters of *Ulysses,* that sort of comedy is associated with humor rather than wit. I define humor in the tradi-

---

Originally written for the 1987 James Joyce Conference in Milwaukee, this essay has since appeared in revised form as a chapter in Zack Bowen, *"Ulysses" as a Comic Novel* (Syracuse, N.Y.: Syracuse University Press, 1989). All quotations are taken from the 1961 Random House text of *Ulysses*.

tional sense, as the product of normal occurrences and foibles that we instinctively recognize as the universal, even if perhaps a bit bizarre, incongruities of human life. Wit, on the other hand, is the product of intellect, of language rather than action, of linguistic incongruities. As such, parody, satire, and its first cousin, the burlesque of style, are the intellectual equivalents of the humorous activities and speech of ordinary people.

In the later episodes of *Ulysses* the speech of institutionalized characters such as the barfly and citizen exists alongside the styles of depersonalized institutions such as the catechism, scientific methodology, and the popular women's magazine. In the earlier chapters such characters as the anglophilic Mr. Deasy represent character prototypes. However, their language is not the center of the narrative focus, but merely spoken or quoted material within the overarching narrative framework. The point is that as the focus shifts to more linguistic variation, the tone of the book becomes more playful and less seriously tragic or painful.

Readers, generally frustrated by the difficulties of comprehending the pyrotechnics of narrative shifts and having to negotiate a new agreement with regard to narrative expectation with every successive episode, attempt to make sense out of the apparently frivolous and search ever more intently for answers to the narrative riddle at the same time they search for ultimate answers to the book. If critics fail to find them, they are apt to call the lack of ultimates a profoundly existential answer in itself. But nowhere in the later episodes of *Ulysses* can I find any form of narrative parody or distortion that produces a serious or tragic reaction rather than a comic one. Comic storytellers, from Chanticleer's erudition to Lucky Jim's paper on "Merrie England," have traditionally attempted parodic narration. Add to that the Irish penchant for mimicry, and you have the portmanteau styles of the later *Ulysses*.

The narration of the Telemachia is controlled by Stephen Dedalus. As we have seen, his are the fictions, the motifs, the correspondences to which we devote ourselves in order to make traditional sense of the rest of the action of the novel. We look for father-son parallels, artist as subject-creator, guilt, and oedipal themes because Stephen has pointed us in those directions. But his is a literary, pattern-seeking mind full of himself and history. Of such narrative stuff is Oxen of the Sun made, only to degenerate into nearly unintelligible babble. Bloom, the allroundman, is a servant of the press, an advertising man who moves among typesetters and political institutions in a world consisting of popular periodicals and clichés. It is traditional to say that he represents a scientific outlook and Stephen a catechismal one.

I'd like to take the observation a step further and declare that all of the narrative patterns of the later episodes are projections essentially of their individual and collective imaginations and experiences.

I wish to deal in this essay with the comic aspects of a fiction-making literary mind that could transform windmills into giants, or, in Oxen of the Sun, a bee sting into the wound of a dragon's spear, and an open can of sardines into "a vat of silver that was moved by craft to open in the which lay strange fishes withouten heads" (*U* 387). If Stephen's actions are not inherently funny, then the literary and ecclesiastical sources of his projections, when used to describe realistic daily existence, can be. The joint sensibilities ultimately compose *Ulysses*. A Bloomean mentality provides the humor of the novel, and a Dedalean one, the wit.

I would like to return to a previous point: the "initial style" provides not only the narrative norm, which is constantly returned to in the latter half of the book, but also the fundamentals of the plot, allowing the reader with some difficulty to piece together a reasonably coherent action despite the narrative distortions inhibiting our easy understanding. All novels contain a covenant of narrative convention between reader and author, a covenant that determines how the novel is to be related and what will or will not be within the parameters of acceptability. For instance, fantasy and science fiction circumscribe their own realms within the first paragraphs. So, too, does the style of most genres announce certain conventions and limitations upon itself, such as the credibility of the narrator. We do not expect violations of these norms, though often they are violated by authorial intrusion and the like. To proceed through six chapters before encountering more than minor shifts in narrative tone, then to have the intruding headlines in Aeolus announce a change before subsequently returning to the initial style for three more episodes, is likely to produce in the reader of the last eight episodes a feeling of betrayal of the narrative convenant. Sirens is really the pivotal chapter in the narrative transformation. Though it contains the verbal innovations of the overture and an abundance of musically allied sounds, Sirens remains fundamentally within the initial style, and although Bloom's mind has already established a prevailing humor for the book, the comedy, that is, wit as well as humor, is not predominant until Cyclops. The only genuinely sustained comic wit in the first eleven episodes is the introduction of the headlines in Aeolus. This chapter foreshadows not only later narrative changes but also a change from a serious to a comic mode.

The narrative variations after Sirens produce increasingly funny reactions right through the comic masterpiece of Ithaca. As the reader's frustration level mounts, so do the comic distortions of reality, until the very covenant itself becomes a prime source of comedy. I had never realized just how funny Ithaca was until I heard a substantial portion of it read aloud at Franklin and Marshall College during a Joyce celebration. It took an actor with a highly developed sense of verbal incongruity to turn tedium to hilarity. Likewise, an older, practiced ear with a penchant for the antique is more likely to appreciate the comic exaggeration of cliché piled on cliché in Eumaeus, simply because of the scope of the exaggeration. Long out of currency, many of the expressions sound more like tired phrases. That is probably why so many Joyceans until fairly recently dismissed the style of the episode as "tired" rather than as spectacular verbal play.

To demonstrate that the narrative perspectives of the later chapters are consistent with one of the greatest comic novels in 380 years, I will discuss a few examples from Aeolus before outlining the comic narrative devices of the second half of *Ulysses*.

AEOLUS

The headlines' break with traditional narration in Aeolus simultaneously introduces a new comic effect. The distancing that results from the late addition of the headlines follows the traditional pattern of comic wit by purposely divorcing the reader from pity and fear, from being caught up in the action. Like the characters in Aeolus, the narrator, fascinated by his own rhetoric, disregards the human drama of Bloom's rejection in the editorial room.

The putative subject of the editorial room conversation, rhetoric and style divorced from meaning, provides the key to comically meaningful depiction of meaninglessness in the last half of *Ulysses*. The characters are talking about rhetoric for its own sake. They praise Taylor's speech, given in rebuttal to Fitzgibbon's earlier rhetorical trumpeting, not for what he said but for the language in which he said it. So the Ten Commandments, certainly a meaningful group of injunctions to many in Western civilization, become less important than the language in which they are couched. The examples the Aeolus characters offer are extended anecdotes designed to prove the rhetorical virtuosity of the speakers themselves. Each one seeks to outdo the rhetorical flourishes of the previous speaker, just as Taylor bested Fitzgibbon on the same ground and subject—language—that night at the College Historical Society. In Hades, the Phoenix Park murders assume less importance than the way Gallaher reported them; the story of the Taylor-Fitzgibbon debate tops that; and, finally, building on Taylor's theme of the Promised Land, Stephen returns the entourage to Dublin and the messianic motif with which the chapter began. But his rendition of a degraded Dublin and the Pisgah sight of two old midwives is designed less to provide a truthful vision than to impress its hearers with Stephen's clever rhetoric.

The whole business is not very funny until the headlines are added. Like the rhetoricians of Crawford's office, the narrator of the headlines seeks distance from the realities of the situation being reported. The headlines, like the modes of rhetoric in the popular press that they emulate, are the products of self-aggrandizement, beginning with the overly formal and proceeding through a staccato barrage to a largely unsuccessful exercise in satiric wit. What is funny about the headlines is not the intentional satire of their descriptions but the pretenses of the headline writer. The narrator of the headlines is just as deluded as everyone else, and in his effort to be increasingly impressive and funny, he becomes the butt of his own joke, even as he seeks to degrade Stephen's attempts at rhetorical self-aggrandizement. For example, the last headline,

> DIMINISHED DIGITS PROVE TOO TITIL-
> LATING FOR FRISKY FRUMPS, ANNE
> WIMBLES, FLO WANGLES—YET
> CAN YOU BLAME THEM?
>
> (U 150)

is almost as long as the text it introduces. The chapter depicts a collection of rhetorical Quixotes, which includes Stephen and the narrator of the headlines. In Aeolus Joyce announces an all-out comic war on the pretensions of narrative method.

SIRENS

In Sirens, the transitional chapter, the tone if not the shape of the narrative changes more radically and consistently than in previous chapters. The emphasis shifts to sound rather than meaning. Like music, the chapter is built around the production, physics, articulation, phonetics, and interpretation of sound. The announcement of a new narrative departure in the overture, which links sounds rather than meanings, is also an announcement that *Ulysses* will explore radically different narrative techniques. Musical, prosodic, and artistic preoccupations will be redefined for the novel genre, previously regarded as the literary form most resembling normal discourse.

Onomatopoeic devices abound in closer, more literal imitation of the nonlinguistic sounds of life: clocks, cash registers, boots scraping the floor, harness bells, door knockers, nose snufflings—all noises announcing only themselves and not linguistic signals of abstract meaning.

Music is the closest artistic parody of purely natural or manufactured sound without meaning. But songwriters were soon joined by lyricists, who domesticated musical sounds with words, as more and more contrivance and artificiality were built into the form to impose meaning upon it. What was once an experiment in emotion-producing mathematical vibrations became inundated with manufactured meaning. Songs became operas, and operas musical comedies as conceit was heaped upon conceit, until the art form became a parody of the lyrics, which themselves parodied life.

In an earlier book, I concentrated for the most part on the meaning of the lyrics in the 158 references to 47 songs in the episode. But the concept of lyrics itself constitutes a form of sirens' song because lyrics are a linguistic distortion of an abstract art, music, to invest it with literal meaning. However, Joyce added still another auditory dimension to the Sirens narrative, a series of verbalized nonverbal sounds, such as the tuning fork call:

> From the saloon a call came, long in dying. . . . A call again. That he now poised that it now throbbed. You hear? It throbbed, pure, purer, softly and softlier, its buzzing prongs. Longer in dying call; (*U* 264)

or Simon's playing the piano trill between the lines of "Goodbye, Sweetheart, Goodbye":

> A duodene of birdnotes chirruped bright treble answer under sensitive hands; (*U* 264)

or the oft-quoted sound of Simon's high B-flat at the end of "*M'appari*":

> It soared, a bird, it held its flight, a swift pure cry, soar silver orb it leaped serene, speeding, sustained, to come, don't spin it out too long long breath he breath long life, soaring high, high resplendent, aflame, crowned, high in the effulgence symbolistic, high, . . . of the high vast irradiation everywhere all soaring all around about the all, the endlessnessnessness. . . . (*U* 275–76)

Joyce's descriptions are as close to representing music tonality as any writer is likely to come. Its excess is comic but its effect, comic truth. The purely auditory functions of the episode are further underscored by a focus on two characters, the blind piano tuner and Pat, the deaf waiter, who manage to exist quite well because of or in spite of their adaptation to their auditory surroundings. Pat is oblivious to most of the noise and the singing, but the piano tuner not only hears better, as Bloom observes, but also is ultimately responsible for the one pure musical sound in the episode by leaving behind his perfect-pitch tuning fork. Thematically, the piano tuner's imperfection, cursing, links him to the croppy boy who "cursed three times since last Easter Day," and hence to Stephen, who, like croppy, failed to pray for his mother's rest. All thematic motifs in *Ulysses* are suspect, slightly off center, and of course there is little reason to associate the piano tuner with Stephen, except for Joyce's numerous hints of a possible musical connection through the motif. Certainly Bloom's helping the piano tuner cross the street parallels later events in the novel, but that is a far cry from the speculations to which Joyce has led us with his linguistic clues linking the tuner and Stephen with the innocent and maligned croppy boy. The perfect pitch emanating from the tuning fork is both a siren's song and an assertion that its message and motif are true. In Sirens, sound seems to be truth and meaning suspect.

The comic aspects of the Sirens' narrative style draw upon all of the above musical and sound devices, though it is not until the end of the episode that the variations on the narrative achieve a fully comic resolution rather than one that is merely pleasing or aesthetically appeasing. The conclusion of Sirens announces a new comic strategy in which four of the six remaining chapters will conclude on comic notes, leaving the reader laughing rather than merely reflective. In Sirens, as in these later chapters, the comic narrative conclusion draws parodic meaning from motifs developed during the episode.

The songs of the Sirens episode have largely been about love in the first half and war and patriotism in the latter part. The two themes coalesce in Robert Emmet's patriotic and sacrificial love for his country and in the love of Christ for man in his sacrifice on Calvary, both juxtaposed against the random sounds of glasses chinking, trams lurching, and Bloom's flatulence:

> Bloom viewed a gallant pictured hero in Lionel Marks's window. Robert Emmet's last words. Seven last words. Of Meyerbeer that is.
> —True men like you men.
> —Ay, ay, Ben.
> —Will lift your glass with us.
> They lifted.
> Tschink. Tschunk.

> Tip. An unseeing stripling stood in the door. He saw not bronze. He saw not gold. Nor Ben nor Bob nor Tom nor Si nor George nor tanks nor Richie nor Pat. Hee hee hee hee. He did not see.
> Seabloom, greaseabloom viewed last words. Softly. *When my country takes her place among.*
> Prrprr.
> Must be the bur.
> Fff. Oo. Rrpr.
> *Nations of the earth*. No-one behind. She's passed. *Then and not till then*. Tram. Kran, kran, kran. Good oppor. Coming. Krandlkrankran. I'm sure it's the burgund. Yes. One, two. *Let my epitaph be*. Karaaaaaaa. *Written. I have.*
> Pprrpffrrppfff.
> *Done.* (*U* 290–91)

In a juxtaposition of hearing and sight, Bloom sees Emmet's picture in the window and reads the hero's last words. When Bloom introduces Mercadante's oratorio in comparing Christ's last words with Emmet's, he adds a musical dimension to the setting. In doing so, he confuses Meyerbeer, a Jewish composer not especially enthralled by the crucifixion, with Mercadante. In any case, music is incongruous to either scene. The idea of Christ warbling the words from the cross is rescued from ludicrousness only if the last words are perceived as the convention of a great work of religious art; and Mercadante's oratorio is not generally regarded as such. It is closer to Monty Python's musical version of Christ's last words, "Always look on the bright side of life," which draws upon the incongruity of a musical crucifixion for its comic effect.

In the conclusion, Sirens' lyrics metamorphose into speech as the song "The Memory of the Dead" is seized upon by the drinkers as a meaningful way to put their patriotism to use as an excuse for another sip of booze. The sound of the clinking glasses, meaningless in itself, is followed by the tiptapping of the entering blind man's cane. The piano tuner, whose hearing, like Pat's sight, has to do double duty, is deprived of Bloom's ability to view the last words of Emmet, just as Pat earlier was deprived of the ability to be moved by the sound of the music from the bar. It is unclear whether when Bloom says "softly," he means softly reading the last words aloud or attempting to fart softly under cover of the passing tram; or whether he is devising some other combination of inspirational language and random noise. Whatever measure of control Bloom has over the volume of his fart, however, it is by no means certain that he is gifted enough to produce such generally accidental occurrences on cue to accompany memorable last utterances.

The fart is probably a happy comic coincidence, sound given meaning through juxtaposition with high sentence, as Joyce mocks excessive and often hypocritical interpretation with the randomness of noise made meaningful. With the word *Done* we see an end to the language of sentimental patriotism and religion and we begin in earnest a new comic attitude for the book and a new flippant source of virtuosity in literature.

CYCLOPS

In Cyclops Joyce takes both the high and low roads, contrasting the meanness of vision and speech of the barfly with the turgidity of an all-enumerating omniscient narrator, who piles list upon list, example upon example, so that excess of expression is matched by the excesses of enumeration. Clearly the duet of narrow-minded, drink-cadging pettiness and overabundant fulsomeness is an apt portrayal of the barroom historians who wax so eloquent in Barney Kiernan's. Mean and unflattering personal histories are mixed with nationalistic diatribes reflecting the spectrum of prejudices, both by the barfly and his drinking cronies. The comedy stems from the contrast between the dual narrative voices, each parodic in its own way. The barfly's observations are a collection of clichés, his descriptions, the hackneyed metaphors of contemporary Dublin pub life. There are so many that their use, excessive as it is, takes on its own comic exuberance. The other voice, as a number of critics have pointed out, is an ever-shifting montage of ceremonial excesses of figures of speech and verbal pretensions that rapidly abandon verisimilitude for linguistic ostentation. If the barfly's sneering descriptions are an intentional parody on that unworthy drinker's part, then the high tone of the hyperomniscient narrator is aggrandizement carried to its extreme. Critics such as Hartman have found fault here with the self-consciously derivative nature of Joyce's parody.[5] But excess is the key to comedy. Hartman's remarks might be appropriate to high, serious fiction, but they are the very source of the debunking quality unique to comedy.

The excesses of Joyce's parody infuse the chapter with a genuine comic energy that is only hinted at in earlier episodes. French is correct that the omniscient narration with all its aggrandizements neutralizes the meanness of the characters and the episode generally.[6] It purposely fails to enhance the importance of the action and instead tends to diminish it comically through comparison to the excesses of Ireland's sentimentalized view of itself. For the reader, jaded with historical rhetoric, it offers paradoxically a comically revitalized sense of the injustices done Ireland even while the advocates of Ireland's grandeur are being made to appear inherently foolish.

There is little need here to reiterate the varieties of parody that have been so systematically cataloged by others or to reiterate that most critics have realized how funny the chapter is. It is enough to say that Joyce, like the comic playwrights of the Dionysian festivals, violated the boundaries of literary decorum with the same exuberance as he rejected the high sentence of tragedy. The result was the sneering corrective of comic reality, again, not far removed from Cervantes. Lawrence points out that the degenerative quality of the hyperbolic lists of guests and ceremonies "is reminiscent of what happens when Don Quixote attempts to use the language of romance."[7]

Joyce again concludes the episode with a comic climactic paragraph blending the two narrative voices and undercutting any more solemn vision of Bloom espousing his doctrine of love to the crucifying rabble:

> When, lo, there came about them all a great brightness and they beheld the chariot wherein He stood ascend to heaven. And they beheld Him in the chariot, clothed upon in the glory of the brightness, having raiment as of the sun, fair as the moon and terrible that for awe they durst not look upon Him. And there came a voice out of heaven, calling: *Elijah! Elijah!* And he answered with a main cry: *Abba! Adonai!* And they beheld Him . . . ben Bloom Elijah, amid clouds of angels ascend to the glory of the brightness at an angle of fortyfive degrees over Donohoe's in Little Green Street like a shot off a shovel. (*U* 345)

The passage is a pastiche of the description of Christ's transfiguration (Matt. 17:1–5) and Elijah's appearance on the mountain. At least one of the words ben Bloom Elijah cries—"*Abba*"—is ascribed to Jesus in Gethsemane, and the capitalization of the masculine third person pronoun is a convention usually reserved for Christ or God. But according to Dowie's throwaway, it is Elijah who is coming, and Elijah also makes a glorious ascension into the firmament. Thus Bloom becomes a combination prophet resembling the dual narrators of the chapter, who have spelled out the evils and delusions of contemporary Dublin.

The last prepositional phrases of the paragraph, beginning with "at an angle," signal a return to the voice of the barfly, whose limited vision of heaven is circumscribed by Donohoe and Smyth, Grocers, Tea, Wine and Spirit Merchants. The last phrase brings us back to earth at the same time it reinforces the incongruity that is the basis of comedy.

NAUSICAA

Nausicaa again uses the device of contrasting narrators, the first a return to Joyce's *Dubliners'* habit of suiting the narration to the mind set of the character described. Like the narration of both barfly and omniscient narrator in the previous episode, the technique in Gerty's half of Nausicaa requires a corrective on the reader's part to extrapolate a more accurate view of the action from the report of an obviously flawed narrator, whose women's-magazine perspective has obviously dominated Gerty's thinking. Distortion here takes on a subtle turn, as Gerty uses the perspective to mask the truth of her own infirmities and to provide a romantic rationalization for her mundane existence. Since pitiable character foibles provide most of the humor, the comic aspect of the stylistic parody seems much more muted than in the previous episode. Statements like "Gerty was dressed simply but with the instinctive taste of a votary of Dame Fashion" (*U* 350) are easy enough to rectify in the reader's mind, and we can move easily between the fantasy of the literary influence and the meanness of her unaffected thought: "Gerty wished to goodness they would take their squalling baby home out of that and not get on her nerves no hour to be out and the little brats of twins" (*U* 357).

Her weakness matches the size of her distortions, which need no comic elaboration, and so wit becomes secondary to bathos. The worship of the Virgin associated with the Star of the Sea church provides only a light comic background for Gerty's romantic distortions.

The counterbalancing palliative is Bloom's stream of consciousness in the latter half of the chapter. Gerty's fantasies provide her relief from her mental distress, but Bloom's masturbation, with all its climactic fantasies of Molly and Blazes and all its voyeuristic fetishism, is an eminently practical solution to the problem of his arousal. As Bloom takes matters in hand so, too, does the narration, as it coincidentally switches from Gerty's fantasy to Bloom's practical perversion. The fulcrum in the shift from Gerty-dominated narration to a Bloom-dominated narrator is also the crux of Gerty's insecurity:

> She walked with a certain quiet dignity characteristic of her but with care and very slowly because Gerty MacDowell was . . .

> Tight boots? No. She's lame! O!
> Mr Bloom watched her as she limped away. (*U* 367)

Thus we instantly learn something that answers a number of problems regarding Gerty's feeling about her companions throughout the entire first half of the chapter, something that the narration, because of its approximation to Gerty's mind, has withheld or distorted beyond recognition. This is not the case with the narration that accompanies Bloom's direct stream of conscious thought. During the rest of Nausicaa, little narration intervenes between Bloom's mind and the reader. Any distortions of reality are not stylistic but purely cerebral on Bloom's part. What few third-person narrator lines there are introduce new stream-of-consciousness paragraphs with a description of Bloom's activity ("Mr Bloom with careful hand recomposed his wet shirt" [*U* 370]). These represent an objective factual return to the initial narrative style, the first of many times that the initial perspective will be reclaimed throughout the rest of the novel. Only in the brief concluding paragraph do we return to Gerty's narrator:

> Because it was a little canarybird bird that came out of its little house to tell the time that Gerty MacDowell noticed the time she was there because she was as quick as anything about a thing like that, was Gerty MacDowell, and she noticed at once that that foreign gentleman that was sitting on the rocks looking was
> *Cuckoo*
> *Cuckoo*
> *Cuckoo* (*U* 382)

The sound of the cuckoo blends the two perspectives into a possible statement about Bloom's mental condition, though critics have often seen it as a statement about his marital condition. If the sound is produced through Gerty's distorted narrative, then the craziness or cuckoldry implied may themselves be suspect. Nothing, after all, in Gerty's previous thoughts has indicated Bloom to be a cuckold or even a little dotty. The time is nine o'clock. The last three *cuckoos* complete the knell previously reported by the initial style narrator, so it is reasonable to assume that Gerty's speculation was broken off before we knew what her conclusion was. The situation at the end of the chapter mirrors that of the middle, when we fail to learn whatever she was going to conclude about herself in the transitional sentence that ended her segment of the episode. All of this is of course linked to Bloom's inconclusive statement etched in the sand. The uncertain conclusion will become a standard throughout the later episodes. The comedy of the conclusion of Nausicaa, like the end of Sirens, stems from the incongruity of combining random noise with supposedly meaningful speculation.

OXEN OF THE SUN

Karen Lawrence offers the following pronouncement on the comedy of language in Oxen:

> One can find comic incongruity in "Oxen" (the sardine tin is an example), but in general the emphatic exuberance and spontaneity of the early chapters are rare in "Oxen," which seems more craftsmanlike in its execution.[8]

Other critics, like Eliot, see Joyce as exposing "the futility of all English styles."[9] Indeed, most of the utility is produced by the reader's having to make repeated correctives to the distortions of successive narrators in order to ascertain the action taking place. Although the sources of the embryonic narratives are "literary" for the most part, and the quality of Joyce's mimetic accuracy has been attested to by numerous scholars, the linguistic genius of the parody and its prototypes obfuscates and distorts the action, leading to the conclusion that the more genius the writer exhibits, the more the writer biases the work. The reader is called upon to negotiate a new compensatory agreement with every shift of narrative parody, enabling the dragons' spears to be translated into bees' stingers, and so forth.

Of course, the assumption of all of this parody is essentially comic: literature, even in its attempt at fictive verisimilitude, has nothing to do with reality but exists as a fictional conceit, shaped by the writer ultimately to glorify its own perceptions. Writers of serious or somber fiction, no matter how distorted their vision of reality may be, do not seek the sort of list-making aggrandizements that undermine their own purpose. Accuracy dictated that Joyce's mimicry of serious styles in Oxen not violate the internal integrity of the parody with comic extravagances of the sort common to Cyclops. The humor of the episode is predominantly ironic, the product of our consciousness of the magnitude of distortion writers build into their narratives.

The speeches of the characters, who burlesque themselves as well as their literary prototypes, make most of the comedy of the episode, at least until the end, when, after the birth of the word, the embryonic specimens of literary artifact become the fully developed word-infants of contemporary dialect. After the utterance of the word, there is a brief literary multistylistic chorus before the coda of multifarious dialects, beginning "All off for a buster . . ." That the next five pages contain even greater distortions than the rest of the chapter is evidenced by the numbers of continuing panels and discussions they inspire at Joyce symposia.

But, ultimately, comic relief from the purgatory of narrative confusion is at hand with Dowie's salvational message:

> Come on, you winefizzling, ginsizzling booseguzzling existences! Come on, you dog-gone, bullnecked, beetlebrowed, hogjowled, peanutbrained, weaseleyed fourflushers, false alarms and excess baggage! Come on, you triple extract of infamy! Alexander J. Christ Dowie, that's yanked to glory most half this planet from 'Frisco Beach to Vladivostok. The Deity ain't no nickel dime bumshow. I put it to you that he's on the square and a corking fine business proposition. He's the grandest thing yet and don't you forget it. Shout salvation in king Jesus. You'll need to rise precious early, you sinner there, if you want to diddle the Almighty God. Pflaaaap! Not half. He's got a coughmixture with a punch in it for you, my friend, in his backpocket. Just you try it on. (*U* 428)

Dowie's speech really doesn't afford much in terms of improving the reader's spiritual well being, but it does indeed provide a coughmixture for linguistic inflamation, a concluding burst of understandable comic exuberance to reinforce the episode's murky comic prognostication that little meaning can ever come from either literature or language in general.

CIRCE

Circe is undeniably a funny episode. The projection of Bloom's aspirations for political and religious leadership, his fears and trials, his fetishism and masochism are all comically objectified during the chapter. However, there is little comedy inherent in the language of the narration. The incongruity lies in the scenes described, such as the construction of the new Bloomusalem construction, a *"colossal edifice, with crystal roof, built in the shape of a huge pork kidney, containing forty thousand rooms"* (*U* 484).

The language of the characters is often comic and exaggerated, but the only narrative voice in Circe consists of stage directions, which, while they may describe fantastic events and scenes, are delivered for the most part in neutral terms, unaffected by variations of parody or aggrandizement. Since the stylistic variations from complete objectivity are so few, it might be worthwhile to comment on the three most obvious:

> *Time's livid final flame leaps and, in the following darkness, ruin of all space, shattered glass and toppling masonry.* (U 583)

This quotation, lifted from Nestor, trivializes Stephen's idea of the significance of his breaking Bella's chandelier by loading the description with his earlier Blakean apocalyptic imagery. Here, at the climactic moment, the stage directions and the mind of a protagonist seem to coalesce. The result is ironic more than comic.

The second variation of the normally bland narrative style of the stage directions appears in

> *They blow ickylickysticky yumyum kisses.* (U 586)

Here the narrator may have merely chosen the most accurate and economical, albeit extralexical, adjectives to describe the whores' solicitations.

The final example is made genuinely comic by adding a musical distortion to the description:

> *The car jingles tooraloom round the corner of the tooraloom lane. Corny Kelleher again reassuralooms with his hand. Bloom with his hand assuralooms Corny Kelleher that he is reassuraloomtay. The tinkling hoofs and jingling harness grow fainter with their tooraloolooloolooloo lay.* (U 608)

It is simply not in Joyce's plan to be perfectly consistent in any narrative agreement. There has to be at least one violation.

There is lots of verbal comedy in Circe. However, the comedy of Circe stems primarily from the incongruity of the concocted visions, the memorably affected comic speeches of Dowie and Mulligan and the rest as projections of Bloom's insecurities, rationalizations, and ambitions, funny because they depict the low-comic, Sancho Panza attitude with which we can readily identify. But the resulting comedy and parody are not produced by the narrative method of the episode and are addressed elsewhere.

EUMAEUS

The confrontation with the unconscious in Circe is the structural climax of *Ulysses*. Despite its humor, the episode arouses an unease akin to the pity and fear of tragedy. In Eumaeus, Joyce allows us to recover from the shocks of the Walpurgisnacht with soothing Bloomian comic platitudes and clichés. Fitzharris's shelter, for all its sinister characters and overtones, has a comfortable lack of clarity about specifics and an overlay of clichés and lies, which plaster the open psychic wounds of the objectified subconscious. Language obscures, like a layer of oily bilge the sailor spreads on the troubled waters of meaning. The comforting message of the three turds, to be read like tarot cards on the floor, is that significance and horseshit are indistinguishable. Yet we persist in extracting meaning from the seeming convergence of completely disparate minds as they make their way to Eccles Street talking of "sirens, enemies of man's reason, mingled with a number of other topics of the same category, usurpers, historical cases of the kind" (*U* 665) to the tune of "The Lowbacked Car," which seems to point to some form of nonexistent unity but which refers merely to the cabman's vehicle.

The chapter is a brilliant exercise in comic obfuscation. It represents the mundane circumlocutions of the sort Bloom would have offered had he indeed written "My Experiences in a Cabman's Shelter." The episode is as much a stylistic projection of Bloom's mentality as Oxen of the Sun was Stephen's, and it has a comic vitality ignored by early critics whose mentalities resemble Stephen's more than Bloom's. The episode provides an encyclopedia of linguistic atrocities. Mixed metaphors, forced puns, excessive pretensions to elegance such as coyness and cuteness, and fastidious identification of pronoun antecedents are overlaid with commonplaces, forced idioms, and tired sayings. But a Nabokovian appreciation of linguistic pop art emerges from the excess of schlock, a comic celebration of the enormity of the violation of sensibility such narrative provides, until ironically we recognize the pretenses of our own violated standards. The narration of Eumaeus has the same comic acceptance of the world as Warhol's can of tomato soup.

The comic aspect of the narrative pretensions is intensified, as it was in Cyclops, by its proximity to an even lower form of literary ineptitude. The funniest sections of Eumaeus are those involving the description and dialogue of W. B. Murphy:

>—Chews coca all day long, the communicative tarpaulin added. Stomachs like breadgraters. Cuts off their diddies when they can't bear no more children. See them there stark ballock-naked eating a dead horse's liver raw.
>
>His postcard proved a centre of attraction for Messrs the greenhorns for several minutes, if not more.
>
>—Know how to keep them off? he inquired genially. Nobody volunteering a statement, he winked, saying:
>
>—Glass. That boggles 'em. Glass. (*U* 626)

Murphy's faith in the power of his own untutored word rivals the narrator's own pretensions. Like *Burke's* in Oxen or *Plastics* in *The Graduate,* the word *glass* takes on its own inane immortality, at the same time it gives an additional dimension to linguistic pretention.

Lawrence[10] and French[11] both assert that Bloom's mind as reflected in his earlier stream-of-consciousness thought passages is incapable of producing anything so egregiously bad as the narration of Eumaeus. Neither seems to understand that were Bloom to attempt to produce a literary artifact, he might well employ the linguistic atrocities everywhere present in Eumaeus. Composition teachers frequently encounter opinionated, slightly inferior students whose language becomes transformed by the literary aspect of their task into exactly the same sort of cliché-riddled pretentiousness as the narrator's in Eumaeus. Bloom had neither the skills nor the background to avoid it. At any rate, Joyce would have enjoyed the prospect of critics disagreeing over whether a fictional character would or would not have had the appropriate skills or lack of them to write a chapter Bloom never had an opportunity to write in the first place. Of such stuff is comedy made, to modify an old adage.

ITHACA

Ithaca comically anticipates our near desperation for answers to the traditional questions of fictive meaning, for relationships between characters and events, and for patterns that will establish some significant artistic intent in order to justify the reader's epic struggle for understanding. We are by this time as much the objects of our own pity and fear as are Stephen and Bloom. Despite Aristotle's notion that the purpose of poetry is to provide pleasure, we are still entranced by our hope for meaningful lessons. Sure that there are truths to be gained from *Ulysses,* we believe that if they have thus far eluded us, it somehow is our fault, and the epiphany will come in the concluding pages.

Here in Ithaca the narrator asks the questions and answers them in cold prose that, if not clear, is at least matter-of-fact. There are answers to questions we would never ask, as well as to ones we want desperately to know about. The relationship between Ithaca's questions and answers is disconcerting, however. To questions demanding speculative interpretation, we get answers of fact, and vice versa, and so many relationships abound that their irrelevancy to what we want to know produces the effect of making them seem like an infinity of microcosmic and macrocosmic meaningless possibilities, even though Joyce has only begun to explore the potential. Once relevancy is divorced from our expectation of meaningful literary patterns of truth, the possibilities are endless, as are the possibilities of the comic sensibility that insists that things, events, people can simply exist without necessarily being aspects of any moral pattern. The essence of tragedy lies in our fitting the characters' actions and circumstances into significant truths about human nature and in the didactic certitude that life, with all its comic accidents and irrelevancy to moral patterns, harbors some deeper, underlying significance. If there is any didacticism in comedy, it is that the tragic view itself is unrealistic.

What makes Ithaca so funny is the purposeful confusion of relevancy and irrelevancy; of human nature and the empirical world we live in; the ratification by the recital of facts seemingly randomly relevant and irrelevant; the whole framed in a catechistic system of questions and answers originally designed to prove with rhetorical certainty the existence of the unknowable. The incongruity of such an assortment, coupled with a plethora of unrelenting details, provides a modern Shandyism that is every bit as funny as it was two hundred years ago. Joyce's reflexive questioning of the process of the novel itself, begun here, entirely pervades his last and admittedly more comic work, *Finnegans Wake*.

If the narration of Oxen obfuscates our understanding of the events by imposing skewed literary interpretations upon their representation, then Ithaca obscures interpretation by providing us with a welter of undifferentiated facts. If literary meaning breeds chaos, so, too, does empirical observation. Joyce's parody of the literary and the empirical points of view provides us with a distancing comic lens that corrects the distortions of any sentiment and profundity we might try to impose on the novel.

The universal truths of serious literature are essentially presented in microcosmographic form. Oedipus's search for the truth about himself, Odysseus's homecoming, and Aeneas's political abandonment of Dido all give us insights into our own individual lives, but those insights are at least partially self-aggrandizing aspirations for significance in a world of random, mundane, and irrelevant detail. Ithaca itself tells us, if anything, that the mundane and trivial are okay, that they are the stuff human experience is really all about, and that insignificance is not shameful.

The comic aspect of irrelevancy is most obvious in Ithaca when Joyce plays with the irrelevancy of language itself. In the series of questions about the differences and similarities between Bloom and Stephen we find the following:

> Did he find four separating forces between his temporary guest and him?

Name, age, race, creed.

What anagrams had he made on his name in youth?
Leopold Bloom
Ellpodbomool
Molldopeloob.
Bollopedoom
Old Ollebo, M.P. (*U* 678)

The silliness of the anagrams foreshadows the narrator's later anagrammatic creations of Stoom and Blephen, in which critics (myself included) have seen much transformative significance. The anagrammatic answer above responds to an irrelevant follow-up question to a potentially meaningful answer. The sequence is comic, and the result, in realistic terms, inane. The anagrams sound like something meaningless that Bloom or any child might make, and the resulting names sound as comical as they are devoid of meaning.

The theme of verbal meaninglessness is picked up again several pages later in a discussion of Plumtree's Potted Meat, when we are admonished about false labeling:

The name on the label is Plumtree. A plumtree is a meatpot, registered trade mark. Beware of imitations. Peatmot. Trumplee. Montpat. Plamtroo. (*U* 684)

Could there actually be four spurious imitators hoping to capitalize on the integrity of the Plumtree label? More likely the comedy is both an exercise in verbal irrelevancy and an admonition not to be fooled by the game any more than the label.

The episode builds again to a comic crescendo in the description of Bloom's reactions to his cuckoldry, then gradually diminishes with an enumeration of Bloom's company in his *Arabian Nights* travels:

With?
Sinbad the Sailor and Tinbad the Tailor and Jinbad the Jailer and Whinbad the Whaler and Ninbad the Nailer and . . . (*U* 737)

Contrary to Lawrence's idea that the names on the list following Sinbad's are merely nonsensical variants produced by the semiconscous mind of Bloom as he drops off to sleep,[12] Tinbad, Jinbad, and Whinbad at least were actually characters in the long-running sequels to the Christmas pantomime. Popular themes were repeated yearly, and the 1892 edition of Sinbad proved so successful that it was revived again and again, sometimes under Sinbad's name and once under the name of Turko, a character in the Sinbad production. The formula remained constant, but the songs, skits, and jokes varied from year to year. Versions of the *Arabian Nights* are still current in contemporary pantomimes. What appears to be nonsense is not always irrelevant, any more than facts always have meaning.

Thus, a chapter that we had hoped would lead us to meaning gives us facts—sometimes false facts—but stubbornly refuses to yield up easy meaning. Since irrelevancy and frustration are hallmarks of comedy, Joyce's circumlocutions in Ithaca inspire a sort of comic abandonment if we will only relax and enjoy ourselves.

PENELOPE

The concluding episode returns to a largely unpunctuated variation of the initial style and to humor from the wit of linguistic fireworks and incongruity. It is funny in its own incongruous sentimentality, suggesting that there is a dominant order to events. But if Molly's eternal affirmation seems apparent, it is also the opening line to the chorus of a comic music-hall song, "YES BECAUSE HE NEVER DID A THING LIKE THAT BEFORE" (*U* 738),[13] and we are on thin critical ice if we apotheosize Molly's observations as the ultimate answers to the modern dilemma, the universe, or whatever questions we think the novel raised. The last soliloquy is a celebration, and the final comic language that of the critics who interpret a series of concluding affirmatives as negatives or extrapolate a positive or negative universe on the basis of whether Molly will cook breakfast in the morning. More problematical than even the culinary dilemma is whether any ultimate conclusions about life's meaning or patterns can ever be confidently extracted from *Ulysses*. For the moment, at least, I am much happier with the view that *Ulysses* is a magnificent comic celebration of life.

NOTES

1. Marilyn French, *The Book as World: James Joyce's "Ulysses"* (Cambridge: Harvard University Press, 1976).
2. Karen Lawrence, *The Odyssey of Style in "Ulysses"* (Princeton: Princeton University Press, 1981).
3. Robert Adams, *Surface and Symbol: The Consistency of James Joyce's "Ulysses"* (New York: Oxford University Press, 1962).
4. Michael Groden, *"Ulysses" in Progress* (Princeton: Princeton University Press, 1977).
5. Geoffrey Hartman, Letter, *PMLA* 92 (March 1977): 307–8.
6. French, *The Book as World*, 140.
7. Lawrence, *Odyssey of Style*, 106.

8. Lawrence, *Odyssey of Style,* 144.
9. Quoted in Virginia Woolf's *A Writer's Diary: Being Extracts from the Diary of Virginia Woolf,* ed. Leonard Woolf (New York: Harcourt, Brace, 1953), 39.
10. Lawrence, *Odyssey of Style,* 170.
11. French, *The Book as World,* 208–9.
12. Lawrence, *Odyssey of Style,* 197–98.
13. Ruth Bauerle recently made this important and as yet unpublished discovery.

5
Murphy, Shem, Morpheus, and Murphies
Eumaeus Meets the *Wake*

SUSAN BRIENZA

Murphy, the braggart sailor in the Eumaeus episode of *Ulysses* who entertains Stephen and Bloom and some drifters in a cabman's shelter, is an enigmatic figure. Curious Leopold Bloom scrutinizes and surmises about him constantly: Bloom is "Sherlockholmsing him up." But one must turn to *Finnegans Wake* for enough details to illuminate this cryptic character; and conversely, the meanings of *murphy* help to explain some passages in the *Wake*. Upon completing his detective work, the reader discovers that Murphy the sailor navigates Joyce into the waters of the *Wake* via various routes: direct connections between Murphy and Shem; indirect links between Morpheus, god of sleep, and Joyce's dreamy book of the dark; and the broadest parallels between Morpheus Murphy and all the Tim Finnegans, the (generalized) Irishmen in the *Wake*.

By examining Murphy as a precursor to Shem and by juxtaposing Eumaeus and chapter 7 of *Finnegans Wake,* we can better understand and appreciate the cleverness of the two characters and the two chapters, especially since Murphy has been deemed a minor, forgettable personage who spins irrelevant tales and since Eumaeus has suffered an undeserved reputation as the only boring episode in *Ulysses*. Instead, with my reading, it is now possible to see this chapter as anything *but* dull; in fact, besides being full of wit and humor, Eumaeus (finished in 1921) functions as one brilliant spark of Joyce's next novel (begun in March 1923). The character and name Murphy provide not just a prototype for Shem but also perhaps an initial inspiration for HCE (another sailor and exile) as protean figure and for the *Wake* as a collective dream of all Irishmen. Significantly, at least three respected Joyce scholars (Senn, Kenner, and Maddox) have written that the *Ulysses* chapter that stylistically most closely approximates and anticipates the *Wake* is Eumaeus.

The more one stares at Murphy, the more he resembles Shem. Both are full of contradictions and paradoxes and are notorious for their dishonesty: Murphy is an unreliable, nay, outrageous teller of tall tales—Bloom finds his postcard and his person bogus—while Shem, repeatedly false and counterfeit (called by his brother "you inconsistency"), was "cuttlefishing every lie unshrinkable about all the other people in the story" (173–74). Each drinks heavily: Murphy carries a flask of rum in each pocket while continuously distilling "potheen" in his stomach; and Shem, who is especially fond of Scotch whiskey, has developed a liver problem. Imbibing from the Tree of Knowledge of evil, Shem also drinks "diodying applejack squeezed from sour grapefruice" and "gulf[s] down mmmmuch too mmmmany gourds of it" (171). Both are exiles and Murphy, a low-life, knockabout mariner, could match Shem in low-down, low-minded nastiness. Most disturbing, each discusses or alludes to cannibalism, which for both Eumaeus and chapter 7 of the *Wake* becomes one metaphor for what Father Boyle would call the Eucharistic artistic process.[1] Similar to Bloom in his disgust with the despicable sailor, the narrator in chapter 7 of the *Wake* repeatedly turns to a question about Shem that sounds like a Johnny Carson routine: How low *is* he? "O the lowness of him was beneath all up to that suck to!" (171). Another answer is that he is low enough to wallow hoglike in the mud: he "was the worst . . . for pure mousefarm filth" (183).

Both characters are wretchedly dirty (Shem, in fact, becomes famous for his foul odor), and both are infested with lice. Scratching his chest hairs for lice provides Murphy with the pretext for opening his shirt, thereby showing his tattoo and telling fantastic tales about it. In the world of the *Wake* everyone acknowledges in Shem "the noxious pervert's perfect lowness" and would consider pitying and forgiving him only "if properly deloused" (175). Significantly, the presence of lice becomes—through Joycean punning—the preponderance of lies, or fictions, and both fabricators are so full of lice/lies that they become the main artist-figures in their respective chapters. Murphy stutters and Shem lisps and sometimes stutters, but no matter how they speak, neither of them tells the truth. With their speech defects, both are thereby associated with HCE and the Russian General, for whom words like *scutterer* and *utterer* contain the meaning of "a passer of counterfeit coins"[2] and, by extension, forgery—and, in Joyce's terms, writing.

These preliminary correspondences lead to a deeper association, since the two antiheroes share a larger identity—James Joyce himself as fiction-maker. Of course Shem's function as a surrogate for Joyce-as-artist has been recognized for decades now, but only lately has Murphy's alias been uncovered, through the work of James Maddox, John Gordon, Ralph Rader, and John Henry Raleigh—and more recently, myself.[3] Murphy is termed "a bit of a literary cove [fellow]" (1439), which relates him to Shem the Penman, and as just one bit of evidence for his relation to Joyce, consider that when the sailor is asked about his son he says that his offspring would be eighteen now, and of course *Ulysses* had grown to eighteen (chapters). Both men carry a stylo (Shem is "brandishing his bellbearing stylo")—the pen as weapon—which connects them back to Stephen Dedalus as "Kinch," the knife blade.

Other apparently surface associations go beyond the superficial. In the Shem chapter, one of the directions for Joyce's "new Irish stew" is the peeling of more "murphies." Irish potatoes are being served up, but if we peel away layers we see more links—sausage links to be exact, that is to say, piggyness. Joyce matches Murphy's slovenly appearance with an overwhelming amount of pig metaphors in chapter 7 of the *Wake*. Shem, with his dirt and stink ("he stank out of sight"), lives like a pig, originally dwelled on *Ph*i*g* Street, and is also one of the three little pigs—"his megageg chin (sowman's son)"—who may have his house of fiction blown down (181). A "supreme prig," Shem answers "to the name of Low Swine" and will tell you his "whole lifelong swrine story" (173). When he drinks he acts like a pig, "retching off to almost as low withswillers" (171), and his face is "a wan phwinshogue" (182). Interestingly, according to the *OED*, the phrase "Murphy's countenance" means a pig's face, hence the family resemblance between Shem and his precursor. In addition, both men are likened to other animals—Murphy to dogs and camels (the latter since both distill "potheen" in their stomachs), and Shem to a skunk, an ape, a fox, and a low dog, leading a "low cornaille [earlier 'canaille'] existence." John Gordon links Murphy to Willie Mulvey, Nora's old boyfriend, then through a chain of metempsychosis to a seawolf, wolf, wolfdog, dog, and eventually to Shem.[4] For my purposes Murphy is most significantly identified, through animal imagery and linguistic parallels, with the horse at the end of Eumaeus. For example, Murphy disturbs some sleeping horses by urinating, and later transmigrates into the roles of both sleepy driver and defecating horse; both the horse and Murphy are modified with the adjective *common* and the adverb *palpably* (a word occurring rarely in *Ulysses* and all four times in Eumaeus, a word further linked to Shem with the description *pulpably* used in chapter 7). This horse has a "proud feathering tail," suggesting the prideful birdman Icarus (an original Joycean artist figure, and echoed when Shem takes the "shipsteam *Pridewin*"), and he produces three "globes of turds" as he passes by Stephen and Bloom. The number three indicates the three sections of *Ulysses, globes* recalls Shakespeare's Globe Theatre (appropriate since Murphy has consumed Shakespeare as well as Homer before he gets transubstantiated into the horse), and turds imply (in both Freud's terms and Joyce's) creation.

In a similar set of associations, the artist Shem is referred to as "the shit" when there is a contract out on his life (179), and his work is condemned as "crap" (185). Icarus-like (compare again the "proud feathering tail" of the productive, cathartic Eumaeus horse), Shem "winged away . . . across the kathartic ocean and made synthetic ink and sensitive paper for [and from!] his own end out of his wit's waste" (185). Justius (Shaun) criticizes his brother for defecating and calling it writing: "even extruding your strabismal apologia, when legibly depressed, upon defenceless paper" (189). It is from this dirty, turdy substance that Shem concocts his "indelible ink," just as indelible as the ink of Murphy's tattoo:

> when the call comes, he shall produce nichthemerically from his unheavenly body a no uncertain quantity of obscene matter not protected by copriright in the United Stars of Ourania or bedeed and bedood and bedang and bedung to him, with this double dye, brought to blood heat, gallic acid on iron ore, through the bowels of his misery, flashly, faithly, nastily, appropriately, this Esuan Menschavik and the first till last alshemist wrote over every square inch of the only foolscap available, his own body. (185)

Here Joyce/Shem, combining the French ("gallic") and Irish ("iron") halves in his nature[5] and in the obscene matter of the *Wake* itself, produces dung that he alchemically transforms into ink, which he then uses to mark his own skin. Murphy also marks his skin with ink, the large tattoo on his chest done, we are specifically told, in *blue* ink. (James Maddox notes this inky link between Murphy and Shem but does not milk it for all it is worth.) The ink's color returns us to Shem, alias Jerry, who we learn at the beginning of the novel has a habit of "making encostive inkum out of the last of his lavings and writing a blue streak over his bourseday shirt" (127). Here again he unites the two strains of his literary heritage, since oakum (compare *inkum*) are fibers used to caulk seams in ships by an Irish method, and the Bourse in *bourseday* is a term for the French Stock Exchange.[6] Literally, Shem is writing with blue ink over his birthday suit. In this he resembles yet another artist, Antonio, who had tattooed his own portrait onto Murphy's chest.

In Shem's chapter, the house of fiction reeks of "stinksome inkenstink" (183); Shem is usually his "squidself" (186) and later the "inkerman" (433); and his house, in which he bottles himself up, is called the "Haunted Inkbottle." Murphy, alias Sinbad the Sailor at the end of Ithaca, presumably also resides in an ink house, since after the question, Where does Bloom, along with Sinbad the Sailor, rest? is asked, the answer supplied by Joyce is a large period at the chapter's end, that is, a spot of ink. All these ancient mariners and alter egos of Joyce are pure fabrications, fictions created out of the nothing—the human waste—of ink.

Questions about Shem's identity and ancestry lead to a statement that implies his evolution from Murphy the sailor with the tattoo inked on his chest: "the answer, to do all the *diddies* in one dedal, would sound: from pulling himself on his most flavoured *canal* the huge *chest*house of his elders (the *Popapreta*, and some *navico, navvies!*)" (179, my italics). My detailed interpretation of the full tattoo that the braggart Skipper so proudly but so cryptically displays joins Murphy the marksman inextricably to Shem the Penman, as I will show with the following short summary of a much longer article.[7] The tattoo consists of the numeral 16, a picture of an anchor, and a portrait of the tattoo artist, Antonio. The 16 is an obvious hint of self-reference to this very chapter 16, which also points to itself in many other ways, for example, in Bloom's fantasy that he will describe this night in a work entitled "My Experiences in a Cabman's Shelter." Pervasive self-recursiveness also links Eumaeus and the *Wake*. Of course every page of *Finnegans Wake* contains some self-reflexive comment about the novel's composition or about how to read its prose: for example, Shem's phrase "*f*ermented *w*ords" in chapter 7 echoes the initials of the book's title and recalls the drunken wake of Finnegan and his ballad; but in particular, Shem's chapter details exactly how he makes his ink and how he writes.

Similarly, the details of Murphy's tattoo embed hints of how *Ulysses* was written. *Anchor* was influenced by the Old French word *ancre,* which recalls (with Joycean bilingual punning) the modern French word *encre,* meaning ink. Ink is the very medium, the foundation, of any book, and indeed the anchor (as a visual pun) serves as the base, the anchor, for the rest of the picture: the numeral 16 and Antonio's face. Antonio is twice identified as Greek, and by explicating one of Murphy's barroom-style antics which Greek Joyce has in mind can be determined precisely.

When Murphy manipulates the skin on his chest he can make the face of Antonio appear to be either smiling or frowning. (Analogously, Shem is termed "the tragic jester" [171]). These two faces suggest the conventional Greek masks for comedy and tragedy, which then recall the literary mode that in a sense supersedes drama—the epic. Antonio emerges as none other than the father of the epic, Homer, and thus Murphy, teller of fictions with a tattoo of the Greek Antonio on his chest, appears as Jimmy Joyce wearing a Homer T-shirt as he constructs his own Odysseus legend. Antonio's yarns also align him with the father of oral epic poetry. Now the sailor says that poor Antonio was eaten by sharks, "ate by sharks after"; in my interpretation, Homer was "eaten," consumed and subsumed by Shakespeare. In episode 9, as Stephen is leaving with Buck and still thinking about his ingenious theory, he imagines how the afternoon will be recalled, musing "One day in the national library we had a discussion. Shaks. After." (463), thus planting the link between *sharks* and *Shaks*. So Homer (Antonio) was devoured by Shakespeare, who in turn was eaten by Joyce. The younger author must "shark up," subsume, be nourished by older writers, by the classical material that is of necessity absorbed by the artist, in this case (since Murphy is associated with the horse at the end of the chapter), digested in the horse's stomach until he has a "full crupper" and is ready to, as it were, produce. This explains why Murphy is chewing lustily throughout Eumaeus and also justifies the references to cannibalism in both chapters under examination.

Shem is a "cannibal Cain" (193) and, in chapter 7, which has a high density of references to Shakespeare as forebear and competitor (and here I am assimilating the work of Vincent Cheng),[8] he destroys the bard. Shem, too, consumes the ideas of others: "he kept on treasuring with condign satisfaction each and every *crumb* of trektalk, covetous of his neighbour's word" (172, my italics). As Harold Bloom shows us, the literary son must escape the anxiety of influence from his elders. In effect, the writer according to Joyce is a violent man who kills his predecessors, his literary fathers, and then cannibalizes their corpses and corpuses, just as some warriors of so-called primitive tribes eat with relish the inner organs of powerful opponents in order to ingest the owner's powers. Shem is accused by his brother of being a "sniffer of carrion, premature gravedigger" (189), and Murphy delights in telling stories about wild peoples consuming the raw livers of dead horses for shamanistic strength. Recall that the horse at the end of the chapter is, through many associations, an artist figure, ready to be cannibalized in a next generation; and horse imagery figures prominently in the letter/litter passage of the *Wake* (111). For Murphy, "his semantics" (*Wake* 173) are again similar to Shem's antics, meanings, and methods.

The vicious competitiveness of Murphy fully reveals itself when he reenacts a celebrated feat of one Simon Dedalus (not to be confused with Stephen's father—or is he?). Dedalus is a circus sharpshooter, a marksman. This word describes a man who hits marks but also, by extension, one who *makes* marks, that is, a writer like Shem and like the would-be artist Bloom, who carries a "marking pen." An artist's "mark" appears in signatures in a book, and a "shooting stick" names a tool used by compositors in letterpress printing to set up type,[9] so in the world of publishing a marksman could again be a writer—or a tattoo artist. This carnival marksman Dedalus can hit two eggs from a great distance and in quick succession, a trick Murphy dramatizes with gusto and shouts of "Pom!" for each shot. Then he sings "bloodthirstily":

> —*Buffalo Bill shoots to kill,*
> *Never missed nor he never will.*

(1363)

As Bill Shakespeare, Murphy sharks up—kills, eats—Homer; as Joyce, he shoots and devours both Homer and Shakespeare. Two eggs: but why eggs as the target?

In *Finnegans Wake* paper is "inked with penmark," and this play on *Denmark* again calls up Shakespeare via Hamlet (as Cheng has documented), thus echoing the father/son motif in the context of writing. Here the biggest egg and grandest daddy of them all is Humpty Dumpty HCE, sometimes alias Shakespeare, whom Shem seeks to kill and replace—in order to usurp the role of King Mark, alias Muster Mark, a marked man. Patrick McCarthy shows that "the fall of the egg represents the overthrow of the father by his sons,"[10] for instance in sentences like "Then old Humphydunphyville'll be blasted to bunboards by the youthful herald who would once you were" (375). Here the old egg is "blasted," and in chapter 7 HCE and other fathers are again destroyed by guns—with the sound "poh!" similar to Murphy's "Pom!"—as Shem is "abusing his deceased ancestors wherever the sods were and one moment tarabooming great blunderguns (poh!) about his farfamed fine Poppamore, Mr Humhum" (173). Significantly, also in Shem's major chapter of the *Wake* Joyce devotes half a page to egg metaphors for the father, who is eaten and thus destroyed by the artistic son: "brooled and cocked and potched in an athanor [an author], whites and yolks and yilks and whotes . . .

(his oewfs à la Madame Gabrielle de l'Eglise, his avgs à la Mistress B. de B. Meinfelde . . . his uoves, oves and uves à la Sulphate de Soude [in the style of sulfur of the south, i.e. deviled eggs] . . . his Frideggs à la Tricarême)" (184). And in the song printed just after the sports competition between All Saints and Belial, between Mick and Nick, we find the line "Broken Eggs will poursuive [follow] bitten Apples for where theirs is Will there's his Wall." Humpty falls off his wall, but Will Shakespeare (the literary father) is also the barrier to Shem's greatness.

In each scenario of the writer's process—that is, in my reading of Murphy and the standard reading of Shem—art is not exactly original but is either creatively forged or plagiarized or both. Shem the Penman becomes "a sham and a low sham," and his writing too is a shameful sham; his words are "too base for printink!" (187). The Joycean artist simultaneously imitates and destroys his models: Shem the Penman, "Maistre Sheames de la Plume [wrote] some most dreadful stuff in a murderous mirrorhand" (177). Shem's technique of writing by plagiarizing is echoed throughout chapter 7: "since it took him a month to steal a march he was hardset to mumorise more than a word a week . . . (trying to copy the stage Englesemen [Shakespeare and other dramatists] . . . Letter purfect!" (181). Murphy's stories seem to Bloom to be "genuine forgeries," and Murphy, as we have seen, is chewing tobacco throughout Eumaeus—chewing up and expectorating material of doubtful origin: his own, Antonio's, and others—just as Joyce is consuming and subsuming Homer and Shakespeare throughout *Ulysses*. Similarly, what did Shem do "but study with stolen fruit how cutely to copy all their various styles of signature so as one day to utter an epical forged cheque on the public" (181). Therefore Shem is as much of an imposter as Murphy, who was "probably" a sailor but who seems unsure of the location of Gibraltar. About Shem, "Who can say how many pseudostylic shamiana, how few or how many of the most venerated public impostures, how very many piously forged palimpsests slipped in the first place by this morbid process from his pelagiarist pen?" (181–82). We must remember, however, that "morbid" elements like shit, and unsavory activities like forgery become positive in Joyce's universe, since they are associated with God-like artistic creation.

Despite their lack of original genius, both artists are megalomaniacs (Shem is "growing meglomane of a loose past" [179]) who think they must be the best (writers) in the world. Like Murphy, alias Buffalo Bill, who always shoots to kill and never misses, Shem blasphemes about "Billy" Shakespeare. He boasts that there is "no other shaggspick, other Shakhisbeard" as good as he is, that he is unique and far superior to the earlier novelists Scott, Dickens, and Thackeray ("scoot, duckings and thuggery" [177]). As artistically competitive as Murphy (who lustily chews the remains of Homer and Shakespeare and "bloodthirstily" enacts shooting the eggs they represent), Shem feels face to face in a boxing match with all the kings of the London literary jungle, starting with the author of *Ivanhoe:* "fux to fux . . . with all the teashop lionses of Lumdrom hivanhoesed up gagainst him" (177–78).

In fact, Shem (with an ego as big as Joyce's) predicts that if he lives long enough, "he would wipe alley english spooker, multaphoniaksically spuking, off the face of the erse" (178). But along with his Murphy-like bravado, he displays a fear that some younger writer, some better marksman with a gunlike pen, will conquer him; thus Shem's avoidance of battles and his aversion to cameras in this chapter: he does not want to be "shot," "captured." The Joycean, unrecognized national hero and self-exile must beware: a "girl with her coldblood kodak shotted the as yet unremuneranded national apostate, who was cowardly gun and camera shy" (171). Like some people from nontechnological cultures, he does not want his *power* stolen, does not want others—photographically or otherwise—to copy *him*.

In discussing the details of his tattoo, Murphy the mariner answers "Ay, Ay" repeatedly. Yes, he is saying "yes," but the sailor's "ay" also sounds like the personal pronoun "I," which announces the author and recalls "double dye" (doubled *I*) in the passage describing Shem's ink. In addition, since the letter *J* was a variant form of *I* in Medieval Latin, a double *I* becomes double *J*, or James Joyce. At the end of the Shem chapter, along with many words that mean "yes" we have "jas jos," another James Joyce[11]—another "Ay, ay," "Yes, yes." Analogously, at the end of Eumaeus Stephen sings a song ("about the clear sea and the voices of sirens" [1447], that is, about the story of *Ulysses*) written by one Johannes Jeep, and these double *J* initials signal our author once more. Throughout the Shem chapter (even more densely than in the *Wake* as a whole—where for example names like Tommy Terracotta appear) alliteration overtly echoes the author's alliterative name, especially in the following description of dirty Shem and his dirty work: "in the *d*earby *d*arby *d*oubled for *f*alling *f*irst over the hurdles . . . the *j*ig*j*agged page, the *f*umbling *f*ingers, the *f*oxtrotting *f*leas, the *l*iabed *l*ice . . ." (180). Many of Shem's ancestors have alliterative first and last names, for example, Horrild Hairwire and an in-law to Mr Bbyrdwood de Trop Blogg. His jealous brother calls Shem "one black mass of jigs and jimjams," which again points to Jim Joyce as the sham.

Both Murphy and Shem also resemble their creator in their varied, paradoxical, and contradictory roles and masks and in their relishing of different poses. Murphy becomes satanic in his disguises and changing, slippery nature: within one page he can be "the impervious navigator," "that rough diamond," or "the old tarpaulin" (1399). Shem, as Nick, who also has the devil in him, is first described as a "hybrid" of impossible oppositions, a misshapen literalization of clichés: "the wrong shoulder higher than the right, all ears, an artificial tongue with a natural curl, not a foot to stand on" (169). As insubstantial as Conrad's "papier-mâché Mephistopheles," he is literally fabricated from the figurative phrases used to describe him. At one point he escapes not within an inch of his life, but "within an inch of its page," since his own body is the paper he writes on; he is a walking book. Through and through, he is a fake (as bogus as Murphy); in fact, he even prefers artificial, canned food to natural nutrients. That is how low *he* is: "his lowness creeped out first via foodstuffs" (170). In every realm, he sets artifice and Art above Nature, and image over reality.

Besides both characters as poseurs, imposters, in Eumaeus Stephen argues that language itself is suspect: "Sounds are impostures . . . like names. . . . What's in a name?" (1361). Murphy has many selves, many roles, and thus in yet another way prepares for the multiple selves, incarnations, and names of Shem (and the other major characters in *Finnegans Wake*). What's in a name like Murphy? It contains the Greek word for form or shape, *morphê*— and Murphy bears in his inked tattoo hints about the self-referential, epic form of *Ulysses*. Of course for Joyce's next epic, HCE represents the quintessential protean multiplicity of forms: Here Comes Everybody, in a thousand shapes. By the time of *Finnegans Wake*, the artist—whether God or Shakespeare—is a Morpheus figure, a shaper: Shaun says of the sinful Shem, "may the Shaper have mercery on him!" (184), and one of Shakespeare's many transmutations is "Great Shapesphere," one who shapes the sphere and reshapes/recreates the world in the Globe.

But there is another family name to be traced, in this case from a generic plaid. Shem, alias Jerry, is "a tarandtan plaidboy" (27), and Murphy has a beard of red and gray mixed, described as a "tartan" beard. The word *tartan* means *a design* of a plaid known by the *name* of the clan, and the name Murphy provides more foreshadowings of the *Wake*'s design, for *Murphy* is the colloquial version of Morpheus, god of sleep and of the forms imagined in sleep—dreams. *Finnegans Wake,* merging the elements of darkness, death, sleeping, dreaming, and waking, contains several direct plays on the word *morpheus,* as well as many indirect nuances. The word *morphyl* in the phrase "every morphyl man of us" is spelled to suggest "Morpheus" as well as "mortal"[12]—with the extra connotation of chlorophyl, perhaps to imply the green of a potato plant, for we must not forget the most mundane definition: that *murphies* is the slang term for potatoes. Justius (Shaun) reminds Shem that "the more Murphies you peel . . . the merrier fumes your new Irish stew" (190). The more layers of a morph, a linguistic form, you peel, the more you enliven the concoction of this Irish epic. In fact, Shem gives as one ingredient of his prose (perhaps borrowing from Murphy and other earlier fiction-makers): "quashed quotatoes" (183).

One clear example of this common meaning of *murphies* is a passage beginning with the root word *tuber*, the botanical term for a type of plant growing from a subterranean stem—for example, a potato: "tuberclerosies I reized spudfully from the murphyplantz Hawkinsonia and berriberries from the pletoras of the Irish shou" (541–42). In Joyce's Irish stew called *Finnegans Wake*, the potato (spudfully, with growths on the outside of an old potato sprouting roots for a new potato plant) provides an especially accurate metaphor for fall and resurrection, for life in death, since potatoes grow underground and must be dug up: they are buried and yet very much alive. As a *pomme de terre*, an apple of the earth, the human being begins tainted by the Fall (original sin), grows, dies (terminates), and is buried in the earth (a terrain) in a grave (a clay terrine?) in order to arise on the last day when called by Christ, so be it: "every morphyl man of us, pome by pome, falls back into this terrine: as it was let it be, says he" (80).

Besides the phrase "the more murphies you peel," the slang *murphy* occurs as food quite plainly in "Change the plates for the next course of murphies!" (625). Furthermore, another indication of change, an occurrence of the word *time*, is frequently in linguistic proximity to words with the root *morph-* or *murph-*: "that dead wash of Lough Murph and until such time pace" (272); "once after males, nonce at a time, with them Murphy's puffs she dursted with gnockmeggs." Potato puffs are dusted with nutmeg, but also the father—the egg—is knocked down by a new form, a new male, to create a renewed time or cycle, dust to dust. The father must "take his medicine," as it were, once after meals, or after males—sons who will usurp his role. Passages containing *morph-* or *murph-* often reveal a four-part structure, suggesting Vico's four cycles of history. Blending together time, four, and "the next course of murphies" produces Vico's cosmos and thus the next ricorso of murphies—or Irishmen, as we shall see later. In a passage that seems to be describing the cad (the bad young kid threatening HCE) as well as all mankind, four sets of

Murphy, Shem, Morpheus, and Murphies

four culminate in a bell that clangs the hour, perhaps the time for the next generation—change plates, pates, faces:

> . . . as to whether he was one of those lucky cocks for whom the audible-visible-gnosible-edible world existed. That he was only too cognitively conatively cogitabundantly sure of it because, living, loving, breathing and sleeping morphomelosophopancreates, as he most significantly did, whenever he thought he heard he saw he felt he made a bell clipperclipperclipperclipper. (88)

Later, a paragraph that conflates food and history, beginning "once in the dairy days of buy and buy," contains a "Sprig of Thyme and a dozen of the Murphybuds" (161), probably here representing the twelve months of the year as well, and the fact that one can sprout a new potato plant from an old potato.

All year round the morphy beings pancreate, create all, by "living, loving," since at least three examples in the *Wake* develop a co-occurrence of mo/urph words and transformations on the word or idea *fornicate*. In the sentence just above the famous geometry diagram of ALP's delta within circles (293), a man is described coming and going in the sexual act and is thereby growing more than just potatoes with his lapis/penis: "murphy come, murphy go, murphy plant, murphy grow, a maryamyyriameliamurphies, in the lazy eye of his lapis." Just below the diagram (depicting, among other things, the two sons seeing the primal scene), we learn that "'twas one of dozedeams," that is, it was one of those daydreams that is more than a wet dream, since it augments, ameliorates, the myriad murphy population; but also one of a dozen dreams, perhaps, and thus back to thyme/time and "a dozen of the Murphybuds," twelve hours in a day, for when the cad tells HCE that it's almost twelve he means that it's time for a new bud to sprout.

A dozen names appear in a long question that asks to know the constituents of the society, recalling the "dour dorty dompling" (the dear dirty Dublin that is also used as one of the headlines in Aeolus), following "Murphy's puffs":

> 7. Who are those component partners of our societate, the doorboy, the cleaner . . . nightly consternation, fortnightly *fornication*, monthly miserecordation and omniannual recreation, doyles when they deliberate but sullivans when they are swordsed . . . Matt and Jakes Mac Carty? (142, my italics)

The twelve names that end this question may stand for many series of a dozen, but just as significant are the generic "doyles" and "sullivans," in other words, the typical Irish. These names and especially the last one recall again Aeolus, specifically the scene where the editor advises Stephen that he can indeed eventually write an Irish epic: "Give them something with a bite in it. Put us all into it, damn its soul. Father Son and Holy Ghost and Jakes M'Carthy." The "answer" to riddle 7 above is "The Morphios!"—the Greek Irishmen, all the Murphys, exiled writers, returning sailors, HCEs, gods of changing form, buried and life-giving murphies—and perhaps language itself.

Of course Joyce/Shem/Murphy finally puts us all into *Finnegans Wake,* all the Mr. Doyles, the common potatoes, all mankind, and even the famous artists like Shakespeare. But then, Joyce as Morpheus, god of transmuting shapes and of dreams, can transform personalities, names, and English and Irish words, because sounds are as mutable as some of Murphy the sailor's stories:

> —Sounds are impostures, Stephen said after a pause of some little time, like names. Cicero, Podmore. Napoleon, Mr Goodbody. Jesus, Mr Doyle. Shakespeares were as common as Murphies. What's in a name? (1361)

As Joyce plays with transformations of murphies, the morphs shift ground; *morphological* comes to be used in descriptions of the body politic or a governing body, or layers of geological time, as well as alterations in the body of language, in words themselves: "these modes carrying us back to the superimposed claylayers of eocene and pleastoseen formation and the gradual morphological changes in our body politic" (165). Toward the end of the novel, the physical body, like the social body, retires; and here the "morphological circumformation" could refer to the circular structure of the dream itself: "a socially organic entity of a millenary military maritory monetary [four adjectives here] morphological circumformation in a more or less settled state of equonomic ecolube equalobe equilab equilibbrium. . . . Nomomorphemy for me!" (599). No more memory for me, or no more morphs, words for me—since the dreamer is asleep, a state of equilibrium between conscious and unconscious, in a world of visions.

Thus, in riverrun routes, we are back to Morpheus, god of sleep—yet another motif that links Eumaeus and the *Wake.* John Bishop discusses a recurrent minor character in the *Wake,* a night watchman on his "night duty" or in "nightwatch service" (576), perhaps on "the vigilance committee."[12] Twice in Eumaeus, once at the beginning of the chapter and once at the end, we meet a nightwatchman named Gumley "wrapped in the arms of Morpheus," that is, sleeping and dreaming; we pass the sentry box "where the municipal supernumerary, exGumley, was still . . . wrapped in the arms of Murphy" (1443). Another minor character in this chapter is a whore, a woman of the night, who suddenly appears around the edge of the *Evening Telegraph* newspaper. She is described as "not exactly all there," a signal of her demented state surely, but also referring to a semiconscious state. Through a set of associations from telegraph to wireless, to thought transference to hypnotism, John Gordon argues that this streetwalker is also a sleepwalker, and thus also "safe in the arms of Murphy."[13] At the end of the episode, the narrator says of the driver in the *sw*eeper car "you might as well call it in the *sl*eeper car" (italics mine).

Throughout chapter 16 of *Ulysses*, Murphy's eyes are "thick with sleep," and in this detail, added to all the other associations, the mariner embodies an influence and inspiration not just for Shem but also for the entire book of the night. At about the midpoint of the *Wake*, the two rivalrous twins, Shem and Shaun, wake up and begin to replay the rises and falls of civilization, warring and fighting in a chaotic state,[14] because they are still foggy-headed from sleep: "put your twofootlarge timpates in that dead wash of Lough Murph" (272). What all of these parallels add up to is that Murphy, far from being merely a minor character in a neglected chapter of *Ulysses*, in the forms and shapes within *morph* and the god of sleep, Morpheus, provides the first genesis (well before Molly's dreamy monologue) to the next book of changing languages and selves within the head of the sleeper. More specifically, through the notion of the liar as a sham, writing as plagiarism, and feces as creation, Murphy becomes one step toward—indeed the prototype for—Joyce's final portrait of the artist as himself, in Shem. In fact, Joyce directly identified himself with Morpheus in a letter to Harriet Weaver after she complained that sections of his *Work in Progress* were "incorrigibly absurd." He slyly answered, "There is no such absurd person as could replace me except the incorrigible god of sleep" (*Letters* 1:252). Morpheus Joyce transforms Murphy into Shem, and ushers in the world of sleep and dreams.

NOTES

1. Robert Boyle, S.J., "Miracle in Black Ink: A Glance at Joyce's Use of His Eucharistic Image," in *Ulysses: Fifty Years*, ed. Thomas F. Staley (Bloomington: Indiana University Press, 1974), 47–60.

2. Kimberly Devlin, "Self and Other in *Finnegans Wake:* A Framework for Analyzing Versions of Shem and Shaun," *James Joyce Quarterly* 21 (1983): 39–41.

3. John Gordon, "In the Arms of Murphy," in *James Joyce's Metamorphoses* (Totawa, N.J.: Barnes and Noble, 1981); James H. Maddox, Jr., *Joyce's "Ulysses" and the Assault upon Character* (New Brunswick, N.J.: Rutgers University Press, 1978), 157–61; Ralph Rader, "Exodus and Return: Joyce's *Ulysses* and the Fiction of the Actual," *University of Toronto Quarterly* 48 (Winter 1978–79): 149–71; and "The Logic of *Ulysses*; or, Why Molly Had to Live in Gibraltar," *Critical Inquiry* 10 (June 1984): 567–78; John Henry Raleigh, "On the Way Home to Ithaca: The Functions of the 'Eumaeus' Section in *Ulysses*," *Irish Renaissance Annual* 2 (1981): 13–114; my article, " 'Eumaeus's' Style and Murphy's Tattoo Means $2+2 \ldots = 16$: A New Reading of Chapter 16 of *Ulysses*," is under consideration. I assume that my audience is more familiar with *Ulysses* than with *Finnegans Wake*, so Eumaeus will be represented with fewer quotations than the Shem chapter. I refer to the Gabler edition of *Ulysses* throughout (New York: Garland, 1984).

4. Gordon, *Metamorphoses,* 152–53.

5. John Gordon, *"Finnegans Wake": A Plot Summary* (Syracuse, N.Y.: Syracuse University Press, 1986), 162.

6. Professor Michael Gillespie, in private communication, informed me of the Irish connection and reminded me of the French echo in this passage.

7. Brienza, " 'Eumaeus's' Style and Murphy's Tattoo," 45 pp.

8. See Vincent Cheng, *Shakespeare and Joyce: A Study of "Finnegans Wake"* (University Park, Pa., and London: Pennsylvania State University Press, 1984).

9. John Paul Riquelme, *Teller and Tale in Joyce's Fiction: Oscillating Perspectives* (Baltimore: Johns Hopkins University Press, 1983), 38, 43.

10. Patrick McCarthy, *The Riddles of "Finnegans Wake"* (London and Toronto: Associated University Presses, 1980), 22.

11. Riquelme, *Teller and Tale,* 10, 36.

12. John Bishop, *Joyce's Book of the Dark: "Finnegans Wake"* (Madison: University of Wisconsin Press, 1986), 80.

13. Gordon, *Metamorphoses,* 143–44.

14. Gordon, *A Plot Summary,* 186.

6
Apostrophes
Framing *Finnegans Wake*

SHARI BENSTOCK

> Apostrophe in the sense in which I will be using it involves the direct address of an absent, dead, or inanimate being by a first person speaker.... The absent, dead, or inanimate entity addressed is thereby made present, animate, and anthropomorphic. Apostrophe is a form of ventriloquism through which the speaker throws voice, life, and human form into the addressee, turning its silence into mute responsiveness.
> —Barbara Johnson, *A World of Difference*

> But apostrophe ... makes its point by troping not on the meaning of a word but on the circuit or situation of communication itself. If we posit for this essay, "Apostrophe," a communicative process linking an "authorial voice" and the readers of *The Pursuit of Signs,* an apostrophe seems to mark a deflection of the message: O mysterious apostrophe, teach us to understand your workings! Show us your varied talents here!
> —Jonathan Culler, *The Pursuit of Signs*

Finnegans Wake.[1] What only certain readers of Joyce's text hear as I say these words is the absence of the apostrophe marking the possessive position of *Finnegan* in relation to *wake*. Others not aware of Joyce's grammatical revisions will hear—rather predictably—the operation of the apostrophe that they cannot see: Finnegan's wake. Although the apostrophe cannot be enunciated, it makes itself heard. It also insists on being seen, precisely because it is not there: helpful editors and printers continue to reappropriate the apostrophe to its (appropriate) place. Indeed, the missing apostrophe of this title announces its presence and finds a life of its own against all efforts to eliminate its subversive workings in the *Wake*.

Apostrophe carries within its wake grammatical and rhetorical effects that structure (and subvert) the literary genre of apostrophe. In particular, apostrophe opens the question of *address*. Grammatically, the apostrophe appears to bind the subject to all that it possesses (Finnegan's wake), but the apostrophe itself opens this assumption to question. Apostrophe is the mark of exclusion, even as its formal claims are to inclusion. As a rhetorical figure, the apostrophe "deflects" its message. According to Quintilian, apostrophe is "a diversion of our words to address some person other than the judge," a strategy whereby words are empowered to the degree that they do not directly address either their subject or their presumed listener. Jonathan Culler comments that apostrophe creates embarrassment: "literary critics . . . turn aside from the apostrophes they encounter in poetry."[2] Critics make the same gesture that the apostrophe itself makes—a turning aside or away from the subject "to repress [the apostrophe] or rather to transform apostrophe into description. Whether this is because writing, in some innate hostility to voice, always seeks to deny or evade the vocative, it is a fact that one can read vast amounts of criticism without learning that poetry uses apostrophe repeatedly and intensely."[3]

The missing apostrophe of *Finnegans Wake* creates discomfort, if not outright embarrassment. It produces a sense of unease, a stepping outside comfortable boundaries of the known and predictable, because it demands a putting aside of familiar reading strategies. By its absence, the apostrophe calls attention to recognition of the *Wake* as a written text, whereas reading strategies make the *Wake* accessible by insisting on the "telling" qualities of its production, thus repressing its written forms.[4] The repression of apostrophe as rhetorical form is bound, almost inexpressibly, to the repression of apostrophe as grammatical marker in *Finnegans Wake*. Apostrophe gives itself to this double suppression through its structure, which both binds and unbinds the subject. The *Wake* traces these "apostrophic" effects through ruptures in traditional grammatical forms, rhetorical conventions, generic limits, and formal textual features.

THE FRAME-UP

Before turning to the effects of the missing apostrophe in *Finnegans Wake*, the framing devices that establish its rhetorical and generic boundaries must be accounted for. Of the four primary textual frames identified by commentators, the most obvious is the title ("Timm Finn again's weak" [93.35–36]), with its references to the mythic hero Finn MacCool, to the Irish song, "Finnegan's Wake," and to the notions of resurrection, awakening, and a wake for the dead. The complexity of allusive levels in this title reveals a compacted linguistic structure that fails to contain the multiplicity of its own meanings and whose borders are overrun by excesses of language. One might claim that such spillage *is* the *Wake,* whose very title is missing the rhetorical and grammatical guide—the apostrophe—that might direct (if not contain) its meanings. What might enclose this text in a specific subject—Finnegan's wake—refuses to take its logical place, to play the expected role, displaced by the linguistic matter (the letters of a name) it cannot possess. Printers who restore the apostrophe, thus fixing the title in an English grammatical structure (possessive pronoun attached to a noun subject), make Finnegan a specific and individual subject and give predominance to the Irish ballad, whose musical story can be told only after Finnegan's presumed death, the song recounting the manner of his death—by a fall from a ladder—as well as his "wake" and his "awakening." When the apostrophe is (properly) missing from the title, however, the song frame is broken. Although the lexical construct of the title retains the shadow of the song frame, the absent apostrophe pluralizes a grammatical structure that opens rather than encloses the text. This effect—of the frame cracked—is rendered by that slight omission of the apostrophe.[5]

The opening words of the *Wake* reveal yet another missing frame, a convention so expected that its absence shocks us into an attitude of not-reading: "riverrun, past Eve and Adam's." The first word of the text, uncapitalized, announces a text with no beginning, a story already embarked on its telling: *riverrun* is both noun and verb, carrying action without commencement. Readers step into a river that is already and has always been running. Because the final page of the *Wake* includes no end-stop, readers have speculated that the *the* of the last page links itself to the *riverrun* of the first page, thereby closing the text in a circle without beginning or ending, a linguistic equivalent to the alpha and omega symbols.[6] The inclusive sweep of "Eve and Adam's," the church past which the river runs, encompasses action, meaning, and myth in the coming together of our first parents; the church reveals their transgression as the first fall away from God's law and love, their tumbling echoed in Finnegan's topple from the ladder. This circularity further suggests that the *Wake* world is sealed, internalized, whole, perfect, and complete, that its movement is cyclic. Its narrative linearity—a function of the printed text itself—constantly turns back on itself to invert its own storytelling forms.

The cyclic structure of the *Wake* is created through a series of rings, or narrative movements, that turn back to question origins and openings. The reading process is a search for the first telling, an effort to "fill in" the missing center of the structure. Peering through the concentric rings of language that envelop the story, we search for a locus of meaning, an illumination of the internal void. Unwilling to accept the possibility that the ring contains "nothing," that the linguistic well may be a bottomless pit, we read more carefully, trying to account for every sentence, every word, and finally every *letter* of the *Wake* in order to complete the figure. Such readings always arrive at the same contradictory stance: there is at once both less and more story than any reading can accommodate. In lieu of one story, there are many; in place of essence there is excess; the *abyme* at the story's center reveals itself to be *supplément*. Rather than sealing the story in an overdetermined structure of narrative closure, a whole, the circular movement of the *Wake* denies the ability to make good on narrative claims: the circle frames a hole, a blank space.

Because there is no entrance as such to the *Wake*, we seem to stand both inside and outside its dimensions, invited to participate in the narrative account while excluded (by the presence of the text itself) from the narration: beginnings are arbitrary and multiple; origins are nonexistent but repeated. There are too many answers to the question, "Where does it begin?":

> the park's so dark by kindlelight. But look what you have in your handself! The movibles are scrawling in motions, marching, all of them ago, in pitpat and zingzang for every busy eerie whig's a bit of a torytale to tell. One's upon a thyme and two's behind their lettice leap and three's among the strubbely beds. (20.20–25)

One of the earliest efforts to untangle the central mystery of the Phoenix Park events, this narrative repeats the conventions of storytelling ("Once upon a time") that situate the story in a dim past ("It was of a night, late, long time agone"—[18.18–19]) whose distance in time and space accounts for the inability to know precisely the origin and development of the recounted events.

If, in total discouragement at the prospect of an ever-fading horizon, readers are heard to whisper, Why is the *Wake* structured like this? the answer echoes back: Because the *Wake* is a dream. In this frame of reading, the dreamer occupies the center of a linguistic field, dreaming versions of the primal scene ("in my serial dreams of faire women" [523.33]) as recounted in a "nat language" (83.12). The dream structure accounts for the cyclical enfolding and repetitive nature of the storytelling and, perhaps more importantly, serves to explain the compounded linguistic patterns of *Wake* language as distortions, or dream effects. This language does not communicate directly, but works—as dreams do—by transfers, ellipses, reversals, and rhetorical displacements. What is excluded and repressed returns in a motion of circularity and circumscription, its convoluted textuality reflecting the larger ring structure of the *Wake*.[7]

A text enclosed and supported by a dream poses questions of entrances and beginnings, of access to information, of lost origins and obscured sources. It also raises queries about the identity of the dreamer in whose kingdom the text situates itself. *Wake* commentators have suggested two possible conceptions of the dream: (1) it is one linguistic fabric, a single dream by one dreamer—Humphrey Chimpden Earwicker—who is himself the subject of the dream; or (2) there are various dreams, many dreamers, and dreams within dreams; HCE is only one of the dreamers, although he may be the central character in all of the dreams. The common denominator of both these frames is the thematic consistency of the dream(s): Phoenix Park is the setting for the compulsive and guilty rehearsal of an indiscretion to which the dreamer(s) may or may not have been party. Both dreamer and reader share the process of "dreaming" or dream "reading"; together we strive to decipher the events held within the dream's grammar. But reader and dreamer are never able fully to participate in the metaphor of textual making or to successfully reconstitute the dream/text. *Finnegans Wake* attests that the night is not only obscure, drenched in darkness, but is pocketed by holes or "blank memory" that result in pockmarked memories (or "m'm'ry" [460.20]). That is, dream frames and textual frames always eventually collapse into one another, erasing the boundary markers that would separate them, eliding recognizable differences. The boundary marker—the slight form of the apostrophe—is markedly and repeatedly absent or misplaced.

THE SCENE OF WRITING

Finnegans Wake—an apostrophe to love? Perhaps. The missing apostrophe of its title marks simultaneously the call to memory and the absence of recall, the vigilance and failure of censorship. It marks repression. That missing apostrophe also directs us toward a double path of elaboration and displacement: Who speaks? Who writes? We begin with a correspondence between doubles, of I and you, the desire of the One for the Other projected through the act of writing. Taking up the doubling effects of *Wake* writing, Jacques Derrida's *La Carte Postale* plots a doubled and divided history: "Our history [story] is also one of twin progeniture, a procession of Sosie / sosie, Atree / Thyeste, Shem / Shaun, S / p, p / p (penman, postman) and more and more I metempsychose myself of you."[8] Writing gives rise to this "metempsychosis" of One and Other that drives the pen and is heard in the practice of all writing, so that the writing of letters—the establishment of a correspondence—creates a set of doubles, doubled. The positions of One and Other hypothesized in the setting of pen to paper are realized in the persons of I and you and manifested in the sender and receiver of the message. Thus authority is problematized by the act that would seem to establish—or underwrite—authority.

In *Finnegans Wake* this condition is examined through twins and doubles (Shem and Shaun, the "sosie sesthers," Issy and her mirror image) and through the effort to establish the omnipotence of the Name of the Father, who is both HCE—the one whose initials are duplicated in nearly every sentence of the text—and Here Comes Everybody, proliferated into everyone and no one. The process of duplication and division that best illustrates this process is the building of the tower of Babel, the attempt to establish a particular language, to reduce all language to one language, to fix a form that cannot be reproduced, to replace the unspeakable (and unwritable) Name of the Father with the name of the son who, by building the tower, establishes a name for himself—he puts his own name in place of the father's. The result is confusion and conflict ("Is the Pen Mightier than the Sword?" [306.18–19]): father is divided against son; son is divided against brother; home—a man's castle—is now a battleground. The pattern of potential strife characterizes the father-son relationship of the Earwicker family, where the father's authority (his name) is threatened by his sons. The possible overthrow of the father is averted only by the division of the language between them. They do not speak the same language, often dividing between themselves (as in the Lessons chapter) the textual space on which their story is told.

This disputation of language between the sons is the father's punishment for their (presumed) attempts to appropriate and displace his name. It appears as the language of the *Wake,* the confusion of Babel. It is also both the interdiction of and demand for *translation.* Derrida writes: "YHWH at one and the same time demands and forbids, in his deconstructive gesture, that one hear (and understand) his proper name in the language; he mandates and erases the translation; he devotes himself to the impossible and necessary translation. And if this *double bind* is first that of YHWH, if each time there is a *double bind* in the structure of the proper name, if there is a 'God,' the name of God, well I let you follow, if you can follow, the writing of the proper name, that of the *penman* Shem, showing himself interminably consigned to the detours and wanderings of Shaun the *postman,* his brother."[9] Derrida poses the question of *Wake* writing in these terms: (1) the need to authorize a text by signing one's name to it; (2) the demand of the father (God, the Master, YHWH, HCE) that one hear and not hear, inscribe and hide, his name in the language, a demand that mandates and erases the translation of his name through the language, a demand that is the double bind of all writing; and (3) the division between language and that which it invokes, between God and "God"; the necessity of language disseminated and dispersed (language *laisser suivre*), made to move from sender to receiver (language *faire suivre*), to fall into the hands of—be translated by—a third party; of necessity, the letter Shem pens is posted through Shaun, following a trajectory that Shaun as carrier rather than Shem as writer determines.[10]

The *Wake* dream letters reveal certain barred correspondences between the unconscious and the conscious—that is, between the unconscious and the law, the double bind of censorship inherent in all writing. *Wake* letters are written to one censor (the ultimate censor, HCE) and conveyed through (the writing of) another censor (ALP), their progress from writer to reader effectively blocking off the crucial events of the dream (letter), allowing the censor no access to that which he has censored. Moreover, the action of censorship (and the transference of censorship) is the action of love: out of love for her husband, Anna Livia does not want (him) to know the ways in which he loves his daughter, who is ALP's own youthful mirror image. The *Wake* censors love letters. Love is imaged as silence, rendered textually through a series of blank spaces—omissions—that require the story to be taken up again at a later point. Silence itself is inscribed dozens of times in the *Wake,* but on four occasions it stops the storytelling, which must recommence again (14.6, 98.2, 334.31, 501.08). These "silences" are not, of course, ascribed to any voice that calls them into being; silence is marked by forms of inscription that must be read but cannot be heard: "(Silent.)"; "silence:"; ("Silents)"; "SILENCE."

Issy, sitting before her mirror image, wants to silence the knowing voice of the Other, the accusing voice heard in the letters and mirror dialogue. The voice mimics the (male) lover, instructing her twin in the art of seduction. Lips and labia are opened and silenced (momentarily) by the sexual act, which is also a form of murder: "Now open, pet, your lips, pepette, like I used my sweet parted lipsabuss with Dan Holohan of facetious memory taught me after the flannel dance" (147.29–31). Voice and vagina are conflated, and kisses promise more illicit pleasures. The Other's voice cajoles, seduces, instructs, and mocks, creating a repressed countertext of sexual-textual slips. The more illicit the love, the less amenable it is to conscious suppression: incestuous longing of father for daughter, daughter for father, sister for sister, slips through the language. At issue are sexual difference, the enforcement of family ties and paternal privilege, and the vulnerability of wives, sisters, and daughters under patriarchal law. In sleep, the norms and forms of family life are transgressed and reinstituted: "O, foetal sleep! Ah, fatal slip! the one loved, the other left, the bride of pride leased to the stranger" (563.10–11). The journey toward desire's truth leads down the memory lane ("mememormee!" [628.14]) of writing: here, the One and Other meet and miss each other.

APOSTROPHIZING M'M'RY

Oh, how it was duusk!

O! O! O! Par la pluie!
—Joyce, *Finnegans Wake*

In the *Wake*'s workings, the "foetal sleep" and "fatal slip" produce a blank space in the text, a gap in the storytelling signaled by the apostrophe. "Finn, again!" (628.14), Anna Livia calls in her final rush to the sea. Her apostrophe to Finn and the separation of "Finn" from "again," marked by the comma of address and directive, turn the narrative back on itself, to the "riverrun" of her wake and his waking. The dream displays its apostrophic effects in the desire to know ("Now tell me, tell me, tell me then!" [94.19]) and the need to forget ("And do you remember, Singabob, the badfather" [94.33]). The apostrophe marks a point of departure and return—a turning point—and its enclosing gesture (') at once binds and unbinds the grammatical construct. A form of address that calls out desire for the Other's voice, a desire for response, apostrophe problematizes narrative authority and subjectivity. Apostrophe is always a call to memory; even in its grammatical status it is an *image* of voice, a calling out and calling up. It *produces* subjectivity. It would make the blank spaces of m'm'ry *speak*. The apostrophes in *m'm'ry* mark the absence of two vowels, E and O, the alphabetic symbols of Earwicker and Anna Livia, the principal players of this drama, male and female, earth and water, dreamer and letter writer.

Of the five *Wake* family members, Anna Livia Plurabelle is most closely associated with apostrophe. She is called up through the O that opens chapter 8, called forth in the gossip of the washerwomen, who read the signs of her sin in the dirty laundry, just as her sons will later discern her private parts—"the O of woman" (270.25)—in their geometry lesson. Anna Livia's chapter is probably the best known of the *Wake,* the one most given to "reading aloud" (as Joyce's own reading attests), the one that argues most seductively for the necessity of "telling" the tale. This O is voice and vagina, sign of the orifices from which ALP's own voice emits the sounds of "babbling, bubbling, chattering to herself . . . the sloothering slide of her, giddy-gaddy, grannyma, gossipaceous Anna Livia" (194.1–4) and from which her "daughtersons" have emerged from the night into the light. The O marks the passageways of female sexuality, and Anna Livia's sexuality is the major topic of conversation in this chapter. The opening apostrophe to her mimes the O that becomes the geometric figure for the vaginal delta through which her children enter the world:

> O
> tell me all about
> Anna Livia! I want to hear all
> about Anna Livia. Well, you know Anna Livia? Yes, of course.
> (196.1–4)

The shapes are doubled in the geometric figure reproduced on page 293, so that the O figures female buttocks, the triangular shape held within the oblong O of the female genitalia. But these O's also reveal a reflected interiority, as if seen through a speculum or reflected inward and downward in the mirror of water, which produces a three-dimensional view. This mirroring effect is available only textually, however. When the invocation of Anna Livia is read aloud, nothing of its graphic spacing or design is communicated except, perhaps, as the double O's echo and mirror in sound what the *Wake* gives to sight. While the missing apostrophe of the title *Finnegans Wake* cannot be heard, its absence unmarked by the voice, the rhetorical status of apostrophe is a call to the voice, producing in the O an image of voice that the *Wake* reproduces textually.

The *Wake* is a reservoir of such effects, and I mention several here (from French) to suggest the ways in which the text of the *Wake* negotiates marked and unmarked languages. When voiced, the phrase O! O! O! *Par la pluie!* carries with it rain *(la pluie)* and umbrella *(par la pluie).* The *l* of *la* is lost, elided, so that rain and an article as protection *against* the rain *(parapluie)* are both heard. Brotfressor Prenderguest's fork ("a pronged instrument," like the various appearances of the capital *E* signifying Earwicker) does damage to a letter he is reading at the breakfast table, the marks of its destruction evident in diacritical markings: "ay ∧ fork, of à grave Brofèsor . . . acùtely profèšsionally *piquéd*" (124.9–10). Read aloud, the markings remain "unvoiced." Precisely because "grave" is missing the adverbial marking of its *accent grave*, it articulates—in speech—an English construction. To the eyes, however, the misplaced *accent grave* (over *a*) changes the article to a preposition (translated into English as "to"). The effect of the French marking troubles the eye but remains unheard by the ear.[11]

A repeated question in the *Wake*, "How do you do, todo, north Mister?" ("How do you do today, my fair/dark sir?"[95.5]) appears intoned through various languages. As rendered "in French," it reads, "Come on, fool porterfull, hosiered women blown monk sewer?" (16.4–5), and although the individual words of this phrase are English, syntactically they find their way to English only through a French *pronunciation*. The English form does not include a "fool," "hosiered women" or a "monk" (see versions at 225, 35, 54, 72, 93, 95, 160, 186, 332, 409, 466, and 511). The old French motto *Honi soit qui mal y pense* offers another example, rendered variously in the *Wake* as "Honeys wore camelia paints" (113.17) and "O'Neill saw Queen Molly's pants" (495.27–28). These recognizable English words appear in a syntactical structure that sounds as if it should make sense (but does not); they echo the French, which both does and does not hold their "meaning." No more does the empty O of the call to Anna Livia hold within it her meaning, the mystery of her origins, the dark secrets of her sexuality or her reproductive capabilities. The O is a call not only to the voice, to *her* voice, but it gives voice to the desire for enclosed meanings, originary powers, safe passage, and the dark sleep of the womb.

Anna Livia is known by the sound of her waters, "lilting on all the time" (627.21); her babbling, bubbling, and "sloothering slide" are calls of seduction to her "devious delts" (197.22). The homophonic connection Jonathan Culler hears in *eau* and O in Baudelaire's poem "Le Cygne" is heard in the call for Anna Livia as well: the washerwomen, working on the banks of the River Liffey, hear Anna Livia's story in the waters as she flows by. The artificiality associated with the O, the trope of apostrophe, allies itself with the waters of nature, a deflection—or a naturalizing—of poetic artifice. The scene along the bank of the Liffey is not, however, a moment of lyric poetry, although lyricism vies with gossip in a pattern of tonal reverses throughout the chapter. This is a scene of narration. It is a story told through the dialogue of two women whose raucous, low Dublin accents contrast with the undercurrents of the river running past. The traditional "I-Thou" relationship of apostrophe is deflected by the opening gesture of the chapter, "O tell me all about Anna Livia!" The O is undirected and undifferentiated; it comes from nowhere immediately identifiable; it is not provided a reading context; it fills a space and silence that do not render a single reading in this gesture. O is neither a call *from* Anna Livia nor *to* her; she is neither the summoner nor the summoned. Anna Livia appears neither through her presence nor through her voice in lieu of her presence. She appears in stories told by the two gossips, whose calls and answers repeat forms common to Issy and her mirror image. The O of address is a plea to narrative ("O tell me all about Anna Livia"), and narrative we know shares *nothing* with apostrophe. Narrative is all that apostrophe denies and resists.

The invocative O is a call, presumably, from one woman to another, from one who listens to one who will speak. This O is also a plea for the Other's voice, and for an-Other voice. The apostrophe proposes a dialogue, but it requires a third party. Barbara Johnson explains that in Baudelaire's poem "Moesta et Errabunda," the opening address ("Tell me, Agatha") "makes explicit the desire for the *other's* voice": "Tell me: *you* talk."[12] Anna Livia, however, is an-Other, an extra, to the dramatic dialogue of this chapter. The two women telling stories about her engage each other in an I-Thou relationship ("You'll die when you hear . . . Yes, I know, go on" [196.5–7]). Anna Livia—as woman, as river—negotiates a space between the two voices that echo and invite her. She does not "tell"; she is "told," albeit in a mimicry, or ventriloquizing, of her voice(s). The O of the chapter marks her absence, a death knell of invocation.

"O tell me all about Anna Livia!" both is and is not apostrophic. Like apostrophe, the call negotiates a terrain between nature and the anthropomorphic (the name "Anna Livia" includes both river and woman). The object of attention exists only in reference to the speaker, to the one who apostrophizes. The call partakes of both direct and indirect address, so that O suggests the absolute impossibility of its endeavor to anthropomorphize the river as woman *exactly* to the degree that it renders the fiction of its own success: we "hear" Anna Livia; (as if) she has responded to the call. Culler argues that apostrophe signals at once a radical interiority (the address is inward, not outward) and fragmentation (the voice, as subject, is disembodied, divided, echoing on the wind). The apostrophe is a net in which its "subjects" are caught in a "time present . . . a temporality of writing" that has nothing to do with the temporal movement of narrative.[13] If, as Paul de Man has suggested, apostrophes are about "an activity of the speaking subject," the speaking subject of the Anna Livia chapter appears to have been divided as a dialogue between I-Thou.[14] Anna Livia is not present in this dialogue in her voice, although the ventriloquist's trick of making us think she is there, speaking through the other(s), seems a quite successful sleight-of-sound maneuver. If she is here, she is recalled through her actions, in a narrative that traces her sexual indiscretions on her "drawers." She is a text, read in the dark as night falls, obscuring the signs of her sin and, as the water flows, washing away the evidence.[15]

The Anna Livia Plurabelle chapter is perhaps the best example of the ways in which *Wake* writing calls to the voice. Its writing vibrates in the tension between the written and spoken word. As the sign of possession, "Finnegan's Wake," the apostrophe is a marker that the reading voice effaces: it disappears. In its presence or absence on the page, this sign is either seen but not heard, or heard but not seen. In its genre, the apostrophe allies an undifferentiated, unmarked O of invocation with the specificity of address ("O wild West Wind," Shelley writes in arguably the most famous of all apostrophes). What is demanded is a voice, and one that is essential, univocal, that belongs to the "one and only." But Anna Livia does not respond in her *voice*, or if she does that voice is registered through the conversation of the two gossips, who mime not only her voice but the voices of all those others who populate their narrative world. Anna Livia's "other" voice, the sound of water, provides an almost unheard undercurrent to the rise and fall of call and answer across the Liffey waters. Apostrophe does not carry the mark of gender, nor does it delineate a genre. It remains suspended between the written and spoken, its genre in question. Apostrophe does not refer to an "essence" of woman that rests in her voice, which is the seductive mode that she has been culturally assigned, as the gaze or reading eye is said to belong to the masculine. Anna Livia is a tributary, a coming together of springs, streams, rivulets, and waterfalls that rush toward the "sloothering slide," the sluice, the delta, her O. The apostrophe, the grammatical marker of possession that is called up every time we call out to the genre of apostrophe, is the sign of this internal difference, of nonpossession, of nonbelonging. Either as river or woman, Anna Livia is not reducible to an essence, a voice: she speaks, if she speaks at all, difference(s).

Earwicker also speaks a form of difference, identifiable in his stutter. His affliction is made worse at guilty moments, and the textual doubling of letters *(ff, kk)* or syllables ("Shsh shake, co-comeraid!" [36.20]) mark an involuntary repetition of sounds. The stutter appears to oppose the O of pure voice (which would overcome absence, even death) by haltingly announcing itself through a failure to communicate. Earwicker's stutter signals his sin ("sinnfinners," with its doubled consonants [36.26]), as the stains on Anna Livia's drawers signify her failings, and both sets of signs mark a sexual fall. The hesitation of Earwicker's speech, however, is manifested through repetitions of words and letters that illustrate the stutter as textual spacing ("that sign of our ruru redemption" [36.25]). This space without meaning, a space of repeated efforts to begin the story (a story that is always a defense of innocence or a pleading against punishment) calls attention to itself as a gap, a loss, a sound without meaning, a formal fault. The stutter marks both absence (of meaning) and excess (of sound). It also calls attention to a difference within; it is a sign of the (failed) effort to make univocal and consistent the multiplicities and inconsistencies of behavior. The stutter makes Earwicker human, but it is more than the sign of presumed guilt or the mark of original sin: it also signifies self-delusion and attempted recompense. Textually, the stutter doubles and divides, opening a space of difference, from self and others, whose effects are apostrophic: "ff, flitmansfluh, and, kk, 't crept i' hedge whenas to many a softongue's pawkytalk mude unswer u sufter poghyogh" (37.20–22). It opens itself to Babel.

The stutter stands against the singularity, the monolinguism of the pure O; it stands against the desire for exact repetition ("woo-woo willing" [36.23–24]); it undoes the logic of the double, the call of One for the Other. The stutter is a *lapsus linguae,* the site of a linguistic falling away, already figured in the fall that opens the way to babelization and Anna Livia's babbling brook. Earwicker's stuttering is the space marked out by the apostrophe we expect to find in *Finnegans Wake,* a moment between waking and sleeping, a place that marks loss and absence. This space enunciates the hope of articulation, full speech, of recall and reappropriation. But the enunciation is delayed and deformed, signifying the failure of its own efforts to signify and producing an aphasic lapse, a "blank memory" or the blanks in *m'm'ry,* a hole. These are moments of significant nonsense, where meaning is denoted not through sense but by absence of sense, a hestitation, a doubling of the consonants and a dragging of the vowels that announce (in their failure to fully enounce) a meaning. They open the way to the "fibfib fabrications" of narrative (36.34).

Earwicker as the "Reverend . . . majesty" of the *Wake* letter is called forth in the magiscule of the letter E, his siglum, sign of his sovereignty and presumed eloquence. The E appears in four different positions: prostrate ɯ , where its erect middle term suggests Earwicker's phallic power ("there was a wall of course in erection" [6.9]), as well as his floundering, bab(b)eling babyishness ("on the flounder of his bulk like an overgrown babeling, let wee peep" [6.31–32]); prone m ("moved contrawatchwise" [119.18–19]), where its form suggests a pronged instrument, perhaps the kitchen fork Brotfresor Prenderguest uses to read the letter (124), or an enfeebled old man walking with a cane ("He who runes may rede it on all fours" [18.05]); finally, "standing full erect" (36.14), pointing in opposite directions, like directional signals or a weathervane ∃ (36.17) and E (51.19, 489.13).[16] Anna Livia is invoked with every appearance of the O, even when it appears in contexts where she is not present ("O.O. Os pipos mios es demasiada gruarso por O piccolo pocchino" [54.16–17]); Earwicker, too, is evoked by the appearance of his siglum, including occasions when the first word of a sentence begins with E: "E'erawhere in this whorl would ye hear sich a din again?" (6.24). Meaning attaches itself to the very movement of these letters, even when the letters are separated from any contextual bearing that would give rise to meaning. The sigla O and E are apostrophic effects that call up Anna Livia and Earwicker, and the separation of these letters from any word *proper* marks their textual exile as alphabetic symbols, cut off by the enclosing stroke of the apostrophe. They are left to float and fly; their effects are disseminated "E'erawhere in this whorl" (everywhere in this world), whirling on the wind, spiraling in the ear.

Symbol of power, the erect E is also a mark of vulnerability. Its power and prestige can be overturned (ɯ) and undermined; the E carries in its wake the possibility of failure and falling. Like the old man walking with a stick (m), it totters along, unsure of its footing, uneasily balanced. The E assumes power because of its placement (at the beginning of a proper name or at the head of a sentence), where a fall from pride of place can change the capital *E* to an *e*, a vowel open to exchange or even exclusion *(aver, ev'ry)*. The space of such a possibility is evident in "*E*erawhere," the apostrophe marking the moment of falling off or falling down. The *Wake* opens with such a fall; it retells the story of the fall of Finnegan (whose initial F already signals the possibility of misstep, an E that has lost its foot as Finn loses his footing): "He stottered from the latter. Damb! he was a dud. Dumb! Mastabatoom, mastabadtomm" (6.9–11). Tim tumbles from the top of the ladder to its foot. His "totter" is also his "stutter," the sound of falling and failing. It will lead to forgeries and fibs, themselves announced by Earwicker's inability to make the fricative *f*: "fibfib fabrications." Finn's fall crashes like thunder, like God's voice proclaiming his omnipotence in sounds that frighten the barbarians into civilization and fear of his name. The fall is announced by a series of thunderclaps, of stutters, that pronounce God's power and open the way to babelian challenges to that power: "bababadalgharaghta-kamminarronnkonnbronntonnerronntuonnthunntrovarrhounawn-skawntoohoohoordenenthurnuk!" (3.15–17). The stutter and stammer have a certain onomatopoeic power, and the fall that brings death to the world is marked in man's speech by the traces of babel, of babbeling, a frightening sort of nonmeaning, a space marked out in the text by the place of Earwicker's fallen *e*: "where he last fellonem" (7.31).

The power of the capital *E* that asserts Earwicker's authority as head of household and state is undermined by the diminutive *e*, especially as the *eh* sound slurs vowels and signification falls away. Unlike the pure *O* of invocation, the *eh/er* is both a defense against the invocative and an impediment to it. A sign of the stutter, the *eh* transposes into textual space and script what can take place only in time and sound ("ah eh oh" [278.10]).The effort to communicate carries with it guttural efforts at enunciation (also the grunts and groans of defecation), sound inf(l)ected with failure, as HCE himself fears the possibility of disease: "he shat the Ructions gunorrhal" (192.2–3, where *shat*, *shout*, and *shot* are associated with guns, oral ruckus, and gonorrheal erections). The small *e* is also the mark of the forger, and the *eh* sound it produces is one of fear or guilt. In references to Richard Pigott, the *Wake* parallels Earwicker's fears of his actions in Phoenix Park with Pigott's attempt to link Charles Stewart Parnell to the Invincibles and the May 1882 Phoenix Park murders of two British government representatives. Pigott was exposed in his effort to frame Parnell when, during a government trial, he spelled *hesitancy* with an *e* rather than an *a*. Parnell's exoneration rested, as did his supposed crime, on the existence of letters, an incriminating correspondence, and, finally, on two (almost interchangeable) letters of the alphabet. Earwicker's feared doom and damnation is spelled in his hesitancy, his stutter, in the titters of local gossips who are tattletales: "But the spoil of hesitants, the spell of hesitency. His atake is it ashe, tittery taw tatterytail, hasitense humponadimply, heyheyheyhey a winceywencky" (97.25–26).

The various repetitions of *hesitencies* in the *Wake* mark Earwicker as a fake, one whose power and authority rest on forged credentials.[17] Earwicker also assumes that a written document (a legal brief, newspaper, or poison pen letter) is circulating among the citizenry, accusing him of unlawful deeds in Phoenix Park. He desires to exchange this document for another, one that will exonerate him. His dream of vindication is marred, however, by the suspicion that forgery may be the very crime with which he is being charged. Thus the intrusive *e* is a mark of evidence that points simultaneously in two directions, toward Earwicker's feared guilt and his hoped-for exoneration. Moreover, this sign of his sin—the exchange of the *e* for the *a*—cannot be heard: *hesitancy, hesitency*. There is a certain hesitancy, an effort that sounds its own labors, in raising the E to its upright and capital position: "his hes hecitency Hec" (119.18), where the capital *H* (which can be made by gathering together the four positions of the capital *E* in a scriptural gesture ∃⊦E) to signify Duke Humphrey ("Him," "Hom," "Hum," "Hurrah" [6.29–33]). He is known by his hesitation, the almost silent sound of breath struggling toward speech, marked by his stutter, the slur, the "trace of his erstwhile burr" (34.36), which is "swift to mate errthors" (36.35).

The *e* and *a* are also inserted in transliterations of the Tetragrammaton, a symbol or substitute for the ineffable name of God: YHWH, which we hear as "YAHWEH" in Hebrew and JHVH, "Jehovah" in the Latin transliteration. But these sigla stand in place of a name, their configuration spacing—and effacing—the name not to be "uttered," which is not to be heard, which is unspeakable. In a *Wake* passage that presumably refers to Shakespeare's habit of writing *m* with four "legs" (which has counterparts in the "fourleaved shamrock" and the "quadrifoil jab" of the Professors' fork, whose marks write a supratext on the morning mail), we also find remarks on the written and spoken forms of YHWH:

> and the fatal droopadwindle slope of the blamed scrawl, a sure sign of imperfectible moral blindness; the toomuchness, the fartoomanyness of all those fourlegged ems: and why spell dear god with a big thick dhee (why, O why, O why?). (122.34–123.2)

The double occurrence of the Hebrew cheth makes a "fourlegged em"; in its singular occurrence the cheth looks like the Greek pi (π), which figures in Shem's geometric drawing of the mother's vagina, where pi is doubled to make two p's, signs of the brothers, who are at war with each other, playing out at one level the Pigott-Parnell controversy. The immediate question, however, is the writing of God's name: "why spell Dear God with a big thick D?" where the "Dear" is a mark of salutation or address, repeated in Anna Livia's missive: "Dear. And we go on to Dirtdump. Reverend. May we add majesty?" (615.12–13). In this version, "majesty" is an afterthought, and although it denotes the majestic, it is not written with a magiscule. The "thick dhee," with its intrusive (but almost unheard) *h* signals the fatal flaw in the majestic scheme; the *h*, which is immediately followed by *e* and *y (why)* is the slur or burr of Earwickean speech. This flawed majestic pattern is summoned by the *O*—"why, O why, O why?"—a call, a prayer to God, to YHWH. Here the *O* of pure sound substitutes for the *A* of Anna Livia, who figures as pure sound in the text. Why spell Dear God with a big thick D(h)ee? Why, O why, O why? Why not spell it as YHWH? Why *spell* YHWH at all?

Apostrophes

This call to God is also a call to script and to scripture. The *e* and *a* exist in sound, in the *ear,* in h*ea*ring. Their existence is, moreover, accidental, since it was the Greek borrowing of the Semitic alphabet, which included signs only for consonants, that gave us signs for vowels, through a Greek economy that used extra Phoenician letter-symbols not needed for consonants to represent vowels. The *e* and *a* presumably existed in sound in this configuration—YAHWEH—before they existed in script, and in script they are the signs of translation and transgression, a space of both absence and excess.[18] These two marks—*e* and *a*—graphically denote the law of apostrophe. In their presence—in YAHWEH—they are excessive; they don't "belong"; they are arbitrary and interchangeable; they signal a historical accident. In their absence—YHWH—they are still "heard," so that their erasure from writing is an erasure of the law that already prohibits their very existence. The law of YHWH is a law of prohibition (God's first commandment: "The Lord thy God is one God. Thou shalt have no other gods before Him"). YHWH prohibits utterance of the Name, which *e* and *a* allow by making the anagram a "name": YAHWEH. The *e* and *a* also mark the impossibility of a *language* or *a* language: they have been seconded into service by a later historical movement, a moment of economy where one sign fills in for another. They give breath and sound to what is extraneous and unnecessary; this very sounding makes a call to the necessary: YAHWEH. Like the apostrophe, *e* and *a* share in what Derrida calls "the event of the mark": "not only what is said in it but its very saying and writing, the mark of its law and the law of its mark."[19] The *e* and *a,* whether present or absent, mark a certain genre.

To insert these (almost mute) sounds in the spaces between the letters of Y—HW—H is to disobey the law of YHWH, to make the name *effable,* to call out sound and difference already inhabiting the name, to transl(iter)ate, to transgress. This law captures Earwicker, who hears of his indiscretions in the scratch of the tree branch at his window (a sound of scripture: "Tip" [8.08]) and in the scratchy whisper of voices, those of the washerwomen, telling the story in the wind, on lips, in slips of the tongue, in kisses and lisps. He hears and does not want to hear; he fears and does not know what to fear; he hopes for a successful forgery and prays for vindication; he hides behind his name but wishes to be dispossessed of it; he recognizes his name and cannot recognize it. In the very act of trying to impose his authority—through his name—he decrees (and is already decreed by) confusion. "Earwicker," that first syllable of the name—*ear, hear*—breeds dissent, conflict, and error enters through the ear, a *Perce-Oreille*: "the mar of murmury mermers to the mind's ear" (254.18).

Sleeping, Earwicker hears the murmur of memories that mar his dream. He hears *memory* and *m'm'ry*, and he chases the *e* and *o* down the whirling, whorling vortex of the O, toward origins.

SUIVEZ LA PISTE

> —Let us consider letters—how they come at breakfast, and at night, with their yellow stamps and their green stamps, immortalized by the postmark—for to see one's own envelope on another's table is to realize how soon deeds sever and become alien.
> —Virginia Woolf, *Jacob's Room*

Resisting the pull of the *E* and *A* toward the whorling vortex of the *O*, the alphabetical configurations *l*, *p*, *s* carry apostrophic (and catastrophic) effects of separation and exclusion. Cut off, these letters stray through the text detached from the parental body: "What's that ma'am, says I" (272, n. 1). "Who'll buy me penny babies?" (273, n. 5). "The small p.s. ex-ex-executive capahand in their sad rear like a lady's postscript" (42.8–9). The confusion of letters as modes of correspondence and alphabetic symbols again overturns any systematic effort to recover what is lost or displaced according to the law of apostrophe. Although all six letters disseminate throughout the text, the vowels *E*, *A*, and *O* gravitate toward origins, sexual unions, the desire for knowledge of sources, and are drawn to the delta of ALP's siglum △. Very generally, this first group evokes the parents, HCE and ALP, and is associated with the vagina and throat. The consonants *l*, *p*, and *s* inscribe the children and are identified with penis and lips. Issy's lisp is heard in the sibilants of her seductive messages, while the doubled threat of her brothers, Shem and Shaun, is apparent in the powers of pen and post.

Following the t(r)ails of these letters, we discover signs of flawed speech and failed communication as the *Wake* traces the alliance of sin and speech, the slur or hesitation in speech that announces sin. The speech defects of father and daughter, whose incestuous coupling is specularized by the dream, are signs of their unlawful desires. His is a "hisshistenency" (146.34) and hers a lisp: "He fell from my lips, for my lisp, for my lewd speaker" (459.28). Wakean *s* sounds are associated with Issy's lips, where they suggest sighs, whispers, the "shimmers" of Nuvoletta's "lightdress" (157.8), the swish of skirts, sounds of the river reeds, and the stir of the air: "The siss of the whisp of the sigh of the softzing at the stir of the ver grose O arundo of a long one in midias reeds: and shades began to glidder along the banks, greepsing, greepsing, duusk unto duusk" (158.6–9). The *s* announces the serpent in the Garden of Eden, the flaw in the immortal scheme, the sound of the tempter's speech as a mark of forbidden knowledge, the sting of death: "hce! O hce!" (291, n. 1). Repeated, the *s* draws itself out in Earwicker's "hisshistenency" (146.34), which carries in its wake the hissing of his detractors, the snake in the grass, the hiss of the asp, and the sounds of micturition. The *s* also traces the flaccid form of the penis, which when erected writes a "capital Pee for Pride" (296.5) in the appropriate place of the woman's anatomy: "in Milton's Park under lovely Father Whisperer . . . making her love with his stuffstuff in the languish of flowers and feeling to find was she mushymushy" (96.10–12).

Bernard Benstock has demonstrated that the *l* and *s* sounds couple "as the gossip crosses and recrosses the river . . . and the seduction of young Anna Livia provides conjecture for the washerwomen: 'Letty Lerck's lafing light throw those laurals now on her daphdaph teasesong petrock' (203.29–31)."[20] The liquid *l*'s and swishing *s*'s combine in the temptresses: the "lilithe maidenettes," "two disappainted solicitresses" (90.16), the "saucicissters" (96.13), "two stripping baremaids" (526.23), *"the Misses O'Mollies"* (106.34), "one dilahah, Lupita Lorette" (67.33) and her "sister-in-love, Luperca Latouche" (67.36). The doubled *l* and *s* combine with the *p* of pepette's "little language" and Issy's baby talk and lisping *s*. Seated at her vanity table, she pens a letter to her lover, her "pettest parriage priest" (458.4). At her looking glass, Issy is also Alice ("Alicious, twinstreams, twinestraines, through alluring glass or alas in jumboland" [528.17–18]), whose narcissism threatens to drown her "in pondest coldstreams of admiration forherself" (526.28–29). She addresses her Other, her rival in love, as "you pig, you perfect little pigaleen" (143.35), practicing a series of poses. The radical shifts in tone move from the seductive ("Tell me till my thrillme comes!" [148.2]) to sadism ("you want to be slap well slapped for that" [148.6]) to vampirism ("Yes, the buttercups told me, hug me, damn it all, and I'll kiss you back to life, my peachest. I mean to make you suffer, meddlar. . . . Bite my laughters, drink my tears" [145.14–19]). She begs for the punishment of the pen ("Pore into me, volumes, spell me stark and spill me swooning" [145.19–20]) and calls for translation and transgression: "Transname me loveliness, now and here me for all times" (145.21). She is a "hot lisbing lass" (553.18) whose teenage sexuality focuses on petting and the "parted lipsabuss" (147.20), where the lisp is a *lapsus,* a "lipsus of some hetarosexual" (120.35).

Imitating her mother before the oval mirror of the makeup table, Issy paints a face that is itself a letter, "of eyebrow pencilled, by lipstipple penned" (93.25). Indeed, the links between *lips* and *letters* are forged throughout the *Wake*. Dion Boucicault's play *Arrah-na-Pogue (Arrah of the Kiss)* is an important Wakean literary source, a play from which Joyce borrowed the character of Sean the Post and in which a secret message is conveyed by a kiss. Joyce's spelling of *pogue* suggests *poke* and *penis* ("poghuing her scandalous" [388.23]), where an earlier reference ("in Arrah-na-pogue, in the otherworld of the passing of the key of Two-tongue Common" [385.3–5]) suggests lingual sexuality, the passing of the letter from mouth to mouth. This image is repeated in the last words of the *Wake*—"Lps. The keys to. Given!"—reminiscent of Molly's passing the seedcake from her mouth to Bloom's, a scene recalled at the close of *Ulysses*. In the play, Sean the Post is called on to sing ("Open the dure softly, / Somebody wants ye, dear"), and the image of the open mouth asking the woman to "open the door" appears variously in the *Wake* as the request to open the lips ("now open your lips" [147.29]; "to ope his blurbeous lips" [477.28]; "what passed our lips" [528.2–3]; *"My Curly Lips Demand Columbkisses"* [105.32]). Miming the image before her oval mirror, Issy "praxis oval owes and artless awes" (458.35–36) while writing a letter. The letter's last request is "kissists my exits" (280.27), prefigured in *Wake* associations between lovemaking and letter writing, the violence of brother battles and wife beating, efforts to read the arabesque script of the Book of Kells ("that last labiolingual *basium* might be read as a *suavium* if whoever the embracer then was wrote with a tongue in his (or perhaps her) cheek" [122.32–34]), and a "lady's postscript" that pleads for financial assistance: "I want money. Pleasend" (42.9–10). Letter writing and lovemaking, letters and labials, are bound together by the *Wake* dreamwork. The *Lps.* of the final line of the *Wake* are both lips and lisp, elsewhere associated with *please*, the plea of the woman to her other and also the *pli* of the envelope that encloses her sexual secrets. The *Wake* seals, stamps, and posts woman through the mails. She is portrayed as a letter whose covering must be slit open and whose message is ravaged in order to be read. The destructive instrument is a fork E whose "therrble prongs" (628.5) ALP fears. Woman's plea is "please stop, do please stop, and O do please stop" (124.4–5).

This plea (and *pli*) contained within the letter return us to the letter's circuit, where Shaun the Post plays a crucial role. As a sign of forbidden desire, the letter traces a tortuous route through the postal system, along a pathway that both leads to and is a diversionary tactic against incest. Entrusted to Shaun, who is the embodiment of canonical and common law, the letter catches him in a double bind: the need to deliver the letter and the desire to suppress it. That is, the postal system itself has an investment in seeing to it that the letter both arrives and does not arrive at its destination. Thus Shaun delivers the letter always into the wrong hands (which are also the right hands), ensuring that it is continually deflected, diverted, displaced and detoured. The diverted plot and scrambled discourse of the *Wake* are at one level *effects* of the letter's nonarrival.

As the letter is carried along the pathway, it meets every possible form of resistance to delivery. Ultimately, it cannot be delivered, for reasons stamped on its envelope: "No such no."; "None so strait"; "Overwayed. Understrumped"; "Too Let. To be Soiled"; "Vacant." The occupants of the various Dublin addresses tracked by the postal system (addresses that once belonged to James Joyce) meet similar fates: "Noon sick parson"; "Exbelled from 1014 d."; "Dining with the Danes"; "Arrusted"; "Drowned in the Laffey"; "Salved. All reddy buried"; "Cohabited by Unfortunates." The letter follows a circuit that either begins or should terminate at "29 Hardware Saint . . . Baile-Atha-Cliath," but even its message despairs of delivery: "Nave unlodgeable. Loved noa's dress. Sinned, Jetty Pierrse." The letter has been opened by "Miss Take," its address "Wrongly spilled," and has been sent "Back to the P.O. Kaer of" (420.17–421.14). Its signature, while nearly illegible, admits responsibility for having "sinned" and "signed," while the signator's name suggests both Jerry (Shem) and HCE, among whose doubles is Persse O'Reilly. The postal system has certain claims on this letter. It has become the property of the post (and Shaun will claim authorship of it), its final resting place to be the dead letter office (the midden heap), where its "penmarks used out in sinscript with such hesitancy by [the] cerebrated brother" (421.18–19) will be pecked at by Biddy the hen. Interrogated by the girls from Saint Bride's school (incarnations of Issy), Shaun first denounces the letter as belonging to "Mr O'Shem the Draper," who put his mother up to writing it ("She, the mammy far, was put up to it by him" [421.35–36]), for which Shem should be "depraved of his libertins to be silenced, sackclothed and suspended" (421.36–422.1).

As Shem's twin, Shaun claims credit for the letter ("Well it is partly my own, isn't it?" [424.23]), accusing his "celebrAted" brother of stealing it from him ("Every dimmed letter in it is a copy. . . . The last word in stolentelling!" [424.32, 35]). Angered by this thievery ("As he was rising my lather" [424.36–425.1], that is, as he was writing my letter), Shaun recognizes the hand of his brother in the letter's "hesitency," whose subject is "HeCitEncy," his excellency, HCE. The letter tells again the episode in the park and conflates the sin of the father with the writing of the letter, as though "righting his name for him . . . after laying out his litterery bed" (422.34–35) were the equivalent of the sexual sin the letter describes. Claiming the authority of the letter for himself, Shaun disclaims his responsibilities as the postman ("innocent of disseminating the foul emanation" [425.10–11]), arguing that under the law he "will commission to the flames any incendiarist whosoever . . . would endeavour to set ever annyma roner moother of mine on fire" (426.2–4). The letter is "incendiary" to the extent that it writes of consuming desire of the father for the daughter or of the son (Shem) for the mother. It is "incendiary" because it inflames desire, but also it risks being put to the flames, consumed, reduced to ashes.

The *Wake* constructs its postal system of desire on the body of Anna Livia, the River Liffey, which traces its route from Sallygap to Dublin Bay. Along this canal the Viking invaders made their way into Ireland, up the vagina of Anna Livia. The sigla of this postal code are a sexual code as well, the doubled *p* signifying the threat of the twin sons and the double identity of the daughter; the *S* and *P* marking the penis in its flaccid and erect forms; the *S* tracing the spiral cone of the vagina, the "commodius vicus of recirculation" (3.2) of the river. The letter/dream of desire starts and ends in the woman's body—the keys to which are given by Anna Livia through her "Lps" located at the mouth of the river, the labia at the entrance of the vaginal canal. Riding the river's wave, the letter rests in the "Gyre O" of the vagina and is buried in the midden heap, the "midden wedge of the stream's your muddy old triagonal delta" (297.23–24). This letter that was never mailed is nonetheless constantly moving through the postal system, retracing the map of desire in "appia lippia pluvaville" (297.25).

The secret of *Wake* writing rests with woman. But how might it be revealed? Shem's triagonal inscription of woman (293) provides no entrance to its hiding place, the place in which this secret writing inscribes itself under the protection of the hymen. The hymeneal fold is marked in Shem's drawing by overlapping circles, which suggest both the virginity of this text (its inaccessibility) and the potential for violation at the point where it can be penetrated. In order to expose the secret text, to deliver the letter and deliver up its message, the woman's body must be violated. In fact, it must be twice violated because the letter is twice concealed, hidden first in the woman's body, where it is protected by the double fold of the hymen, then concealed by the "everydaylooking stamped addressed envelope" of its "feminine cloithering" (109.31) that covers the female body. The reading involves first stripping the woman (writing and reading are forms of "secret stripture" [293, n. 2]), then pentrating her body. Reading constitutes a kind of rape, a desire to impose authority and uniformity through violence, to appropriate the secret at all costs, to expose a textual/sexual vulnerability. "Form" is broken in the effort to extract "meaning" from the text, emptying it, making it bleed, erasing, effacing, blanking out, or "rewriting" certain of its forms and norms. Submitted to the light of day, rescued by the reading process from its dark hiding place, the letter is rendered transparent. The hymeneal veil that supports *sin* and *sign* as double signatures of dream and letter, each bearing the mark of the other, is broken. The writing is pronounced unreadable.

THE GENRE, APOSTROPHE

Thus I apostrophize. It is also . . . a genre and a tone.[21]

What can one say about the genre, apostrophe? And what are the links—if any—between its rhetorical and grammatical status? Certainly the double movement of apostrophe, to enclose and exclude: apostrophe marks excess and default. It is an address that turns away from the addressed, making a movement that in English is called an "aside." Turning away, apostrophe calls attention to what it would hide—a longing, a(n) (unspoken) desire. The darkness of apostrophe obscures its movements. Situated in the blackness of night, of death, of absence, apostrophe cannot tolerate the light. It resists narrative and "telling"; its desire is for the dramatic: to apostrophize. Juliet, calling out to Romeo in the night's darkness, addresses herself to Romeo's name; she calls to Romeo *in* his name and *through* his name. She awaits his response, but he turns aside (the stage directions tell us), pausing in that gesture to reflect on whether he should speak ("Shall I hear more, or shall I speak at this?"). He turns away from her, but in the darkness she cannot see the turn of apostrophe, and he speaks to himself and to us. He asks us—the audience, we who are outside the drama "proper"—for an answer. None comes, and she continues to apostrophize his name, declaring that his name is her enemy.[22] That name stands as barrier to the union of the lovers, to her membership in his family and his membership in hers. We "overhear" this nonexchange; we trespass—as the apostrophe insists we must—on an intimate, secret, hidden territory. Apostrophe forces a trespass. It calls out to curiosity, to voyeurism, and turns away from the storytelling we so desire, calling attention to the loss of the very story that apostrophe calls out to be told.

The movement of apostrophe problematizes the series of oppositions its doubling movement invokes: sound/silence, here/there, me/you, speaker/listener, internal/external, address/response, living/dead, presence/absence, and so forth. Apostrophe resists and enforces these oppositions even as it traverses them. It is the mark of difference, a difference within that precedes such categories and brings them into existence: apostrophe announces the silences within speech, providing in the announcement graphic evidence of the power of that silence: O! As a genre it calls out to the voice, which is represented through an image *of* voice, an image only available textually. Apostrophe undoes the effects of time (including the end of all time, in death) by apparently enforcing something like a "timeless present," which Jonathan Culler remarks is "better seen as a 'temporality of writing.' "[23] Apostrophe insists on a "now" that is impossible, apostrophe calling out to and also exposing this impossibility. The action of apostrophe should exist outside writing, it makes claims to existing outside writing, but its effect is to put into question the status of voice *within* writing. Apostrophe turns aside to insist on calling attention to itself, to its effects. These effects register the resistance to any kind of mastery. Apostrophe compromises systems, bodies (including the human body), origins, delivery points, and points of departure. It undoes the structure of hierarchies and resists closure—this last a way of resisting the narrative drive from origin to closure. That is, apostrophe calls the question of genre to account. As a grammatical marker, apostrophe marks all that it cannot fully account for.

Finnegans Wake also sketches that which cannot be fully accounted for and in so doing subverts *accounting* itself: it overstates, in a rush of words, letters, sounds, songs, all that cannot be stated as such. Narrative *in general,* not a specific genre, is called to account. The effort to tell the story, from beginning to end, with all false starts and loose ends carefully tied together under the generic imprint "narrative" is undone by the turn (') of the apostrophe and the apostrophic turning aside. *Finnegans Wake:* a turning that confuses subjects and objects, waking and sleeping, borders and boundaries, definitions and explanations, genders and genres. Apostrophe, the mark of genre that marks the impurity and impossibility of genres. Apostrophe, an impurity that contaminates the pure sound of O or the moment of pure presence or the pure present. Apostrophe is at work even when we cannot see it or hear it: Finnegan's wake. *Finnegans Wake.*

NOTES

1. Portions of this paper were first read at two James Joyce Conferences (University of California, Riverside, 15 May 1987; Marquette University and University of

Wisconsin, Milwaukee, 15 June 1987). I have not erased certain "spoken" qualities of this essay as a reminder that the apostrophe form itself works the boundaries between the spoken and written.

All references to James Joyce, *Finnegans Wake* are to the Viking Press edition (New York, 1947), included parenthetically by page and line number. All references to Jacques Derrida, *La Carte Postale,* are to the French edition (Paris: Flammarion, 1980). I have not relied solely on the English translation of *La Carte Postale,* in part because I want specifically to work the boundaries between French and English. The act of translation constitutes one of the various "border crossings" examined by *La Carte Postale.* Unless otherwise indicated, translations are my own.

2. Jonathan Culler, *The Pursuit of Signs* (Ithaca: Cornell University Press, 1981), 135, cites Quintilian, *Institutio Oratoria* 4.1.63.

3. Culler, *Pursuit,* 136.

4. The privileged spoken word of the *Wake* is examined by Philippe Sollers in "Comme si le vieil Homère," *Le Nouvel Observateur* (6 February 1982): 73–74: "Joyce? It is sufficient to hear his voice. More precisely, his recording of a fragment of *Finnegans Wake.* . . . Unreadable, this book? Untranslatable? Listen, listen. Immediately, from the depths of the night, rises this strangely assured, even emphatic voice, cunning, hardened by hundreds and hundreds of troubles, but always melodious; this voice, blindly firm, separating the branches and the blinds of sleep; it is as if Homer, an old man, but one always young, comes toward us through the weave of a thousand adventures, a thousand stories, a thousand and one languages encountered in his underwater wanderings, syllables respond and illumine each other, vivified by a new breath." (Translation my own.)

The notion that the *Wake* is somehow more available, more understandable, when read aloud, that its language frequently empowers aural rather than visual techniques of wordplay, has long been a commonly held assumption. Indeed, a standard method of teaching *Finnegans Wake* is to read it aloud, which suggests that what is *heard* in the *Wake* may be more evident, even more trustworthy, than what is *seen*. What apostrophe—in all its forms—suggests is not merely that the opposite might be true (writing takes precedence over telling in the *Wake*) but that the relationship between telling and writing is far more complex than we have so far thought. In its genre, apostrophe invokes *through* writing an image of voice that is possible only in writing. That the writing effects of the Wakean use of the vocative have been systematically overlooked, even denied, is the inescapable effect of the *Wake*'s own law, wherein the difference between telling and writing is *inscribed*.

To hear Joyce (or anyone else) read the text—and Joyce reads from the Anna Livia Plurabelle section, which is itself an apostrophe—is to hear the effects of the apostrophe *undone*. The O of the apostrophe, the voice's image, can exist only in writing; the O on the page gives evidence of the impossibility of apostrophe's own invoked effect. The O attests to the nonexistence of the voice that the apostrophe would call into sound: there remains only the O, only the sign, the marker. In calling up that which is dead, absent, or silent, apostrophe can only acknowledge death, absence, silence. There is a space between the O—the invocation—and its intended and resultant effects. That space is writing, and I shall come back to it in the specificity of its Wakean moment.

5. This essay examines three functions of the apostrophe, as defined by the *Oxford English Dictionary*:

1. A figure of speech in which a writer suddenly stops in his discourse and turns to address pointedly some person or thing, present or absent; an exclamatory

address. Modern use has extended the apostrophe to the *absent* or *dead,* but it is by no means confined to these, as is sometimes erroneously stated. [Note that the OED definition places the apostrophe as a written rather than spoken form.]

2. Omission of one or more letters of a word *(don't).*
3. A sign of the modern English genitive or possessive case *(woman's).*

6. Such a reading would be: "A way a lone a last a love a long the riverrun, past Eve and Adam's." An extended analysis of the effects of this circularity is Jacques Aubert's "riverrun," in *Post-Structuralist Joyce: Essays from the French,* ed. Derek Attridge and Daniel Ferrer (Cambridge: Cambridge University Press, 1984). Aubert suggests that *riverrun* is unreadable because it is *undifferentiated:* "Reading is obstructed by lack of difference" (69). Further, *riverrun* is "unhearable," not corresponding "to any vocable which the ear can honestly claim to recognize," and a common reading—"River, run!"—inserts a "pause, a silence" (by resituating the comma that follows "riverrun"). What might confer meaning—the comma—is absent. This reading, which makes of *riverrun* both an apostrophe and a directive, owes its sense to an (unmarked) silence. I return to this place that is "missing"—the place of pause and silence.

7. John Bishop's reading of the *Wake* draws together sleep, dreams, and memory to suggest ways of Wakean obscurity, its language serving (in Joyce's words) to "reconstruct the nocturnal life." (*Joyce's Book of the Dark* [Madison: University of Wisconsin Press, 1986], 4). Bishop's particular interest is in "blank memory," the realm of dreamless sleep: "if we think of sleep (as opposed to 'dreams') as that part of the night which cannot be remembered, this would mean finding a way of 'reveiling' (220.33 [note the occluding 'veil']) an interval of life inherently barred from 'mummery' (535.30 ['memory'])" (7).

Bishop's study does not concentrate on dreams, per se, and thus he extends the dream frame to mark the internal boundary between sleep and dreams, between the "hole" and the "whole," continually passing the bar between that which is barred from memory and that which is available only in dream. His entrances to the *Wake* are those which mark a falling asleep (presumably the opening pages) and the coming awake (the closing pages). Postulating that the clearest renderings of *Wake* themes and structures are available here, Bishop rigorously tries to reconstruct through his reading what the "night" is like. His readings try to render a comprehensive, literal interpretation of the text, which the text itself defeats.

8. Derrida, *La Carte Postale,* 155.
9. Ibid., 179.
10. Derrida rightly suggests that "the writer, Shem, is the inheritor of H.C.E., Here Comes Everybody" (*La Carte Postale,* 154). It is through writing that Shem takes his father's name, disseminating and dispersing it through the letter that he scripts for his mother. The act of writing is at the heart of the brother battle in the *Wake,* which both links the twins (as penman and postman) and pits them against each other in their efforts to possess the letter—that is, to possess the other in their efforts to possess the letter—that is, to possess the father's name, to be his inheritors. Although Shaun is the father's favored son, Shem has access to powers of language (powers that frighten both his father and brother) and thereby threatens the father's sovereignty. Derrida "translates" YHWH as "he war" (HCE's war), a war of language that divides father from son and turns sons against each other, a war inscribed by the pen: "his penisolate war" (3.6). The pen divides. See *La Carte Postale,* 154–55.

11. Derrida has examined this tension between the written and spoken in Joyce's work. See his explanation of the effects of "gramophony" in *Ulysse gramophone* (Paris: Galilee, 1987), where among other concerns he takes up the workings of Molly's "yes." The English version is "*Ulysses* gramophone: Hear say yes in Joyce," trans. Shari Benstock, in *James Joyce: The Augmented Ninth,* ed. Bernard Benstock (Syracuse, N.Y.: Syracuse University Press, 1988), 27–75. In the prologue to *Feu la cendre* (Paris: éditions des femmes, 1987), a text printed and also available on cassette tape, he describes this "polylogue" of a double-columned text through which is heard/read a variety of voices, including voices from other texts, notably *Dissemination,* trans. Barbara Johnson (Chicago: University of Chicago Press, 1981); *Glas,* trans. John P. Leavey, Jr., and Richard Rand (Lincoln: University of Nebraska Press, 1986); and *La Carte Postale.* These writing voices are both masculine and feminine, a "tangle of voices" whose number is indeterminate. Of particular concern in *Feu la cendre* (7) is the status of the word *la,* in the phrase *il y a là cendre.* This word changes grammatical status and function depending on whether or not it carries an accent grave *(la):* "*Là* writes itself with an accent *grave: là, il y a cendre, il y a, là, cendre.*" One, of course, cannot "hear" the accent; this grammatical marker of adverbial status, making for "a certain indecision between writing and voice," Derrida describes as a "vibration of grammar in (of) the voice." And the uncertain status of the *là,* with its unheard *accent grave,* is present in the English translation of the phrase as well: "There, there is ash" (or "There, there are cinders"). The movement from *là* as adverb to *la* as definite article is felt in English, where the first *There* is an adverb and the second an introductory expletive. Unlike the apostrophe, which marks an absence, *there*—as in "there is ash"—marks a deficiency; its presence fills in an implicit absence or supplements the syntactical structure. In English, the difference between *There* and *there* in the translation of *là, il y a cendre, il y a, là, cendre* is even more indefinite: there is nothing, no accent mark, nothing that can be either seen or heard to distinguish the repetitions of the word from each other.

This text also makes "a call to the voice" (as does apostrophe, which in its grammatical role also cannot be heard); it is a *mise en voix*—a "voicing." But that *voix* can be heard through several variant spellings—*voie* (way), *vois* (to see)—and carries with it perhaps the expression, *mise en scène,* to stage: this tension dramatizes itself. This tension between the written and the spoken also has its effects on translation, which has been rigorously problematized in Derrida's most recent texts (as it is by *Finnegans Wake*): that which remains to be translated of the *la* (ˋ) is precisely that which cannot be translated; in its silence it calls out for translation.

12. Barbara Johnson, *A World of Difference* (Baltimore: Johns Hopkins University Press, 1987), 185.

13. Culler, *Pursuit,* 148–49.

14. Paul de Man's argument concerning the speaking subject is found in *Allegories of Reading* (New Haven: Yale University Press, 1979), 29. Culler outlines several levels of apostrophe involving the "I-Thou": the constitution of the object *(thou)* as another subject "with whom the poetic subject might hope to strike up a harmonious relationship. Apostrophe would figure this reconciliation of subject and object" (Culler, *Pursuit,* 143); the O of apostrophe as trope that might parody apostrophic procedures, so that the O is an "invocation of invocation" (144); the apostrophic fiction implicit when the poet dresses Earth, "that the things of earth function as *thous* when addressed" (this claim would find approximation in ALP as river [145–46]); that the call to the O of the address "which seems to establish relations between the self and the other can in fact be read as an act of radical interiorization and

solipsism" (146). Culler reads apostrophe "as sign of a fiction which knows its own fictive nature . . . to stress its optative character, its impossible imperatives: commands which in their explicit impossibility figures events in and of fiction" (146).

15. The double mark of reading and washing that obliterates the text is taken up elsewhere in the *Wake,* importantly associated with ALP as her letter both repeats and refutes the charges against Earwicker. I have examined elsewhere these reading/writing effects. See my "Nightletters" in *Critical Essays on James Joyce,* ed. Bernard Benstock (Boston: G. K. Hall, 1986), 221–33.

16. There are seven sigla for the Doodles Family (299, n.4). Of these, I emphasize only the ⊓ for Earwicker and the △ for Anna Livia. Shem's sign ⊏ provides an association with Cain, and Shaun's ∧ repeats part of the form for the mother. Issy's sign as Isolde ⊥ is a mirror image of the alphabetic symbol earlier used to designate Tristan ⊤. In a letter to Harriet Shaw Weaver on 24 March 1924, Joyce wrote out a more inclusive set of signs than the set of seven, among them the capital *S* (for Snake) and *P* (for S. Patrick). My own interest has to do with alphabetic symbols that are associated (through a movement of disassociation) with the family characters: *E, O, A, L, P, S.* For information on the use of sigla, see Roland McHugh, *The Sigla of Finnegans Wake* (London: Edward Arnold, 1976), 8, 133.

17. Various references to documents that include incriminating evidence appear throughout the *Wake.* The most important of these focuses on two documents involved in the founding of the Irish Free State in 1921 ("ducomans nonbar one" [368.30]; "deckhuman amber too" [619.19]). The controversy centered on the first document brought back from London, a typewritten draft, which was altered by a variety of amendments. De Valera submitted a second draft, one positing a looser connection between Ireland and Britain than offered by the first document. According to John Garvin, "in 1932, when Mr. de Valera formed his Government, he disinterred the original Treaty showing the penmarks of excision, revisions and so on, to suggest unseemly haste and indecision on the part of the signatories." See *James Joyce's Disunited Kingdom* (Dublin: Gill and Macmillan, 1976), 141. Excisions, revisions, and penmarks contaminate all documents in the *Wake,* especially the letters.

An early reading of the document in the *Wake* includes references to false documentary evidence against Alfred Dreyfus, the Jewish army captain charged with leaking French state secrets: "Closer inspection of the *bordereau* would reveal a multiplicity of personalities inflicted on the documents or document and some prevision of virtual crime or crimes might be made by anyone" (107.23–26). Other references are at 356, 358, 369, 390, 482, 528, 619. Appearances of forged evidence (as in the Parnell and Dreyfus cases) are included as forged checks (181.16) and "piously forged palimpsests" (182.02).

18. This sketchy (and profoundly suspect) development of the alphabet cannot take up the various problems in the movement from oral to written cultures, nor does it mean to suggest that the boundary between the two is clearly marked and strictly drawn. Indeed, this border area is of great interest. In his critique of the Saussurian "ethnocentrism privileging the model of phonetic writing" and of the "epigenetist" concept of writing held by Lévi-Strauss, Derrida points to the implicit failure of the effort radically to distinguish language from writing: "This [distinction] allows [Lévi-Strauss] to consider the passage from speech to writing as a *leap,* as the instantaneous crossing of a line of discontinuity: passage from a fully oral language, pure of all writing—*pure,* innocent—to a language appending to itself its graphic 'representation' as an accessory signifier of a new type, opening a technique of oppression." See

Of Grammatology, trans. Gayatri Chakravorty Spivak (Baltimore: Johns Hopkins University Press, 1976), 120. A writing that extends beyond this "usual" or "narrow sense" of writing is already present "in the differance or the archewriting that opens speech itself" (*Grammatology,* 128). This movement of *e* to *a* in *differance* is seen but not heard (written differently, but spoken as though it were the same), a movement already apparent in YHWH, which carries the trace of this "archewriting." This trace leads us toward apostrophe and the mark of genre.

19. Jacques Derrida, "Two Words of Joyce," in *Post-Structuralist Joyce: Essays from the French,* ed. Derek Attridge and Daniel Ferrer (Cambridge: Cambridge University Press, 1984), 155. Derrida takes up the question of Babel in the *Wake* (a subject also explored in *La Carte Postale,* 154–55, 257–58), with particular attention to the words *he war* (258.12): a version of YAHWEH, in which *he war* "exchanges the final *R* and the central *H* in the anagram's throat" ("Two Words," 154); "he declared war in language and on language and by language, which gave languages, that's the truth of Babel when YAHWEH pronounced its vocable, difficult to say if it was a name" (146). That is, "the law enounced in the performative dimension is also the ban on the very principle of translation, the ban *in* the very principle of translation, intertranslation as one and the same experience of language: of the one language as one God" (155). So that to translate *he war* "into the system of a single language . . . is to erase the event of the mark" (155). The apostrophe marks such an erasure: Y'HW'H, where the supplied vowels are *a* and *e*, as in *he war* and *Earwicker.* (Note that the apostrophe to mark contraction as well as possession is peculiar to English; it is not "translatable.") 'YAHWEH, HE WAR,' declares war on individual language and on translation, as does *Finnegans Wake*: "And how war your maggies? Answer: They war loving" (142.30–31).

20. I follow Benstock's close reading of the *l, p, s* movements in *Joyce-again's Wake* (Seattle: University of Washington Press, 1965), 148–55. He includes many more examples than is possible here, but it is important to note the echoes of the serpent's "hiss" that pervade the *Wake,* as Phoenix Park is an analogue for the Garden of Eden. Issy's lisp allies her with the snake: she is a "liss in hunterland" (276, n. 7), and her lisped, "Liss, liss! I muss whiss!" (148.26) suggests as well an alignment with Lilith, apocryphal precursor of Eve, and Lily Kinsella in the *Wake.* The yolking of the *ls* sound with *p* also *(pee)* suggests urination, as does *p-q* inversion (the Prankquean), which combines in the yonic shape of the letters both urination and invagination. Benstock includes a detailed discussion of these references on pages 152–54 and suggests that "*P-q* becomes a leitmotif . . . not just by dint of incorporation into proper names of the two seductresses or the single Prankquean figure ["Peena and Queena" (377.18); "prunktqueen" (250.29), among others], but in the very flow of language" (153–54). The patterns of coupling *(pq, ps, ls,* etc.) these alphabetic characters seem to establish are undone by the movement of the letters themselves, which appears to be random, establishing accidental contacts. Their effect is divisive, destructive of patterns and motifs. As well, they enforce meaning even when they appear where they should not be or in "contexts" where their placement seems out of place or irrelevant. Stated differently, these "symbols" refuse symbolic status. Carried along as part of the Liffey's litter, they find no resting place. They are metonymic, transgressive, and hold within them revolutionary acts.

21. In French, the verb *apostropher* means "to speak brusquely or brutally to someone." The effect is carried by "tone," as Derrida suggests (*La Carte Postale,* 8). No such meaning inheres in the English "apostrophize," where the word carries only the marker of genre: to apostrophize something or someone.

22. Relevant here is Derrida's discussion of theater, time, written and spoken words, and proper names in Shakespeare's *Romeo and Juliet,* where the title entombs heroes whose very names bear the mark of cliché, of a certain critical embarrassment. See "L'aphorisme a contretemps," in *Psyche: Inventions de l'autre* (Paris: Galilee, 1987), 519–33.

23. Culler, *Pursuit,* 149.

7
"The bawk of bats" in Joyce's Belfry
The Flitter-mouse in the Feminine

VINCENT J. CHENG

"Can't hear with bawk of bats, all thim liffeying waters of" (*FW* 215.33-34).[1] This famous line from the Anna Livia Plurabelle section of *Finnegans Wake* suggests a connection among woman (Anna Livia, the gossiping washerwomen), water (Anna Liffey, washing), talking (gossip, bawk), and bats. By the waters of the babbling Liffey, the washerwomen babble on, remembering Zion, Babylon, and all "gossipaceous" (*FW* 195.04) histories, as evening falls and bawking bats emerge. By the waters of Sandymount Strand, Gerty MacDowell, Edy Boardman, and Cissy Caffrey—like their counterparts washing undergarments in the *Odyssey*—chatter on in the Nausicaa episode of *Ulysses* as evening falls and a squeaking bat emerges. There had been, of course, "batlike souls" already in chapter 5 of *A Portrait of the Artist as a Young Man*. I was tempted, while writing about vampires and panthers in Joyce (see Cheng 1987), to view the bats as merely a variation in *Ulysses*'s pattern of nocturnal beasts—vampires, panthers, lemurs, hyenas, and so on. But I began to realize that bats were a very special case, repeatedly allied with the female, while vampires were generally and more frequently allied with the male. Or were they, rather, part of the Joycean motif of winged, flying creatures, a variation of the bird imagery that commentators have explicated so lucidly?

What have other critics made of these bats? Only William York Tindall, Elaine Unkeless, and Patrick A. McCarthy seem to have attempted to make any sense of them—all in very brief passages recognizing their attachment to women. Unkeless cites Tindall's speculations and then tries to suggest correlations between bats and vampires in *Ulysses;* McCarthy, citing Unkeless, suggests links to Joyce's vision of prostitution; but I'd like to return to the basic, still-unanswered questions surrounding Tindall's speculation (he is talking about the early, pre-*Ulysses* works): "In Joyce's iconography the bat implies darkness, secrecy, blindness, and loneliness. For that reason it is associated at times with the artist. When Stephen breaks his glasses, and incurs the pandy*bat*, he is blinded entirely [one might say he was blind as a]. Joyce was never certain whether women and artists were birds or bats" (Tindall 1954, 217; my emphasis). One suspects that Joyce, however, knew exactly what he was doing and that the ambivalence may have been intentional: if the artist figure is both the soaring Dedalus and the mad, bat-blind Shem ("*When He Is Going Batty*," the "acheseyeld from Ailing" in *FW* 177.29 and 148.33), so also perhaps women may be depicted simultaneously as both birdlike and batlike.

What is a bat? "Messer Brunetto" (*U* 194) Latini, Stephen's source on basilisks, panthers, and hyenas (del Greco Lobner 1978, 134; Cheng 1987, 168-75), says nothing about bats in his medieval bestiary. Skeat's *Etymological Dictionary*, which Stephen read "by the hour" (*SH* 26), and which Joyce, too, perused frequently (Whittaker 1987), defines a bat as a "winged mammal"—from "Dan. *bakke* or *aften-bakke*, evening-bat" and "M. Swed. *natt-backa*, lit. 'night-bat' " (Skeat 1882, 50)—suggesting only that Joyce would no doubt have associated bats with evening and night (I will, however, return to the Scandinavian source later). The *OED* is more detailed:

> from Danish, *aften-bakke* ('evening bat'). An animal, a member of the Mammalian order *Chiroptera* and especially of the family *Vespertilionidae*, consisting of mouse-like quadrupeds (whence the names *Reremouse, Flitter-mouse*), having the fingers extended to support a thin membrane which stretches from the side of the neck by the toes of both pairs of feet to the tail, and forms a kind of wing, with which they fly with a peculiar, quivering motion; hence they were formerly classed as birds. They are all nocturnal, returning by day to dark recesses, to which habits there are many references in literature.

The *OED* goes on to cite a number of such references, such as that "a bat is a night-bird (nihte-bird, a bakke)"; in its very habits and etymology, then, the bat (as suggested by both Skeat and the *OED*) is to be seen as a night version of the "bird," bird and bat being day and night versions of the same creature. (Joyce may or may not have read the *OED*—volumes A to P were out by 1910; in any case, he was likely aware of these points.)

So what did Joyce make of this? The early works provide some interesting keys, especially around the figure of Emma Clery as she is collectively portrayed in *A Portrait, Stephen Hero*, and *Chamber*

Music. In *Chamber Music* the girl (who is Emma's parallel), Tindall argues (1954, 85-86), is "compared once or twice to a bird, but toward the end of the sequence, in poem XXXI, becomes a bat, not only a kind of vampire but a symbol of Ireland." This is a lot to infer from the single unremarkable line in question—"When the bat flew from tree to tree"—and Tindall's conclusions make sense only in the larger, composite context of Stephen's reactions to Emma in *Stephen Hero* and especially in chapter 5 of *A Portrait* ("a figure of the womanhood of her country, a batlike soul" [*P* 221]). But there is a wide-angled sense to Tindall's collective perspective (1954, 218), seeing the whole forest for the trees: "The flittering of the bat from tree to tree in XXXI suggests the girl's inconstancy. That trees are men is made plain by Joyce's use of the image in XXXIII, where the deserted lover sheds leaves, in 'Tilly,' the first poem of *Pomes Penyeach,* where Joyce weeps for his torn bough, and in *Finnegans Wake,* where Shem is a tree. Compare *Ulysses* [377], where Bloom thinks: 'Bat . . . Thinks I'm a tree.'"

The parallel moments in *Stephen Hero* (187-210) are more detailed and even more interesting. As Bonnie Kime Scott notes about these meetings between Stephen and Emma, "Stephen is tempted by her physical appearance once again. He sees her in a perfect moment, contrasted to the decay around her, and posed against the trees in the rain, conditions which have proved alluring to him in the past" (1982, 75). At the end of their meeting in *Stephen Hero* (187-89), Stephen bids goodnight to Emma "in the shadow of the leafless trees" and is greeted instead by the "Goodnight, love" of a woman in the shadows wearing "a black straw hat" (*SH* 189), clearly a prostitute (in *Ulysses* [290] Bloom notices that the "whore of the lane" is wearing a "black straw sailor hat," and again on page 632 he sees the "streetwalker . . . under a black straw hat"). Stephen is thus led to draw a contrast between the whore in the black straw hat ("Who have I to help me except the woman in the black straw hat?") and "the virgin" (Emma) who rebuffs his advances (*SH* 192). Stephen is tempted to draw generalizations about their sex from these two poles, for "he wished to avenge himself on Irish women" (*SH* 200). In fact, he later tells Lynch that all women are whores of a sort, the black-hatted one perhaps of a more generous sort: "The woman in the black straw hat gave something before she sold her body to the State. Emma will sell herself to the State but give nothing" (*SH* 203). In this way, Stephen is led to a further generalization about the promiscuous and animal voracity of the female: "By brooding constantly upon this he ended by anathemising Emma as the most deceptive and cowardly of marsupials" (*SH* 210). If Emma is repeatedly described in *A Portrait* as a bird, innocent and light (e.g., "simple and strange as a bird's life . . . simple and wilful as a bird's heart" [P 216]), she is also a marsupial in *Stephen Hero*—or, in *A Portrait*, a bat. As Richard Brown notes (1985, 119), "Stephen calls girls 'marsupials' and, since all women are obliged to sell their bodies in one way or another, in his scheme Emma is 'the most deceptive and cowardly of marsupials' "; in fact, in Stephen's mind women are *both* marsupials and "birds" (another popular term, after all, for "girls"—like "chicks," "hens," and so on), both whores and virgins.

In *A Portrait*, the marsupial image for women is replaced by the bat. Women have, for Stephen, marsupial- and bat-like, rodent-like association related to sexual promiscuity. They are agents of entrapment, betrayal, and sin. In *A Portrait*, after Davin tells Stephen the story of the peasant woman who invited him in for the night, Stephen thinks of her "as a type of her race," "a batlike soul waking to the consciousness of itself in darkness and secrecy and loneliness and . . . calling the stranger to her bed" (P 183). When Stephen grows to suspect Emma of flirting with the "young priest," he similarly concludes "that she was a figure of the womanhood of her country, a batlike soul waking to the consciousness of itself in darkness and secrecy and loneliness" (P 221). Finally, thinking of both the women "who had all but wooed [Davin] to her bed" and of Emma, Stephen wonders how these Irish "daughters . . . might breed a race less ignoble than their own": "And under the deepened dusk he felt thoughts and desires of the race . . . flitting like bats across the dark country lanes, under trees by the edges of streams and near the poolmottled bogs" (P 238: the natural elements of both Nausicaa and Anna Livia Plurabelle are here already—dusk, bats, trees, water, and women allied with this batlike flitting).

In Stephen's misogyny, then, he is led to conclude that women are a race of marsupials or bats. He has a brief moment of doubt, wondering whether, "he had judged [Emma] harshly": "If her life were a simple rosary of hours, her life simple and strange as a bird's life. . . . Her heart simple and wilful as a bird's heart?" (P 216). McCarthy (1982, 98) notes that "in contrast to the image of the bat or the prostitute, the bird image suggests innocence and simplicity," but then further points out that Stephen connects the cries of the birds on the library steps with "the squeak of mice" (P 224), a rodentlike squeaking (like the bawk of bats) that he has previously associated with sin and prostitution: "his sins, the jeweleyed harlots of his imagination, fled before the hurricane, squeaking like mice" (P 115). As McCarthy (99) argues, "The mouse squeaks that connect the birds to 'the jeweleyed harlots of his imagination' provide a link between birds and bats—innocent and degraded images of women—and suggest, again, the ambiguity of Stephen's view of Emma."

As in Tindall's suggestion about *Chamber Music,* then, the portrayal of femininity here moves from innocent and virginal to promiscuous and sexual, from bird to bat—or, more accurately, to the dark bat inside the white bird, to the night-bird. This movement (exfoliation, unveiling of a reciprocal nature) is already suggested in Stephen's epiphanic vision of the birdlike girl on the beach (once again we have dusk, woman, water), whose virginal, birdlike qualities ("beautiful seabird . . . delicate as a crane . . . pure . . . ivory . . . soft white down . . . dovetailed . . . bosom as a bird's . . . dark-plumaged dove") are balanced by her overt sexuality ("long slender bare legs . . . thighs, fuller and softhued . . . bared almost to the hips . . . her waist . . . her bosom"). Even more notably, the rhythms of the prose reflect Stephen's state of charged, suppressed, erotic excitement: "Long, long she suffered his gaze and then quietly withdrew her eyes from his and bent them towards the stream, gently stirring the water with her foot hither and thither. The first faint noise of gently moving water broke the silence, low and faint and whispering, faint as the bells of sleep; hither and thither, hither and thither: and a faint flame trembled on her cheek" (*P* 171). Well might Stephen's soul cry out "in an outburst of profane joy"—"Heavenly God!"—for it is already ironically profaned by the suppressed eroticism of the binary "hither and thither" rhythms. These are reminiscent of the similarly sexually charged descriptions of Emma on the tram—"She came up to his step many times and went down to hers . . . and once or twice stood close to him for some moments on the upper step, forgetting to go down, and then went down. His heart danced upon her movements like a cork upon a tide" (*P* 69)—and of the barmaid/siren Lydia Douce's hand motions on the phallic beerpull in *Ulysses*: "On the smooth jutting beerpull laid Lydia hand lightly, plumply, leave it to my hands. . . . Fro, to: to, fro: over the polished knob . . . her thumb and finger passed . . . passed, repassed and, gently touching, then slid so smoothly, slowly down, a cool firm white enamel baton protruding through their sliding ring" (*U* 286).

"Hither and thither" seems to be a motif frequently associated with women and with birds. As Stephen gazes at the birds on the library steps and listens to their cries ("like the squeak of mice"), "there flew hither and thither shapeless thoughts from Swedenborg on the correspondence of birds to things of the intellect" (*P* 224). John B. Smith (1980, 153-54) notes the hither/thither imagery of *A Portrait* and argues that "The indecisive oscillation between polar opposites, implying no sense of resolution, is one form of the hither/thither motif";

while this may be partly accurate, in my reading of bats and birds I see the related hither/thither motif of linear, binary movement as suggestive of sexual activity, promiscuity, and sin ("his sins, the jeweleyed harlots of his imagination . . . squeaking like mice" [P 115]). Indeed, most of its occurrences suggest just such a context. In chapter 3, thinking of his sexual appetites, Stephen "had sunk to the state of a beast. . . . Forms passed this way and that through the dull light. And that was life. The letters of the name of Dublin lay heavily on his mind, pushing one another surlily hither and thither with slow, boorish insistence. His soul was fattening and congealing into a gross grease" (P 111). In the bird-girl passage, "hither and thither" occurs thrice; of the ten occurrences of the motif in *A Portrait* (see Hancock 1967, 58), only one other passage contains more than one occurrence; it, too, contains "hither and thither" three times and is, significantly, Stephen's vision of sin and hell (P 137-38): "A field of stiff weeds. . . . Creatures were in the field; one, three, six: creatures were moving in the field, hither and thither" (P 137). These "Goatish creatures with human faces" look forward to the beasts in the whorehouses of Circe, "as they moved hither and thither, trailing their long tails behind them" (P 137). Tailed like the devil or like a beast, these field creatures speak a soft babble (like the bawk of bats) and suggest a hell of sin and "luxury" (in the archaic sense): "Soft language issued from their spittleless lips as they swished in slow circles round and round the field, winding hither and thither through the weeds, dragging their long tails amid the rattling canisters. . . . That was his hell: God had allowed him to see the hell reserved for his sins: stinking, bestial, malignant, a hell of lecherous goatish fiends" (P 138). Aware of the triple use of the hither/thither motif in this passage to denote the movement of sin and lechery, it becomes impossible for us to read its triple occurrence in the bird-girl vision without sensing the suggestive sinfulness and sexuality underneath the description of the dovelike girl stirring the water with her foot. The suppressed rhythms in the bird-girl passage unsuccessfully hide the whore beneath the virgin, the bat beneath the bird. The suppressed sexuality of *A Portrait* will become overt in *Ulysses,* the bird becoming a bat; as Fritz Senn writes, "In the vision of *A Portrait,* a 'wild angel had appeared' [P 172]; in 'Nausicaa' a bird, a bat, and a dark stranger appear" (Senn 1974, 294). Or, as McCarthy suggests, "Joyce completed his thread of associations between virgin and prostitute—girl as bird, girl as bat—in the 'Nausicaa' chapter of *Ulysses,* in which Bloom's onanistic reaction to Gerty MacDowell's exhibitionism ironically recapitulates Stephen's vision of the girl on the strand"(1982, 99).

This movement of bird to bat is even more resonant if we recall that, as Unkeless (1978, 128) first pointed out (also McCarthy 1982, 97), "bat" is a slang term for prostitute—a very special kind of nocturnal creature. The word is listed in Partridge's *Dictionary of Slang and Unconventional English* (37) as meaning, since the seventeenth century, "a prostitute favouring the night"; a further nineteenth-to-twentieth century slang meaning of "spoken language . . . speech, word" (as in "to sling the bat") also seems appropriate in the context of the bawk of bats, chittering washerwomen, gossip, and girl talk. Joyce reminds us of this bat/whore association when he describes Bridie Kelly, the whore who performed Bloom's sexual initiation, as a chittering bat in the brothel episode: *"With a squeak she flaps her bat shawl"* (U 441). This attaches additional sexual significance to the description of Emma in the early works as a "bat" *(Chamber Music)*, a "marsupial" *(Stephen Hero)*, and a "batlike soul" *(A Portrait)*, for Emma, too, like the bat-winged whore Bridie Kelly, always seems to be wearing a shawl—as Joyce takes pains to remind us four times (P 82, 141, 222, 248). If Bridie's bright name suggests both bride and birdie, the fact that she is in fact a whore by night suggests an equation of bird and bat as bawd. This oscillation (hither, thither) between bird and bat lends even more resonant significance to *Ulysses*, where the women of Dublin can find their daytime selves transformed into "night-birds," into the "bats" of Nighttown in the Circe episode.

Jean-Michel Rabaté writes that "the Sirens are primarily winged beings, like sea-birds, and they belong to the long series of bird-like women met and loved by Ulysses: Circe, a hawk-owl; Calypso, a nocturnal bird of prey; Penelope, a teal, daughter of Ikarios, the partridge; and the Sirens, possibly cormorants" (1986, 85). In this litany of Ulyssean women a winged correlative to Joyce's Nausicaa might be a bat. As Fritz Senn notes about the Nausicaa episode, "The immersion in this female world coincides with the oncoming of night" (1974, 282). It is evening, the time of vespers, and the time that *Vespertilii* (Lat., bats) emerge. And so, in Nausicaa: "there in the gathering twilight, . . . the touching chime of those evening bells and at the same time a bat flew forth from the ivied belfry through the dusk, *hither, thither,* with a tiny lost cry" (U 363; my emphasis).

Much has been justly made of the many parallels between Nausicaa and Stephen's vision on the strand (and again we have dusk, water, women), between the bird-girl's "sufferance" of Stephen's gaze (leading to his intellectual orgasm) and Gerty MacDowell's sufferance of Bloom's gaze and masturbation (see, for example, Senn 1974, 284-86)—and I don't intend to recapitulate these comparisons. There are, however, some other interesting parallels in the context of birds and bats. Gerty has some batlike qualities and even imagines herself in the alter ego of a "bat," conscious that (like a whore) she has made the stranger sin: "he had erred and sinned and wandered. Should a girl tell? No, a thousand times no. That was their secret, only theirs, alone in the hiding twilight and there was none to know or tell save the little bat that flew so softly through the evening to and fro and little bats don't tell" (*U* 367). We have again here the batlike motifs of talking/telling and (as on *U* 363) flitting hither/thither ("to and fro"). If bats don't tell, they certainly talk or bawk, as Cissy and Edy do, chattering among themselves; as the "tittering daughters" (*FW* 215.29), the gossiping washerwomen, do in *Finnegans Wake*: chattering, too, is a trait frequently associated with women that supposedly drives men bats.

Gerty, on the other hand, refrains from much talking with the girls, imagining herself to be a little bat that doesn't tell. Just then a real bat had flown out, an emblematic or objective correlative to Gerty—and Bloom notices it: "Ba. What is that flying about? Swallow? Bat probably. Thinks I'm a tree, so blind. Have birds no smell? Metempsychosis" (*U* 377). Hearing the bat's bawk/squeak ("Ba"), Bloom at first mistakes it for a bird (swallow), and then recognizes it as a bat, emerging now that it is evening. Gerty, too, metamorphoses at dusk from her daytime self to her night-self's sexual awareness: her menstrual cycle begins, and she becomes a sexual object, a prostitute-bat, recognizing in Bloom her phallic "tree." Bloom, though, doesn't recognize the femininity of the bat: "Ba. There he goes. Funny little beggar" (*U* 377).

Bloom signifies the bat by its bawk: "Ba." The nature and movements of bats suggest to Bloom both birds and rodents: "Ba. Again. Wonder why they come out at night like mice. They're a mixed breed. Birds are like the hopping mice. . . . Who knows what they're always flying for?. . . Birds too never find out what they say. Like our small talk" (*U* 377-78). As a woman, Gerty, too, is—like a "bat"—a mixed breed, hovering between bird and rodent, making small talk but not telling. Finally, Bloom remarks on the flittering, to/fro movement of the flittermouse—and both its rodentlike nature (like Stephen's sins, "jeweleyed harlots . . . squeaking like mice" [*P* 115]) and its binary movements recall the lecherous field beasts in Stephen's vision of hell, moving "hither and thither": "Bat again. . . . A bat flew. Here. There. Here" (*U* 382). In "Here. There. Here" we find the sexually suggestive hither/thither from the parallel bird-girl vision and the vision of the creatures of hell linked to Gerty-as-bat.

Finally, Joyce underlines the link between Gerty and the "bat," between the virgin and the whore, as a "mixed breed," in the description of her clothing: although she was dressed "simply but with the instinctive taste of a votary of Dame Fashion," she "wore a coquettish little love of a hat of"—none other than—"wide-leaved nigger straw" (*U* 350). Here we have Gerty (like Bloom's "whore of the lane" also) dressed in the signal identification of the whore of *Stephen Hero*, whom Stephen endows with a giving generosity; Gerty has, in the same sense, been generous to Bloom—"coquettish," literally like a *coquette*.

Bloom muses further about the bat: "Wonder where he lives. Belfry up there. Very likely. Hanging by his heels in the odour of sanctity" (*U* 377). Ironically, the bat comes from the belfry of the nearby Star of the Sea church, associated with the Blessed Virgin Mary and whence the Litany of Our Lady of Loreto is emanating—and Joyce's "symbol" (in his own designations) for the Nausicaa episode is the Virgin: ironic because, like the Virgin Mary who tempts men to follow her ways, and like Stephen's equation (in *Stephen Hero*) of the virgin Emma with the woman in the black straw hat as universal whores, Gerty is—simultaneously—literally a virgin and figuratively a whore, a "bat." In Nausicaa Joyce's "symbol" is The Virgin; in Circe, it is The Whore. In fact we see that, as night falls, the two are interchangeable: Gerty is only one of a number of women who, respectable by daylight, emerge (like bats) at night into the phantasmagoria of Nighttown and the Circe episode to take their roles as prostitutes-in-fantasy, virgins as whores: birds by day, bats by night (one might even suggest that Nausicaa and Circe blur the distinction between ego and id). Molly Bloom, *Ulysses*'s fullest portrayal of the feminine, has, as we might expect, the same dual nature, too—for on her commode, we are told in Ithaca, "rest[s] a lady's black straw hat" (*U* 730); John Gordon (1981, 142-43) even suggests that the whore of the lane, that "streetwalker . . . under a black straw hat" (*U* 632), is an alter ego for Molly. And all of these characteristics seem now intimately related in the binary duality of Joyce's women; day cedes to evening, to darkness, to poor vision, to blindness, to nocturnal bats (who are blind), to the bawk of bats, to vampire bats (the devil, the Prince of Darkness), to hell, to sin, to sex, to lecherous creatures moving hither and thither in the night.

At last we are ready for the *Wake*'s "bawk of bats." Clive Hart's *A Concordance to "Finnegans Wake"* lists a number of references to bats. There are, first of all, other types of bats (besides the winged type) in *Finnegans Wake*, as in the other novels—pandybats, cricket bats, bolo bats—yet even these seem relatable, for the "bawk of bats" becomes the "pock" of bats in *A Portrait* (the "pock puck" of the cricket bats [*P* 41, 44, 45, 59]) and the "squak" of "bolo the bat" in

Finnegans Wake (151.22-23). Bats also suggest madness and going bats, and in this context the word is applied twice to the mad artist, Shem ("Sh! You are mad!" [*FW* 193.28]), in the episode by his name: *"When He Is Going Batty"* (177.29), Shem has "the rats in his garret, the bats in his belfry" (180.27; "rat" was also slang for "priest"). (Joyce himself must have been full of bats, rats, and hither/thither in his own belfry, till he was perhaps "Hitherzither! Almost dotty!" [*FW* 360.01]). But the contexts of most of the bats in *Finnegans Wake* reinforce and expand the associations already discovered from the other works. Bats are related to dusk and darkness: "Aught darks flou a duskness. Bats that?" (*FW* 276.20)—and to vespers: "Dogs' vespers are anending. Vespertiliabitur" (*FW* 276.11; Lat., *vespertilio*); they are rodentlike: "the rats in his garret, the bats in his belfry" (*FW* 180.26–27); they are related to woman, and to water—in a section that joins birds ("chicks"), bats, Nausicaa, sex, kissing, and Bloom kissing Molly's rump (cheeks): "positively cover the two pure chicks of your comely plumpchake with zuccherikissings . . . that I'd scare the bats out of the ivfry . . . upon the mingling of our meeting waters" (*FW* 446.09-14; "ivfry": the "ivied belfry" of Nausicaa, whence the "bat flew forth" [*U* 363]).

And, of course, there are the washerwomen. Women near water (as with Stephen's bird-girl and Nausicaa's bat) suggest "hither and thither": "Hither-on-Thither . . . watery world . . . Tell mother that" (*FW* 452.27-32). The washerwomen of Anna Livia Plurabelle are prefigured in the Nuvoletta section of the Mookse and Gripes story. Young "Nuvoletta in her lightdress" (*FW* 157.08) by the riverbank recalls Gerty ("a votary of Dame Fashion") by the waterbanks; as in Nausicaa and the bird-girl epiphany, it is dusk by the water's edge, a young lass ("Nuvoletta, a lass" [*FW* 159.05]) is present, and darkness is falling: "shades began to glidder along the banks . . . duusk unto duusk, and it was as glooming as gloaming could be. . . . Oh, how it was duusk! . . . It was so duusk that the tears of night began to fall. . . . O! O! O! Par la pluie!" (*FW* 158.07-24). Like Nausicaa and her handmaidens washing their undergarments, the two washerwomen come down to the banks to wash an apron and a handkerchief (Mookse and Gripes): "Then there came down to the thither bank a woman of no appearance . . . and she gathered up his hoariness the Mookse . . . her boshop's apron" (*FW* 158.25-30); "And there came down to the hither bank a woman to all important . . . as blow it to a hawker's hank, she plucked down the Gripes" (*FW* 158.31-35). The "hoariness" is not only the Mookse but her own "whoriness," for we have here all the attendant qualities assigned to the "bat" (whore): women, water, nightfall, hither-thither, sex, washing, and phallic trees—"And there were left now an only elmtree and but a stone" (*FW* 159.03-4).

All are found also in Anna Livia Plurabelle:

> His tittering daughters of. Whawk?
> Can't hear with the waters of. The chittering waters of. Flittering bats, fieldmice bawk talk. Ho! Are you not gone ahome? What Thom Malone? Can't hear with bawk of bats, all thim liffeying waters of. Ho, talk save us! My foos won't moos. I feel as old as yonder elm. A tale told of Shaun or Shem? All Livia's daughtersons. Dark hawks hear us. Night! Night! . . . Night now! Tell me, tell me, tell me, elm! Night night! Telmetale of stem or stone. Beside the rivering waters of, hitherandthithering waters of. Night! (*FW* 215.29-216.05)

It is nightfall by the river as the bats emerge. By now this passage should shine with a number of new meanings, since all the accumulated elements associated with Joyce's bats come together in this famous conclusion to the Anna Livia Plurabelle chapter—as the "tittering daughters of" Anna Livia, in the form of the washerwomen, recall and repeat stories (like Blake's fabling "daughters of" memory), two "old bats" talking across the riverbanks like the bawking bats: women, water, talk/chatter, bats, trees, birds, dusk, darkness, and night. The gossiping women can't hear one another clearly for both the babble of the river and the bawk of the bats, and so the various sorts of incomprehensible speech become equated and coalesce into a feminine Babel: women's gossip (like the chatter of the young girls in Nausicaa), the bats' bawk (like the "squeaking" of Bridie Kelly in Circe, the bat in her "*batshawl*," and the "Ba" of the bat who doesn't tell in Nausicaa) and the "Quoiquoiquoiquoiquoiquoiquoiq!" (*FW* 195.06)—the mad, quacky, aqueous babbling—of Anna Liffey. We recall that *bat* is slang not only for prostitute but also for "spoken language . . . speech, words"—as in "to sling the bat." Even more appropriately, *bawk* (conflating *bat*, *hawk*, and *talk*) suggests not only talk and sound but the etymological source of *bat*, Danish *bakke*—so that the two words *bawk* and *bat* both (and neatly) suggest the other, through etymology and slang.

The bats are "flittering" in the night air like birds ("hawks"), but bawking like the rodents they are ("fieldmice bawk talk"): flittering and mice in combination self-reflexively suggest their combination, the flittermouse (Ger., *fledermaus*)—like the "mixed breed" Bloom imagines the bat to be, "hopping mice," both bird and rodent (like the birds in *A Portrait* with their "squeak of mice"). These images collectively evoke the chain of rodent images for the feminine in Joyce's works: women first as "marsupials" in *Stephen Hero*, metamorphosed as "batlike souls" in *A Portrait,* as bats in *Chamber Music,* and as "bats" flittering (hither and thither) in the streets of Nighttown in *Ulysses.* Even more, "fieldmice" (as in Stephen's sins, "jeweleyed harlots . . . squeaking like mice") should again suggest the lecherous field creatures in Stephen's vision of hell, "moving in the field, hither and thither" (*P* 137) with the hither/thither of feminine sexuality, the night side of woman in Joyce's works.

And so the combined elements of talk, women, bats, water, and sexuality are developed in this Anna Livia Plurabelle passage within a suggestive and progressive series of verbal echoes and equations: the "tittering daughters" of feminine gossip are also the "chittering waters" of the babbling Liffey and the "flittering bats" of female promiscuity, the "liffeying waters" and the "rivering waters" revealing themselves finally, when night falls, as the sexually engendered "hitherandthithering waters." As night falls, the women's voices talking merge with the bats' bawking; and women emerge as bats, flighty creatures animated by the hither and thithering waters of their sexual natures, their batlike, night-bird selves—as night falls and the rivers babble on and the bats bawk on and the women talk on by the rivers of Babble-on.

NOTE

1. In page references to James Joyce's works, I have used the following abbreviations: *CM* for *Chamber Music,* *FW* for *Finnegans Wake,* *P* for *A Portrait of the Artist as a Young Man,* *SH* for *Stephen Hero,* and *U* for *Ulysses.*

WORKS CITED

Brown, Richard. 1985. *James Joyce and Sexuality.* Cambridge: Cambridge University Press.
Cheng, Vincent J. 1987. "Stephen Dedalus and the Black Panther Vampire." *James Joyce Quarterly* 24:161-76.
del Greco Lobner, Corinna. 1978. "The Metamorphoses of Brunetto's Basilisk in 'Scylla and Charybdis.'" *James Joyce Quarterly* 15:134-37.
Gordon, John. 1981. *James Joyce's Metamorphoses.* Dublin: Gill and Macmillan.
Hancock, Leslie. 1967. *Word Index to James Joyce's "Portrait of the Artist."* Carbondale: Southern Illinois University Press.
Hart, Clive. 1963. *A Concordance to "Finnegans Wake."* Minneapolis: University of Minnesota Press.
Joyce, James. 1954. *Chamber Music.* New York: Columbia University Press.
———. 1939. *Finnegans Wake.* New York: Viking Press, Reprint, 1959.
———. 1964. *A Portrait of the Artist as a Young Man.* New York: Viking Press.
———. 1944. *Stephen Hero.* New York: New Directions, Reprint, 1963.
———. 1934. *Ulysses.* New York: Random House, Reprint, 1961.

Latini, Brunetto. 1948. *Li Livres dou Tresor de Brunetto Latini: édition critique par Francis J. Carmody.* Berkeley: University of California Press.
McCarthy, Patrick A. 1982. "The Jeweleyed Harlots of His Imagination: Prostitution and Artistic Vision in Joyce." *Eire-Ireland* 17, no. 4:91-109.
The Oxford English Dictionary. Compact ed. 1971. Oxford: Oxford University Press.
Partridge, Eric. 1961, 1967. *A Dictionary of Slang and Unconventional English.* 6th ed. New York: Macmillan.
Rabaté, Jean-Michel. 1986. "The Silence of the Siren." In *James Joyce: The Centennial Symposium,* edited by Morris Beja, Phillip Herring, Maurice Harmon, and David Norris, 82-88. Urbana and Chicago: University of Illinois Press.
Scott, Bonnie Kime. 1982. "Emma Clery in *Stephen Hero*: A Young Woman Walking Proudly through the Decayed City." In *Women in Joyce,* edited by Suzette Henke and Elaine Unkeless, 57-81. Urbana and Chicago: University of Illinois Press.
Senn, Fritz. 1974. "Nausicaa." In *James Joyce's "Ulysses,"* edited by Clive Hart and David Hayman, 277-311. Berkeley: University of California Press.
Skeat, Walter William. 1882. *An Etymological Dictionary of the English Language.* Oxford: Clarendon Press.
Smith, John B. 1980. *Imagery and the Mind of Stephen Dedalus.* Lewisburg, Pa.: Bucknell University Press.
Stoker, Bram. 1897. *Dracula.* Reprint. New York: Modern Library, 1932.
Tindall, William York. 1954. "Introduction and Notes." In James Joyce's *Chamber Music,* edited by William York Tindall. New York: Columbia University Press.
———. 1959. *A Reader's Guide to James Joyce.* New York: Farrar, Straus, and Cudahy.
Unkeless, Elaine. 1978. "Bats and Sanguivorous Bugaboos." *James Joyce Quarterly* 15:128-33.
Whittaker, Stephen. 1987. "Joyce and Skeat." *James Joyce Quarterly* 24:177-92.

8
James Joyce
The Olfactory Factor

BERNARD BENSTOCK

> "And you'll nose it, O you'll nose it,
> without warnward from we"
> —Joyce, *Finnegans Wake*

The genesis of this inquiry into the Joycean method of olfactory perception is twofold: an item from *A Portrait of the Artist as a Young Man* intended for "Inscribing James Joyce's Tombstone," an item retrieved from the cutting-room floor and now pressed into service, and an anecdote some twenty years old that (as far as I know) has never been publicly aired—and probably shouldn't be. The *Portrait* incident comes from chapter 2, where Stephen, in despair over what he considers Emma's defection, runs through the Dublin streets until he comes to the city morgue:

> He saw the word *Lotts* on the wall of the lane and breathed slowly the rank heavy air.
> —That is horse piss and rotted straw, he thought. It is a good odour to breathe. It will calm my heart. My heart is quite calm now. I will go back. (P 86)[1]

The anecdote derives from that other kind of fiction we know as real life: in Ohio sometime in the sixties a colleague reported having met an Irishman who claimed to have attended the University in Dublin with James Joyce. When asked what he remembered of Joyce, the old man (with red-rimmed horny eyes) said, "He stank." Perhaps we were too intent in the 1960s on separating James Joyce from Stephen Dedalus for the odiferous anecdote to have its full potency, but recent critical tendencies, while insisting on the death of the author, have also focused attention on Joyce as a person, as a character in that "other fiction."

We have long since learned to accept the hydrophobic Stephen, aware of his sensitivity to the bullying behavior of Wells, the rituals of the Catholic church, and the demise of Icarus—and if he has not bathed in eight months, have we ever stopped to question what could have occurred in October of 1903 for him to have bothered to bathe then? There has been no speculation to date on what Stephen smelled like on the warm day of 16 June 1904, primarily because no one within sniffing distance ever recorded an olfactory verdict. The primacy of the two dominant senses, sight and sound, is an aspect of conventional narrative presentation that has rarely been challenged even by modernist and avant-garde writers, primarily because they are so much the property of all readers, whereas the tactile, gustatory, and olfactory are far more personal and subjective. Stephen Dedalus was born with and in infancy developed all five senses, as we are aware from the opening segment of *A Portrait*: he can see his father's hairy face, taste Betty Byrne's lemon platt, hear "the wild rose blossoms" song, feel the oilsheet get cold, and smell the degree of niceness that differentiates his mother from his father (*P* 7). These basic capacities are essential for the forging of the artist within him, the tools of even the most ordinary artist, and yet we suspect that an extraordinary sixth sense will distinguish the extraordinary artist, a sense that is a confusion of the senses, the artistic deployment of synaesthesia. At the brink of artistic self-discovery, schoolboy Stephen muses on his love for the color of words:

> No, it was not their colours: it was the poise and balance of the period itself. Did he then love the rhythmic rise and fall of words better than their associations of legend and colour? Or was it that, being as weak of sight as he was shy of mind, he drew less pleasure from the reflection of the glowing sensible world through the prism of a language manycoloured and richly storied than from the contemplation of an inner world of individual emotions mirrored perfectly in a lucid supple periodic prose? (*P* 166-67)

Compensation for the weakened sense of seeing has always been assumed of the purblind author, as well as the concomitant stress on the aural, the making of "soundsense and sensesound kin again" and the making of "singsigns to soundsense" (*FW* 121.15-16; 138.7),[2] these being the operative dicta of *Finnegans Wake*. Yet the penman in the *Wake*, the alchemistic Shem, makes the ink he needs from his own feces and urine, and one can only wonder how foul the laboratory in his ink-bottle house on Brimstone Walk—a haunted house with a doorplate reading "SHUT" (*FW* 182.33)—must smell. One can only wonder, since no olfactory judgment is rendered here, either. Shem started out cooking eggs in his "lithargogalenu fowlhouse" (*FW* 184.13), and it would take only one rotten egg for it to reek of sulphur; one of his recipes is "à la Sulphate de Soude" (*FW* 184.29). Yet even his *"stercore turpi"* (*FW* 185.24) is credited with no particular smell in a text that remains odor-innocent. The incantation for the alchemical process is of course in Latin, or more likely in a kind of Latin used by Rabelais and designated as *latin de marmite;* Joyce depicts his younger Shem, the Glugg of the Mime: "He stanth theirs mun in his natural, oblious autamnesically of his very proprium, (such is stockpot leaden, so did sonsepun crake)" (*FW* 251.4-6). In the saucepan and stockpot, language undergoes its chemical metamorphoses, so that even the naked micturating mute (*mun* melds the Irish words for dumb and urine) will have the soundsense from which to create his literary art.

* * *

The privileging of the ear and the eye, that interplay between the "ineluctable modality of the visible" and the "ineluctable modality of the audible," sustains most forms of realistic fiction, with only occasional forays into the domains of the minor senses. Sexual longing provokes tactile-laden thoughts for Stephen Dedalus, who, having once experienced the hands of Eileen Vance, "long and white and thin and cold and soft" (*P* 35), first over his eyes and then with his hand in his pocket (*P* 43), later (in Proteus) fantasizes on a "Soft soft soft hand. . . . Oh, touch me soon, now" (Pr 434-5).[3] The gustatory in the Joyce canon can perhaps be represented by an extreme case of individuated palatal taste: when Stephen accuses Lynch of eating "pieces of dried dung" (*P* 205), Lynch admits it with delicious glee, so that Stephen, visualizing his companion as reptilian, allows that "we are all animals. I am an animal too" (*P* 205). He also applies an aesthetic analysis of such individual savorings:

> The desire and loathing excited by improper esthetic means are really unesthetic emotions not only because they are kinetic in character but also because they are not more than physical. Our flesh shrinks from what it dreads and responds to the stimulus of what it desires by a purely reflex action of the nervous system. (*P* 206)

Just as Lynch's flesh did *not* shrink from eating dried dung, so the recipient in *Finnegans Wake* says a grateful thanks to Kate the Slops's offer of a "plateful" of "*Shite*"—"Tak" (*FW* 142.7). Between the sexual tactile and the cloacal gustatory, the ineluctable modality of the smellable has its important moments in the works of James Joyce, and particularly in the ultrasensory and extrasensory *Ulysses*.

The publication in 1986 of Patrick Süsskind's novel *Perfume* has momentarily brought to the surface and given individual honors to the sense of smell, as well as allowing the author to comment throughout on the phenomenon and to argue its newly established position of dominance. Süsskind's protagonist, Grenouille, was born with a supernatural sense of smell as well as no perceivable body odor of his own. His creator compares with him several of the most heinous villains of history, noting that "it was not because Grenouille fell short of those more famous blackguards when it came to arrogance, misanthropy, immorality, or, more succinctly, to wickedness but because his gifts and his sole ambition were restricted to a domain that leaves no trace in history: to the fleeting realm of scent."[4] Historical restoration fails to take the olfactory into consideration—no time capsules buried for later recuperation contain a retrievable whiff of the odor of the times—yet each work of fiction is posterity-proof. No captured smell specified in *Ulysses* is ever lost in the rereading or fails to register its full pungency for every new reader. Although Süsskind maintains that the fleeting realm of scent leaves no trace in history, he also acknowledges that "there are scents that linger for decades. A cupboard rubbed with musk, a piece of leather drenched with cinnamon oil, a glob of ambergris, a cedar chest—they all possess virtually eternal olfactory life." Against such more permanent odors he contrasts the transitory ones: "lime oil, bergamot, jonquil and tuberose extracts, and many floral scents—evaporate within a few hours if they are exposed to the air in a pure, unbounded form."[5]

In the fleeting realm of scent the transition from life to death plays itself out as Stephen recalls his dead mother, conjured up by "her wasted body within its loose brown graveclothes giving off an odour of wax and rosewood, her breath, that had bent upon him, mute, reproachful, a faint odour of wetted ashes" (Te 103-5). This dream vision, first returning to him when Mulligan accuses him of failing to kneel when the dying Mrs. Dedalus begged him "with her last breath," is recapitulated soon after, once Stephen is alone atop the tower. As is so often the stylistic finesse in *Ulysses,* the repetition is almost exact, except for a few rearranged words, and in the second instance "mute, reproachful" is amended to "with mute, secret words" (Te 272), as Stephen attempts to find the *language* of the impalpable experience. The ghostliness of the extended recollection amplifies into "Her hoarse loud breath rattling in horror" (Te 275). Breath as aspiration bridges the gap between the intangible odor that cannot be recuperated in language and the insistence on giving recordable speech to that which is inarticulate. The Stephen who will hours later announce that his vocation is that of a reader of "Signatures of all things" (Pr 2) is already at work blending the visual and the auditory into language, "The twining stresses, two by two," as he gazes out to sea and listens to his sounds: "Wavewhite wedded words shimmering on the dim tide" (Te 245-47). The memory of his mother that follows immediately focuses on "Her secrets: old featherfans, tasselled dancecards, powdered with musk, a gaud of amber beads in her locked drawer" (Te 255-56). He has conjured up "Phantasmal mirth, folded away; muskperfumed" (Te 263), corroborating Süsskind's observation on the persistence of olfactory memories in "a cupboard rubbed with musk . . . a glob of ambergris." The transitory and immediate sensation of "a faint odour of wetted ashes" nonetheless gains supremacy over the lingering musk that is "Folded away in the memory of nature with her toys" (Te 265).

The basic dichotomy set up in Süsskind's *Perfume* and emphasized in Joyce's *Ulysses* is reconciled in Süsskind's conclusion that "the perfumer counteracts this fatal circumstance [that is, the pure, unbounded form that will quickly evaporate] by binding scents that are too volatile, by putting them in chains, so to speak, taming their urge for freedom—though his art consists in leaving enough slack in the chains for the odor seemingly to preserve its freedom, even when it is tied so deftly that it cannot flee."[6] Süsskind's eponymous perfumer stands in the same relationship to the creation of a work of art as does Stephen Dedalus's artist, as expounded to Lynch in *A Portrait*: "to try slowly and humbly and constantly to express, to press out again, from the gross earth or what it brings forth, from sound and shape and colour which are the prison gates of our soul, an image of beauty we have come to understand—that is art" (P 207). In characterizing the art and defining the domain of art in beauty, Stephen tends to privilege the two major senses, while lumping the three ancillary senses together as he interprets Aquinas's *visa* "to cover esthetic apprehensions of all kinds, whether through sight or hearing or through any other avenue of apprehension" (P 207), adding the Platonic definition of beauty as "beheld by the imagination which is appeased by the most satisfying relations of the sensible" (P 208). Yet Stephen's immediate perceptions, leading to his process of intellectuation, include apprehension of his immediate environment: "A crude grey light, mirrored in the sluggish water, and a smell of wet branches over their heads seemed to war against the course of Stephen's thoughts" (P 207). Only a few hours earlier he had "walked down the avenue and felt the grey morning light falling about him through the dripping trees and smelt the strange wild smell of the wet leaves and bark," acknowledging that "his soul was loosed of her miseries." On the basis of this olfactory apprehension begins the linked associations for him along literary-aesthetic lines:

> The rainladen trees of the avenue evoked in him, as always, memories of the girls and women in the plays of Gerhart Hauptmann; and the memory of their pale sorrows and the fragrance falling from the wet branches mingled in a mood of quiet joy. (P 176)

Stephen's susceptibility to sensory perceptions is obviously associative, leading often from the kinetic to the static, from loathing and desire to that "stasis called forth, prolonged and at last dissolved by . . . the rhythm of beauty" (P 206). That *ideal* Stephen, however, is all too frequently grounded in "the gross earth," not always able to see himself as the "artist forging anew in his workshop out of the sluggish matter of the earth a new soaring impalpable imperishable being" (P 169). As he admits when his recitation of his aesthetic ideas is interrupted, "His mind, emptied of theory and courage, lapsed back into a listless peace" (P 216). As an adolescent Stephen had found in the odor of "horse piss and rotted straw" the balm for his disquieted heart, once he had run aground at the morgue, where the odors lingered from the wagon that had carried the dead. This experiencing of desire and loathing finds its eventual translation toward the end of the aesthetics recitation, as Stephen arrives at "luminous silent stasis of esthetic pleasure, a spiritual state very like to that cardiac condition which the Italian physiologist Luigi Galvani . . . called the enchantment of the heart" (P 213). An appreciation of horse piss and rotted straw is not the privilege solely of the potential aesthete, nor is it always palpably kinetic; so neutral an observer of the olfactory scene as Leopold Bloom can walk by a masticating horse and objectively record the "sweet oaten reek of horsepiss" (Lo 215) without any apparent cardiac effect.

It should come as no surprise that it is Bloom who has a particularly active and sophisticated nose—odors are an important human factor for him. He calls attention to himself immediately by having a rare predilection for "a fine tang of faintly scented urine" (Ca 4-5), with which he endows grilled mutton kidneys, revealing a synaesthetic conflation of the gustatory and the olfactory, the rarefied relationship between taste and smell. As he ventures out into the morning world, imaginary scents vie with those of the tangible world; he identifies, classifies, savors, and accepts them: "water scented with fennel" (Ca 91) of exotic cities; "whiffs of ginger, teadust, biscuitmush" (Ca 107) from O'Rourke's pub: "the lukewarm breath of cooked spicy pigs' blood" (Ca 143-44) from Dlugacz's butcher shop. When his imagination produces oranges and citrons, Bloom contemplates holding "cool waxen fruit" in his hand and lifting them to his nostrils to "smell the perfume . . . heavy, sweet, wild perfume" (Ca 207-8). Such olfactory fantasies are luxuries for him, while others come closer to home and are self-protective: when a cloud hides the sun and his thoughts are suddenly of "poisonous foggy water. Brimstone," his mind retreats to the smell of "gentle smoke of tea, fume of the pan, sizzling butter" (Ca 221, 238), aligned with anticipation of Molly's "ample bedwarmed flesh" (Ca 239). The arrival of Boylan's letter intrudes, however, and, mingled with the "fragrance of the tea she poured," the bedroom odor offends him: "Rather stale smell that incense leaves next day," he notes. "Like foul flowerwater" (Ca 306-7, 315-16). But the audience with Molly is cut short by her sensing "a smell of burn," the "Pungent smoke" (Ca 380, 384) of his burned pork kidney. Molly's defection makes the anticipation of lunch not nearly as potent as that of breakfast had been, and an afternoon cloud also intervenes on his mood.

As he converses with Mrs. Breen, Bloom is assaulted by the smell of a potential meal ("Hot mockturtle vapour and steam of newbaked jampuffs rolypoly poured out from Harrison's" [Le 232-33]), but once freed of Mrs. Breen and in search of a place for lunch his "smile faded" as "a heavy cloud" (Le 475) hid the sun, and he feels "as if I had been eaten and spewed," all the while hoping for "liver and bacon" (Le 495, 498). Unable to keep Molly out of his thoughts as he surveys lingerie in a shop window—and affected by midday hunger—he is prey to a potent confusion of appetites:

> A warm human plumpness settled down on his brain. His brain yielded. Perfume of embraces all him assailed. With hungered flesh obscurely, he mutely craved to adore. (Le 637-39)

(Those famous structured sentences are chiasmatic, the running against each other of urges for food and sexual gratification, balanced in the concept of perfume.)

> Duke street. Here we are. Must eat. The Burton. Feel better then.
> . . . Perfumed bodies, warm, full. All kissed, yielded:
> . . . His heart astir he pushed in the door of the Burton restaurant. Stink gripped his trembling breath: pungent meatjuice, slush of greens. (Le 640-42, 650-51)

Nowhere else in *Ulysses*—not until the rancid environment of Circe—is there as defined a locus of olfactory putrescence as at the

Burton, where Bloom's scented fantasies and delicately balanced perfumes of desire are demolished by the reality of human stench. And yet Bloom lingers in the doorway, surveying the disgusting scene, before relying on a subterfuge in order to escape, apparently fascinated by Burton's as a paradigm of the human condition.

Bloom's receptivity to the entire range of olfactory sensations, his tolerance for the rank odors and his pleasures in appreciating the most fragrant, consists of both human effluvia and manufactured scent. He is as attuned to the odors of the living body as he is to those of its waste products, to the individual and the communal, those offered openly and those kept hidden. Human odors contain both social stigma and social acceptance, what both differentiate and mutually identify. Patrick Süsskind characterizes the contradiction by asserting:

> That aura . . . the highly complex, unmistakable code of a *personal* odor, was not perceptible for most people in any case. Most people did not know that they even had such a thing, and moreover did everything they could to disguise it under clothes or fashionable artificial odors. Only that basic odor, the primitive human effluvium, was truly familiar to them; they lived exclusively within it and it made them feel secure; and only a person who gave off that standard vile vapor was ever considered one of them.[7]

The France of the seventeenth century that Süsskind evokes in *Perfume* has its corollary in Joyce's Circean Nighttown, into which Bloom the outsider—both alien to the "primitive human effluvium" and integrated within it—wanders, his nostrils alerted and mind attuned to interpreting the essences he is there to read. Throughout the day and night he is navigating and adrift, confronted by smells that are common to all flesh and seeking his own individual olfactory identity.

* * *

The Nighttown into which Bloom emerges is a miasma of *"stagnant fumes"* that *"arise on all sides"* from *"drains, clefts, cesspools, middens"* (Ci 138–39)—those of the city slum paralleling the drains, clefts, cesspools, and middens of the human body. His first gesture is to look at himself in the distorting mirrors of the hairdresser's windows, mirrors both concave and convex and already reflecting the images of Nelson, Gladstone, and Wellington, distortions reflexive and self-reflexive as well for the sense of smell. The aroma of *"birdseye cigarettes"* soon assails him: *"The odour of the sicksweet weed floats towards him in slow round ovalling wreaths"* (Ci 652-53), wreaths that announce "Sweets of sin" (Ci 655), thereby locating Bloom's personal perfumes of embrace. In *"a dark stalestunk corner"* (Ci 667) he gives away to the dog the food he had bought for himself, having pronounced his verdict on the animal: "Stinks like a polecat" (Ci 661). On the doorstep of the brothel he encounters Zoe Higgins luring him inside, but his fantasies protect him with an outdoor image of gazelles and a *"womancity"* that is *"nude, white, still, cool, in luxury,"* and from the cedargroves *"Aroma rises, a strong hairgrowth of resin"* (Ci 1325-28). Zoe herself, however, emits a different aroma as she bites his ear, *"a cloying breath of stale garlic"* (Ci 1340)— Bloom had rather ambivalent reactions to garlic as he stood outside the Burton: repulsed by animals eating animals he considers the values of a diet without meat ("After all there's a lot in that vegetarian fine flavour of things from the earth garlic of course it stinks after Italian organgrinders crisp of onions mushrooms truffles" [Le 720-22]). As Zoe is leading him into the house Bloom feels himself drawn *"by the odour of her armpits,"* and he assumes that in the folds of her clothes *"lurks the lion reek of all the male brutes that have possessed her."* The MALE BRUTES respond by *"exhaling sulphur of rut and dung"* (Ci 2015-19).

Inside the Bella Cohen establishment Bloom finds an even greater concentration of the malodorous. Florry Talbot is characteristic, *"A female tepid effluvium leaks out from her"* (Ci 2167), and Bella herself is "all of a mucksweat" (Ci 2750). Her foot, personified as THE HOOF, invites Bloom to "Smell my hot goathide" (Ci 2820). As Bello, the Madam promises her newly feminized and recruited Bloom that he will be "perfumesprayed" and "ricepowdered" and that one of the newly rechristened whores will be provided with a "nice scent" (Ci 2974, 2980), but this fantasy advertising soon is replaced by Bello's threats that Bloom will now be washing "our smelling underclothes also when we ladies are unwell" (Ci 3065-66). In his own nostalgic fantasy, Bloom reverts to adolescent appreciation of "the mingling odours of the ladies' cloakroom and lavatory" (Ci 3319-20), and as someone well acquainted with his own flatulence (twice during the day he credited his own to such scented beverages as Burgundy and cider), Bloom seems to believe in a product that promises a "noiseless, inoffensive vent" (Ci 3276). Throughout Circe he is propelled back and forth between an inoffensive Pollyanna existence and the Malebolgean depths, THE NYMPH rescuing him amid a "pall of incense smoke" that "screens" and then "disperses" (Ci 3232-33), while his tenure as Bello's Ruby Cohen inures him to the Nymph's disintegration in *"a cloud of stench escaping from the cracks"* (Ci 3469-70), so he can insist that he cannot be fooled. His nose reads the Circean world: *"(he sniffs)* Rut. Onions. Stale. Sulphur. Grease" (Ci 3477-78). Two external voices serve as a conscience for him, that of Reverend Dowie denouncing Bloom as "this stinking goat of Mendes" (Ci 1755), and that of his grandfather, Lipoti Virag, caustically commenting on insects "lured by the smell of the inferiorly pulchritudinous fumale" (Ci 2413-14). Perhaps it is just as well that, upon entering Nighttown, Stephen Dedalus had armed himself against the lure of fragrance, insisting that "gesture, not music not odour, would be a universal language" (Ci 105-6), denying the odorous, the malodorous, the melodious.

Stephen had of course undergone his own initiation (in *A Portrait of the Artist as a Young Man)* and secured his own protective strengths. Although he reacted to the "cold and slimy" water of the square ditch (P 10) into which Wells had shouldered him, he records no reaction to its smell, nor of the cow yards into which youthful enthusiasms later led him: "foul green puddles and cloths of liquid dung and steaming brantroughs sickened Stephen's heart" (P 63), yet he continues his tours with the milkman and eventually feels "no repugnance" (P 64). In effect, Stephen is inuring himself to the stink of hell—and well he needs to. Father Arnall spares none of the sensory avenues of perception in his Hell Open to Christians, and the olfactory is awarded its share: "the dark smoke of burning brimstone," "its awful stench," "a vast reeking sewer," "its intolerable stench," "a pestilential odour"; "The very air of this world," he notes, "that pure element, becomes foul and unbreathable when it has been long enclosed. Consider then what must be the foulness of the air of hell." He considers: "dense smoking fumes . . . sickening stench . . . reeking darkness . . . the horror of the stench of hell" (P 120). In the "foul laneways" of the brothel district Stephen had found among the "leisurely and perfumed" the prostitute with a "perfumed head" (P 100), who initiated him into adult sexuality: her lips had "pressed upon his brain as upon his lips," a pressure that he acknowledges as "darker than the swoon of sin, softer than sound or odour" (P 101), a foreshadowing of the "warm human plumpness" that "settled down on [Bloom's] brain" in Lestrygonians.

* * *

We become aware, however, that for Stephen it is the *heart* that is the receptive center of his olfactory sensations: the cow yards that had "sickened" his heart prepared him somewhat imperfectly for the "sickening stench" conjured up in the sermon, where he is reminded that he has trampled on "the sacred and loving heart" of Jesus (P

134). It remains only for his own conjuring up of hell, a region reminiscent and redolent of the cow yards, for his torment to be complete: "An evil smell . . . curled upwards sluggishly out of the canisters and from the stale encrusted dung" (*P* 137). His nightmare of a personal hell is "stinking, bestial, malignant," and he leaps from his bed, "the reeking odour pouring down his throat." After vomiting, he opens the window, "the air sweet to breathe . . . and amid peace and shimmering lights and quiet fragrance he made a covenant with his heart" (*P* 138). After confession and absolution, "his prayers ascended to heaven from his purified heart like perfume streaming upwards from a heart of white rose" (*P* 145), and yet in the processes thereafter of mortifying his senses, Stephen finds that the one sense that defies efforts at mortification is the olfactory: "he found in himself no instinctive repugnance of bad odours, whether they were the odours of the outdoor world such as those of dung or tar or the *odours of his own person* among which he had *made many curious comparisons and experiments*. He found in the end that the only odour against which his sense of smell revolted was a certain stale fishy stink like that of longstanding urine: and whenever it was possible he subjected himself to this unpleasant odour" (*P* 151, emphasis added). This tendency toward ichthyphobia reflects suspiciously on the longstanding religion of Stephen's upbringing, and once he has separated himself from it, he can walk through Dublin and at once see and turn "his eyes coldly for an instant towards the faded blue shrine of the Blessed Virgin" and smell "the faint sour stink of rotted cabbages" (*P* 162).

As much as the mature Stephen may discount the language of odor in favor of a universal language of gesture—his own in Circe is the smashing of the lamp chimney in an act of exorcism, only to have it countered by the aggressive gesture of Private Carr—it is the denial of an active sense that remains without him, within him, inexorably with him. His ironic intellect exonerates his hydrophobia by asserting that "All Ireland is washed by the gulfstream" (Te 476); he does not, however, indicate whether it is also fumigated and deodorized by the gulf stream, and one may well wonder what sort of "comparisons and experiments" Stephen had made with his own body odor. "Odors have a power of persuasion stronger than that of words, appearances, emotions, or will," Patrick Süsskind claims. "The persuasive power of an odor cannot be fended off, it enters into us like breath into our lungs, it fills it up, embues us totally. There is no remedy for it."[8] Leopold Bloom would undoubtedly concur, but often only unconsciously. That it has wafted its way into works of literature gives it a dubious distinction, as Jane Heap was aware, when in an article in *The Little Review* she noted:

> You can talk about or write about or paint or sculpt some parts of the body but others must be treated like the Bad Lands. You can write about what you see that you don't like, what you touch, taste, or hear; but you can't write about what you smell; if you do you are accused of using nasty words. I could say a lot more about the geography of the body, and how its influence goes all the way through until the censor makes a geography for your mind and soul.[9]

Jane Heap, who was to go on to a disastrous showdown with the censor, in this instance was talking not about *Ulysses* but *A Portrait of the Artist as a Young Man,* yet one can assume that a whiff of *Ulysses* was already in her nostrils.

The vocabulary determined by the olfactory is extensive and probably indicative of what Süsskind maintains, that "our language is of no use when it comes to describing the smellable world." The range of English nouns (with the usual borrowings) extends along a rainbow of pleasant to unpleasant: perfume, fragrance, bouquet, essence, scent, aroma, redolence, odor, smell, effluvium, stink, stench, reek, putrescence, fetor, mephitis, miasm—the more malodorous, the more esoteric. The smellable world divides itself between the pleasant and the unpleasant, as well as the natural and the artificial, each of the second two categories intersecting with each of the first two. Life odors derive from the living human body and from the natural world; death odors from the putrescence of the human corpse and the body's waste, as well as from the by-products of human activity. In the Ulyssean atmosphere, the participating characters apprehend and resist olfactory sensations, sensibly choosing the life preserving and avoiding the death dealing, although the persistence of odors is often irresistible: they waft democratically in the air and approach any passerby. Stephen Dedalus may well have his defenses in place, whatever the olfactory equivalent of "silence, exile, and cunning" may be, but he is nonetheless subject to unexpected and uninvited smells.

Stephen's nose makes class distinctions in the classroom as he reads his students in terms of a "sweetened boy's breath. Welloff people" (Ne 24) and surmises that their girls also have breath "sweetened with tea and jam" (Ne 37)—Molly will corroborate when she says, "I love the smell of a big rich shop" (Pe 1554). When he enters Deasy's office it is the olfactory that provides the overture ("Stale smoky air hung in the study with the smell of drab abraided leather" [Ne 199-200]), but Stephen has no ostensible reaction. He had been rather oblivious to the "cloud of coalsmoke and fumes of fried grease" (Te 316-17) that choked Mulligan in the confined tower room, Stephen apparently interested only in his breakfast. Yet later, in a hypothetical mode, he turns away from thoughts of Uncle Richie's aria to prefer the natural air of Sandymount Strand, deciding that "This air is sweeter" (Pr 104).

The reign of the malodorous is universal and common to everyone. In Proteus, Stephen's olfactory sense as he watches the dog sniffing, especially as it sniffs the carcass of a dead dog, is sharply awakened. The dog's owners, the cockle-picking gypsies, evoke for Stephen the brothel slums of the city, a "shefiend's whiteness under her rancid rags" and "the tanyard smells" (Pr 379-80)—the Nameless One in Cyclops characterizes the Citizen as "All wind and piss like a tanyard cat" (Cy 1311-12). Stephen soon conjectures on the body of the drowned man in odor-conscious terms:

> Bag of corpsegas sopping in foul brine. A quiver of minnows, fat of a spongy titbit, flash through the slits of his buttoned trouserfly. God becomes man becomes fish becomes barnacle goose becomes featherbed mountain. Dead breaths I living breathe, tread dead dust, devour a urinous offal from all dead. Hauled stark over the gunwale he breathes upward the stench of his green grave, his leprous nosehole snoring to the sun. (Pr 476-81)

Bloom turns up his nose at the putrid. He takes in stride the smell of the jakes, smells that both cover and conceal, "the stench of mouldy limewash and stale cobwebs" (Ca 496-97); in the newspaper printing plant he accepts the "Heavy greasy smell" (Ae 223-24); and in Lestrygonians his gullet is actually tickled by the "heavy noonreek" (Le 237) that awakens his appetite for lunch, although at the Burton the "Smells of men" and "sweetish warmish cigarettesmoke, reek of plug, spilt beer, men's beery piss, the stale of ferment" (Le 670-71) offend him, "tightening the wings of his nose" (Le 678-79). Bloom has a large degree of stench tolerance, as befits his strong odor curiosity. When he undresses late that night he derives satisfaction from the pickings of his toenail, recapturing the same pleasure that he had as a youth (*A la recherche* . . .) and attributing the smell of dead skin (his own) to the "odour of the quick" (It 1490)—a satisfactory association with life.

* * *

Bloom approaches the smells of this world with equanimity as well as tolerance and curiosity and does so with a certain element of interest and enthusiasm. He sniffs his hat, "inhaling his hairoil" (Lo 21); he holds the *Freeman's Journal* "against his nostrils, smelling freshprinted ragpaper" (Lo 50)—both of these gestures are disguise, concealment. At the chemist's he inhales "slowly the keen reek of drugs, the dusty dry smell of sponges and loofahs" (Lo 487–88), but he mostly appreciates the "Nice smell" of the soaps (Lo 501), one of which he takes with him, and he employs it to counteract the printing shop odor: "He took out his handkerchief to dab his nose. Citronlemon? Ah, the soap I put there" (WR 226-27). He remembers with satisfaction that Molly was "smelling herself" that morning (Lo 495), and Molly's perfume has already become an intrusive question in his mind, courtesy of Martha Clifford's letter. "Do tell me what kind of perfume does your wife use" had immediately sent him to sniff at the flower enclosed in her letter, but he is disappointed as he "smelt its almost no smell" (Lo 258, 260). At the chemist soon after he seems to answer the question for himself ("What perfume does you? *Peau d'Espagne*" [Lo 500]), the answer perhaps deriving from his image of her, "the darkness of her eyes . . . Spanish, smelling herself" (Lo 494-95). In her own right Molly disqualifies that particular scent as she recalls the experience with Mulvey in Gibraltar and the handkerchief into which she "pulled him off" (Pe 809): "I kept the handkerchief under my pillow for the smell of him there was no decent perfume to be got in that Gibraltar only that cheap peau dEspagne that faded and left a stink on you" (Pe 863-65)—the translation of the living odor into a dead smell. The smell of sex, the redolence of desire, has sustained itself in Molly's nostrils, as it has in Bloom's mind as he teases, tortures, tantalizes himself with the perfumes of *Sweets of Sin*:

> Warmth showered gently over him, cowing his flesh. Flesh yielded amply amid rumpled clothes: whites of eyes swooning up. His nostrils arched themselves for prey. Melting breast ointments *(for him! for Raoul!)*. Armpits' oniony sweat. Fishgluey slime *(her heaving embonpoint!)*. Feel! Press! Chrished! Sulphur dung of lions! (WR 619-23)

This wild confusion of "melting breast ointments" and the "sulphur dung of lions" (shades of Circe!) has its presumed linkage in the "armpits' oniony sweat," itself an odd intrusion into the sexually blissful smells that Bloom evokes from *Sweets of Sin*. Unfortunately, an external inference presents itself in the presence of the bookstall keeper whom Bloom has been unable to avoid: "Onions of his breath came across the counter out of his ruined mouth" (WR 596-97). The shopman's oniony breath imposes itself on the ointments of the text, adding the stench of the body to the sweets of sin. Raoul's living representative in Bloom's life, Blazes Boylan, puts his finger on the sexual effluvium in Circe as *"he holds out a forefinger"* and invites Lenehan to "Smell that." Lenehan, with a capacity for equating the olfactory with the gustatory, *"smells gleefully"* and announces, "Lobster and mayonnaise. Ah!" (Ci 3751-53).

The linking of love and death complements the linking of love and life. At the cemetery Bloom muses over the thrill of sex in a graveyard and also speculates on the swollen belly of Father Coffey:

> What swells him up that way? . . . Air of the place maybe. Looks full up of bad gas. Must be an infernal lot of bad gas round the place. . . . they have to bore a hole in the coffins sometimes to let out the bad gas and burn it. Out it rushes: blue. One whiff of that and you're a doner. (Ha 606-12)

(Bloom's "bad gas" floats on the same winds as Stephen's "bag of corpsegas.") Yet not all creatures react against the graveyard air, and in conjunction with his observations that "the Chinese say a white man smells like a corpse," Bloom considers the flies of the field of the dead who "come before he's well dead. Got wind of Dignam. They wouldn't care about the smell of it. Saltwhite crumbling mush of corpse: smell, taste like raw white turnips" (Ha 983-94). The flies, like Lenehan, are extrasensory in regard to the confluence of taste and smell.

Body scent, natural and artificial, articulates the language of sexual desire, odors like sounds traveling on the air across space to communicate, to close up the gaps of space. In reviewing *Perfume* in *The New Yorker*, John Updike concluded that "along with the existential nausea is the proposition, borne out by modern scientific studies, that we are more sensitive and responsive to odors than we realize—that the great buried language of smell is still being spoken, subconsciously, by our brains," corroborating the more succinct comment of Paul Valéry that "scents have immense powers on our memory and thus on our emotions."[10] Gerty MacDowell, who has a nose for the "nice perfume" of "good cigarettes" (Na 144-45), comes prepared with her calling card, "a piece of cottonwool scented with her favourite perfume" (Na 153), which she puts to use for Bloom's benefit. Bloom is unimpressed by Gerty's cheap perfume, comparing it with Molly's "opoponax . . . with a little jessamine mixed" (Na 1010-11). He is, in effect, answering Martha's question, which still lingers in his mind, with what he knows is Molly's perfume, not with the false Peau d'Espagne that he used in Lotus Eaters, probably as a mental blind to put Martha off the trail. When he returns home and sniffs Molly's "outsize" drawers, he discovers that they are "redolent of opoponax, jessamine, and Muratti's Turkish cigarettes" (It 2093-94)—Boylan has added his message to Molly's. The human animal leaves its calling card much like the canine, as Stephen has observed: "He stopped, sniffed, stalked round it, brother, nosing closer, went round it, sniffling rapidly like a dog all over the dead dog's bedraggled fell. Dogskull, dogsniff, eyes on the ground, moves to one great goal" (Pr 348-51).

It is Leopold Bloom, however, who has elaborated most extensively on the vast olfactory world, qualifying as a priest of olfactory imagination. His long reverie in Nausicaa is a disquisition on the subtleties of odors, differentiating between the contrasting scents of Gerty and Molly, establishing the fragrance that drew Molly and Blazes together, remarking on the delayed reactions of wafting aromas, linking human and animal factors, searching for the locus of fragrant desire in the feminine body, and transposing his criteria for the masculine body as well, until he seeks and finds the essence of his own self:

> That's her perfume. Why she waved her hand. I leave you this to think of me when I'm far away on the pillow. What is it? Heliotrope? No. Hyacinth? Hm. Roses, I think. She'd like scent of that kind. Sweet and cheap: soon sour. (Na 1007-10)

(Bloom's process of deduction begins as one of elimination, since the specific scent does not communicate itself directly. His inclination first to heliotrope is self-identifying, given his tendency to turn toward the sun. The alliterative process then leads him to hyacinth, until something closer to direct contact leads him to roses—belatedly.)

> Why Molly likes opoponax. Suits her, with a little jessamine mixed. Her high notes and her low notes. At the dance night she met him, dance of the hours. Heat brought it out. She was wearing her black and it had the perfume of the time before. Good conductor, is it? Or bad? Light too. Suppose there's some connection. For instance if you go into a cellar where it's dark. Mysterious thing too. (Na 1010-15)

(Bloom has arrived at an olfactory version of his morning speculations on black clothing as a "conductor" of heat, still pondering the operative process, but now in less objective terms: sexual infidelity engenders the value judgments associated with alluring fragrances in terms of good and bad, light and dark.)

> Why did I smell it only now? Took its time in coming like herself, slow but sure. Suppose it's ever so many millions of tiny grains blown across. Yes, it

> is. Because those spice islands, Cinghalese this morning, smell them leagues off. Tell you what it is. It's like a fine fine veil or web they have all over the skin, fine like what do you call it gossamer, and they're always spinning it out of them, fine as anything, like rainbow colours without knowing it. Clings to everything she takes off. Vamp of her stockings. Warm shoe. Stays. Drawers: little kick, taking them off. Byby till next time. (Na 1015-23)

(Further "scientific" speculation distracts Bloom from the sexual matter at hand, especially since interest in Molly reflects uncomfortably her luring of Boylan. The fragrance that fails to last, the scent that turns sour, affects his mood; the death smells, from Chinese to Cinghalese, were already present in the stale air of the Bloom bedroom, as his association with her discarded clothing attests.)

> Also the cat likes to sniff in her shift on the bed. Know her smell in a thousand. Bathwater too. Reminds me of strawberries and cream. Wonder where it is really. There or the armpits or under the neck. Because you get it out of all holes and corners. Hyacinth perfume made of oil of ether or something. (Na 1023-27)

(The fleetingness of aroma makes the association with the gustatory an essential, even when it is as ludicrous as strawberries and cream with bathwater. The quest for the corporeal essence of odor is quickly deflected away from the instinctive answer, the genital area, to the armpits associated with the bookstall encounter but Bloom has no qualms about locating the phenomenon in the animal kingdom.)

> Muskrat. Bag under their tails. One grain pour off odour for years. Dogs at each other behind. Good evening. Evening. How do you sniff? Hm. Hm. Very well, thank you. Animals go by that. Yes now, look at it that way. We're the same. Some women, instance, warn you off when they have their period. . . . Potted herrings gone stale or. Boof! Please keep off the grass.(Na 1028-33)

(Although in his potent example of animalistic functions Bloom chooses the menstruating woman, he has first linked himself to the sniffing animal as he gives the same responses to inquisitive dogs that he had himself had to Gerty's scent: "Hm. Hm.")

> Perhaps they get a man smell off us. What though? Cigary gloves long John had on his desk the other day. Breath? What you eat and drink gives that. No. Mansmell, I mean. Must be connected with that because priests that are supposed to be are different. Women buzz round it like flies round treacle. Railed off the altar get on to it at any cost. The tree of

forbidden priest. O, father, will you? Let me be the first to. That diffuses itself all through the body, permeates. Source of life. And it's extremely curious the smell. Celery sauce. Let me. (Na 1034-41)

(As investigative as he insists on being, and as valiantly as he turns away from externals, his search for the essential odor that distinguishes the male from the female is faulted by an element of prudery, his reluctance to explore the "Bad Lands." Bloom resists the operative vocabulary that Molly employs with abandon, at least in the privacy of her own thoughts. His use of the celibate priest as guinea pig is mired in confusion: Do women flock to priests because of a smell of celibacy? Is it their presumed virginity that is the source of that attraction? If so, what bodily fluid causes their odor if that of semen is not present? Given the tentativeness and timidity of the speculation, it is not surprising that Bloom should return to the aromatic realm of food, and if the female effluvium for Lenehan is the rich lobster mayonnaise, then the masculine for Bloom is the prosaic celery sauce. Yet he does eventually turn to himself for the male essence, even if the result is inconclusive, based as it is on an external scent.)

Mr Bloom inserted his nose. Hm. Into the. Hm. Opening of his waistcoat. Almonds or. No. Lemons it is. Ah no, that's the soap. (Na 1042-43)

* * *

All breathing creatures are subject to the invasion of whatever odors are in the wind, although some, like Stephen Dedalus, may try to resist them, or at least *select* what they take in, while others, like Leopold Bloom, are overly receptive to whatever passes near. By accumulating his own body odor Stephen may build up a resistance to alien odors; by his fastidiousness Bloom may accelerate his receptivity. One can wander unconsciously through Dublin and be circumscribed by the odors received, as was Father Conmee in his stroll through northeast Dublin: incense, bacon, and a woman's perfume accost him, characterizing him in terms of his religion, his belly, and his submerged fascination with Mary, first countess of Belvedere, on whose scent he has been for years. Molly Bloom reveals the reflexive/self-reflexive emphasis of two lovers drawing one breath (the amorous cliché), of the odors that attract and repel, as she prosaically replays her love scenes with Boylan: "I hope my breath was sweet after those kissing comfits" (Pe 1140-41), revealing the artifice that she had used, having wondered about Boylan's: "he smelt of some kind of drink not whisky or stout perhaps the sweety kind of paste they stick their bills up with some liqueur" (Pe 125-27)—inadvertently accounting for Boylan's odd choice of sloe gin at the Ormond bar. (By contrast it was the natural odor of flowers that gave its fragrance to young love on the Rock of Gibraltar and the Hill of Howth.) Molly is wondering simultaneously whether Boylan is dreaming of her and where he got the flower he sported, suggesting an affinity between the language of odors and the language of dreams.

Who dreams in *Ulysses?* Stephen Dedalus for one, Leopold Bloom for another. And their dreams have affinities and similarities that merge them, so that Bloom becomes the guide for Stephen into the harem, and Molly the object of their desire. When he first reclaims his dream in Proteus, Stephen is watching the dog smelling a rock and remembers: "The melon he had he held against my face. Smiled: creamfruit smell" (Pr 367-68)—yet when he replays the dream scene, having seen Bloom on the library steps, the vision is odor free: "A creamfruit melon he held to me" (SC 1208). In Circe, where dreams subsume dreams, he merely notes: "I dreamt of a watermelon" (Ci 3922). It remains only for Bloom to locate the creamfruit upon getting into bed with Molly: "He kissed the plump mellow yellow smellow melons of her rump, on each plump melonous hemisphere, in their mellow yellow furrow, with osbcure prolonged provocative melonsmellonous osculation" (It 2241-43). To which Molly adds her somewhat cantankerous yes: "Ill tighten my bottom well and let out a few smutty words smellrump" (Pe 1530-31)—and Molly is usually granted the last word.

NOTES

1. James Joyce, *A Portrait of the Artist as a Young Man,* rev. ed. (New York: Viking, 1964). Further references cited in text as as P.
2. James Joyce, *Finnegans Wake* (New York: Viking, 1939). References are to page and line numbers.
3. James Joyce, *Ulysses,* rev. ed. (New York: Vintage, 1986); references are to chapter and line numbers: Te-Telemachus; Ne-Nestor; Pr-Proteus; Ca-Calypso; Lo-Lotus Eaters; Ha-Hades; Ae-Aeolus; Le-Lestrygonians; SC-Scylla and Charybdis; WR-Wandering Rocks; Si-Sirens; Cy-Cyclops; Na-Nausicaa; Ox-Oxen of the Sun; Ci-Circe; Eu-Eumaeus; It-Ithaca; Pe-Penelope.
4. Patrick Süsskind, *Perfume,* trans. John E. Woods (New York: Pocket Books, 1987), 3.
5. Ibid., 223.
6. Ibid.
7. Ibid., 182.
8. Ibid., 150-51.
9. Jane Heap, *The Little Review* (September 1917).
10. John Updike, review of *Perfume, The New Yorker,* 15 December 1986, 125.

9
Wilde... Joyce... O'Brien... Stoppard
Modernism and Postmodernism in "Travesties"

RICHARD CORBALLIS

Stoppard is a postmodernist with an old-fashioned conscience, and in *Travesties* Joyce helps to prop up both sides of his personality. The Joyce who appears in the play is a postmodern creation, a collage of attitudes and sayings, its paratactic nature enhanced by the way it is filtered through the leaky sieve of an unreliable memory (Henry Carr's). But this diffuse, fragmented portrait is set within a carefully ordered framework that owes much to the structure of *Ulysses,* and, like *Ulysses* (though in a much more rudimentary way), the play as a whole attempts to probe personality (especially Carr's and the Lenins') and to grapple with such modernist problems as the relationship between politics and art and between form and content.

The idea that modernism and postmodernism are deliberately juxtaposed in *Travesties* gains credence from the fact that other playwrights were experimenting with much the same juxtaposition at much the same time. Sam Shepard's *Tooth of Crime,* first performed in London in 1972, can be interpreted as an allegory of postmodernism's victory over modernism.[1] Whereas Stoppard focuses on literature, Shepard focuses on music. Hoss is a traditional rock-and-roll singer who can trace his art through the southern slums and the cotton fields to the jungles of Africa:

> It come down a long way. It come down by every damn black back street you can move sideways through. 'Fore that even it was snakin' thru rubber plants. It had Cheetahs movin' to its rhythm.[2]

Crow (who, like Stoppard's Lenin, appears only in the second of the play's two acts) is a punk rocker with no concern for his roots. He is

"Nothin' but flash. No heart,"[3] but his aggression carries the day in the musical duel-to-the-death that closes the play.

There is an analogous but less conclusive contest between a modernist painter and a postmodernist photographer in Alma de Groen's *Going Home* (1976). More relevant to Stoppard is *No-Man's Land,* a play written by his friend Harold Pinter in the same year that *Travesties* was first produced (1974). Here an old-fashioned poet (Hirst) has his authority usurped by a brash and cynical young upstart (Foster).

Stoppard's version of postmodernism is less sinister than either Shepard's or Pinter's. To him it seems to represent innocent carnival rather than naked power.[4] Moreover, modernism and postmodernism do not really come into conflict. Lenin (who embodies the former) and Joyce (the latter) scarcely ever share the stage. They are juxtaposed rather than opposed, Joyce dominating proceedings in act 1, Lenin, in act 2.

Ostensibly, however, it is Old Carr who controls both acts, since most of the action takes place inside his head. After a brief, zany induction that serves to introduce the other principals, Old Carr has a long monologue, in which he lays great emphasis on photographs as he struggles to recollect the famous figures—Joyce, Lenin, and Tzara—that he knew (or did not know) in Zürich some sixty years before. Lenin he can visualize only with "the benefit of historical perspective and the photograph album."[5] Joyce he knew rather better, but he still has to think his way back beyond the days when "publication and fame" had "turned him into a public monument for pilgrim cameras more often than not in a velvet smoking jacket of an unknown colour, photography being in those days a black and white affair" (22).

These references help us to see that what Stoppard (through Old Carr) gives us in act 1 is in effect a series of snapshots of Joyce, some realistic, some quite bizarre—like a collection of Angus McBean portraits. These snapshots are assembled principally from the pages of *Ulysses* and Richard Ellmann's biography of Joyce. Unlike these two works, however, Stoppard's photomontage in no way evokes the "real" Joyce. His method may be described as allegorical insofar as he is "rewriting a primary text [James Joyce] in terms of its figural meaning," at the same time distancing us from that text, emptying it of "resonance . . . , significance . . ., authoritative claim to meaning" and investing it (particularly at the end of act 1, where Carr recalls Joyce's death and burial in Zürich) with that trace of melancholy that Craig Owens (following Walter Benjamin) associates with postmodern allegory.[6]

The first snapshot in Stoppard's photomontage is of Joyce in the

Zürich Public Library, composing one of the most recondite sections of *Ulysses,* the opening of the Oxen of the Sun. Stoppard—or rather Old Carr, who is supposed to be remembering this—is taking liberties here, of course; the Oxen of the Sun was begun in Trieste in 1919, not in Zürich in 1917-18. (And, anyway, one doubts if the historical Carr ever read it.) Presumably Stoppard chose this section of *Ulysses* simply because it is so recondite. Like *Dirty Linen, Travesties* begins with an induction in which hardly a word of standard English is spoken, the effect of which is to startle the audience and prepare them for the eccentric collage to follow. He wanted to give Joyce phrases as abstruse as those uttered by Tzara (who recites—in the form of a limerick that makes some sense in *French—English* words drawn randomly from a hat), by Lenin and Nadya (who speak nothing but Russian), and by Cecily (who says nothing but "Ssssssh!")

At the end of the induction Joyce leaves the stage "at a strolling pace," crooning the opening lines of "Galway Bay"—snapshot number two: Joyce as stage Irishman, Bing Crosby vintage. Immediately the scene changes, and we find ourselves in Old Carr's room.

The ensuing snapshots are separated not by scene changes—"the Room" remains the ostensible setting for the rest of act 1—but by "time slips" and mood changes in the controlling memory of Old Carr. The matter is elucidated in an early stage direction:

> The scene (and most of the play) is under the erratic control of Old Carr's memory, which is not notably reliable, and also of his various prejudices and delusions. One result is that the story (like a toy train perhaps) occasionally jumps the rails and has to be restarted at the point where it goes wild. . . .
> It may be desirable to mark these moments more heavily by using an extraneous sound or a light effect, or both. The sound of a cuckoo-clock, artificially amplified, would be appropriate since it alludes to time and to Switzerland; in which case a naturalistic cuckoo-clock could be seen to strike during the here-and-now scene of Old Carr's first monologue. At any rate the effect of these time-slips is not meant to be bewildering, and it should be made clear what is happening.

It is worth observing, I think, that the sound of a cuckoo clock alludes not only "to time and to Switzerland" but also to the close of the Nausicaa section of *Ulysses,* where the phrase "Cuckoo, Cuckoo, Cuckoo" is thrice repeated. Since Nausicaa immediately precedes the Oxen of the Sun, these "cuckoos" are contiguous with the passage quoted in Stoppard's induction. It is remarkable how often Stoppard borrows more-or-less consecutive passages from either *Ulysses* or Ellmann; his reading of both seems to have been somewhat selective.

The first snapshot of Joyce in Carr's room depicts "an Irish nonsense" spouting limericks (one of them irregular[7]—a misprint?) along with the rest of the cast. Though Stoppard himself composed all these limericks, he knew from Ellmann (and perhaps from the Aeolus section of *Ulysses*) that Joyce was fond of the form.

Joyce subsequently returns looking more like his historical self. His outfit (unmatching jacket and trousers—subsequently swapped for "the other halves" of this outfit) is presumably based on the fact, reported by Ellmann, that "he never wore a complete suit, always the jacket of one and the trousers of another."[8] (Ellmann mentions this detail unemphatically in a list of Joyce's personal eccentricities. Stoppard, as usual, suppresses the human aspect and explains the trait in terms of hard, cold logic. Joyce explains:

> My wardrobe got out of step in Trieste, and its reciprocal members pass each other endlessly in the night. [96])

This Joyce, aided and abetted by his amanuensis (Gwendolen), gives us in quick succession snatches of "Bahnhofstrasse" and "Mr Dooley," a reference to *Exiles* and his contributions to "the neutralist press," a quick description of his eye troubles (including the famous account of himself as "an international eyesore") and an introduction to the activities of the English Players. All this—even the poems—Stoppard found in chapters 25-27 of Ellmann. To the Ellmann material he added a couple of quips drawn from the early sections of *Ulysses*. Mr. Deasy's definition of "an Englishman's . . . proudest boast: *I paid my way*"[9] becomes Joyce's "An Irishman's proudest boast is—I paid back my way" (50). And—in response to Tzara's contention that "making poetry should be as natural as making water"—Joyce adapts Mulligan's line from Telemachus: "God send you don't make them in the one hat."[10]

There follows a loose travesty of the Ithaca section of *Ulysses*, toward the end of which Joyce begins performing conjuring tricks (for which there is, as far as I know, no warrant in either Ellmann or *Ulysses*). His pièce de résistance is the production of a rabbit from his hat.

This grand flourish serves to accentuate the impact of a grand speech Joyce has just delivered in defense of the artist as magician and of art that leaves "the world precisely as it finds it" (63)—art for art's sake. This speech was not in Stoppard's original draft. The director, Peter Wood, persuaded him to add it during rehearsals, and Stoppard based it on Georges Borach's account of a conversation with Joyce, transcribed by Ellmann. Snatches of Ellmann's surrounding commentary also make their way into Stoppard's version.[11]

This speech (which Stoppard has since called "the most important . . . in the play")[12] simply makes explicit the "figural meaning" that underpins the diverse snapshots of Joyce displayed previously in the act: Joyce the arcane wordsmith (in the induction); Joyce the composer of limericks, of symbolist poems, of neutralist poems and articles; Joyce the magician; even, I suppose, Joyce the crooner of "Galway Bay"—these are all simply variants of Joyce the artist, Joyce the capricious champion of play (that most postmodern of activities).

To further reinforce the playfulness of act 1, Stoppard chose to assimilate his characters to the design of that most playful of plays, *The Importance of Being Earnest*. It was, of course, a production of this play in Zürich in 1918 that brought Joyce (the business manager) and Carr (a leading actor) into contact with each other and led to their famous quarrel over tickets and trousers. This coincidence gave Stoppard a convenient excuse for building his characters into the fabric of Wilde's play; he surmised that the 1918 production would have remained Carr's most vivid memory of Zürich (thanks to his successful portrayal of Algernon and his subsequent litigation with Joyce), so that as he grew older—and Old Carr is *very* old—all his other memories would be subsumed and perverted by it.

Two other coincidences helped to establish the roles of Joyce and Tzara within the Wildean scheme. Joyce's middle name was (as the result of a clerical error at the time of his baptism) Augusta, which is also Lady Bracknell's first name. And Wilde's Jack was played in 1918 by Tristan Rawson, so it was easy for Old Carr to slide another Tristan—Tristan Tzara—into the role.

Stoppard insists that he discovered these two coincidences after he had cast Joyce and Tzara as Lady Bracknell and Jack, respectively.[13] But his veracity on this point is open to doubt, since the very chapter in which Ellmann describes the 1918 production states clearly that Tristan Rawson played Jack. Joyce's odd middle name is also prominent in Ellmann; it is discussed in the first chapter.

I mention this point simply to indicate the ephemeral matters that often affect Stoppard's artistic decisions. His tricky, mercurial attitude toward creation is indicated by these remarks from an early interview with Mark Amory:

There is a secret in art, isn't there? And the secret consists of what the artist has secretly and privately done. You will tumble some [allusions] and not others. The whole process of putting them in . . . gives art that texture which sensibility tells one is valuable.[14]

It is worth pausing a moment to note how much Stoppard's notions of "texture" and "sensibility" differ from standard modernist definitions of those things. Modernism aspires to the kind of mystic unity of form and content Beckett found in *Finnegans Wake:*

> Here is direct expression. . . . Here form *is* content, content *is* form. You complain that this stuff is not written in English. It is not written at all. It is not to be read—or rather it is not only to be read. It is to be looked at and listened to. His writing is not *about* something; *it is that something itself.*[15]

The same could be said of Orghast, the language Ted Hughes invented for the play of the same name, performed by Peter Brook's International Center for Theatrical Research at the Shiraz Festival in 1971. Orghast is an onomatopoeic language; the sense of each word is indicated by its sound. Stoppard found it obscure and unconvincing and proceeded to invent a language of his own (Dogg), whose meaning could be deciphered only by attention to usage and "philological clues."[16]

What is true of Dogg is true in a larger sense of the greater part of Stoppard's oeuvre. Sound, tone, mood, and style contribute nothing to meaning. All the characters speak in the same voice (just as Wilde's do—at least in *The Importance of Being Earnest*), and interpretation becomes a purely intellectual exercise; the audience must solve a series of more or less arcane puzzles. The "sensibility" of which Stoppard talks really amounts to intellect, and the "texture" is two-dimensional, like a mathematical progression. This approach yields art that is more akin to a cryptic crossword than to a well-wrought urn.

The allusions discussed so far were not difficult to "tumble." More ingenuity is required to see why Stoppard turned Wilde's Cecily into a librarian. On the face of it, the Meierei Bar or one of the Zürich cafés—the Odeon, Terrasse, or Voltaire (which was, of course, in the Meierei Bar)—might seem to be a more theatrical venue for the encounters of Joyce, Tzara, Lenin, and Carr. Stoppard probably wanted to allude distantly to the Scylla and Charybdis episode of *Ulysses,* but he had a more immediate reason for choosing the library over which Cecily presides as the scene for these meetings.

In Wilde, Algernon finds out about Cecily from an engraved cigarette case left behind by Jack on a previous visit. In *Travesties,* Carr finds out about her from a library card similarly abandoned by Tzara. This contretemps over a library card seems to have been suggested by the row that ensued when Joyce tried to borrow his brother Stanislaus's card in Trieste in 1911.[17]

Here, then, are three factors—a love of cryptic conundra, an emphasis on play, and an impulse toward allegory—that distinguish the author of *Travesties,* act 1, as a postmodernist. Joyce is the central character of the act and therefore the focus of Stoppard's postmodernism. It is tempting to close the circle by surmising that Stoppard got his postmodernism from Joyce in the first place, but I can find little evidence for this. Wilde—often classed as a prepostmodernist—was an important model, of course. And so, I think, was Flann O'Brien.

Stoppard professed admiration for O'Brien's first novel, *At Swim-Two-Birds,* in an early interview,[18] and there are clear signs that *Lord Malquist and Mr Moon* (Stoppard's only novel to date) was written under its influence. *At Swim* is about a student who writes a novel about a novelist who is eventually taken over and killed by his own characters; Stoppard—somewhat less ambitiously—writes about a latter-day Boswell (Moon) who is chronicling the day-to-day activities of his patron (Malquist) and is eventually killed by the repercussions of those activities. Besides this self-reflexiveness, the two novels share a predilection for "ready-made" characters, often of a bizarre kind—"nigger skivvies" in O'Brien's Dublin, a black Irish Jew in Stoppard's London, and cowboys in both.

At Swim may even have a roundabout connection with *Travesties.* Graham Greene's oft-quoted comments on the book included the remark that he "read it with continual excitement, amusement and the kind of glee one experiences when people smash china on the stage."[19] It is possible that this was the source of the episode late in act 1 where Tzara reinforces his notion that artists are "vandals and desecrators" by smashing "whatever crockery is to hand" (62).

But there is a larger-scale parallel between O'Brien and Stoppard, which leads me into the second part of this discussion of Stoppard's relationship with Joyce. Unlike Wilde, who moved from something like a modernist sensibility in his early society dramas to a prepostmodernist playfulness in *Earnest,* O'Brien quickly repudiated the surface brilliance of *At Swim* in favor of a more serious (if still bizarre) exploration of the workings of conscience in *The Third Policeman.*

Similarly, there is a deeper Stoppard, who has become increasingly evident in recent years—at least since 1977, when he wrote *Professional Foul* and *Every Good Boy Deserves Favour,* and arguably since 1972, when he completed *Jumpers* and married Miriam Moore-Robinson. This Stoppard is interested in human emotions (but, like Henry in *The Real Thing,* he is diffident about his ability to depict them). He believes that there are moral imperatives that cut across the postmodern conviction that "playing is the attainment of freedom."[20] He is, moreover, something of a snob, an enthusiast for the traditional ways of the English gentleman: prep schools, cricket, fly fishing and—most important for our purposes—the great humanistic tradition of English literature in which Joyce can, with some sleight of hand, be incorporated.

The portrait of Joyce in *Travesties* may be, as I have suggested, remarkably un-Joycean, but the play as a whole—especially those sections of it in which Joyce does *not* appear—owes a good deal to *Ulysses* and often looks to be emulating that work's peculiar strengths. Three large-scale parallels between the play and the novel spring immediately to mind. First, both use the same kind of raw materials—a preexisting literary work *(The Odyssey; The Importance of Being Earnest)* and events from a historical time and place (Dublin, 1904; Zürich, 1917-18). Secondly, they employ analogous narrative methods. Like *Ulysses, Travesties* is an interior monologue punctuated by other narrative modes. Most of act 1 is set inside Old Carr's head, but in act 2 several characters bypass Carr and talk to each other and/or the audience directly. Lenin and Nadya are the most prominent of these, but Cecily also has a couple of important solos (one as Young Cecily and one as Old Cecily), and Old Carr himself speaks out several times instead of simply unraveling his memories.

Thirdly there are verbal and structural similarities. In the first of Old Carr's monologues—immediately after the induction in the library—a connection with the early stages of *Ulysses* is established. Carr describes Zürich as

> the bustling metropolis of swiftly gliding trams and greystone banking houses, of cosmopolitan restaurants on the great stone banks of the swiftly-gliding, snot-green (mucus mutandis) Limmat River, of jewelled escapements and refugees of all kinds. (23)

The passage fairly bristles with puns that may or may not have been inspired by Joyce, but there can be little doubt that the description of the "snot-green ... Limmat River" is a conscious echo of Buck Mulligan's reference to "the snotgreen sea" in Telemachus.[21] The addition of "mucus mutandis" may mean that Stoppard was also glancing at the moment, near the end of Proteus, when Stephen picks his nose.

These early echoes should encourage us to watch for other connections with *Ulysses*. We duly get—a little early for comfort if we are looking for strictly parallel developments—the Ithaca travesty. And the library setting for act 2 (and the first few pages of act 1) may allude to Scylla and Charybdis. (The way Tzara and Carr invade the Lenins' space here is vaguely reminiscent of the encroachments of Bloom and Mulligan on Stephen's patch in the National Library.) Finally, there is the introduction of a new character—a woman—to oversee the closing section of the play. Although there is no obvious resemblance between Old Cecily and Molly Bloom, Stoppard makes us associate the two of them by having Cecily (almost) quote the closing words of Molly's monologue: "yes, I said yes when you asked me."

Of course, the closing words of *Travesties*, which follow soon after, are given to Carr, not to Cecily, but again their source is Joycean in a curiously roundabout way. This is what Carr says:

> I learned three things in Zurich during the way. I wrote them down. Firstly, you're either a revolutionary or you're not, and if you're not you might as well be an artist as anything else. Secondly, if you can't be an artist, you might as well be a revolutionary. . . . I forget the third thing. (98-99)

Earlier Stoppard had used the same tactic to close a play called *Dogg's Our Pet;* Charlie, who is some kind of caretaker of some kind of school, says,

> Three points only while I have the platform. Firstly, just because it's been opened, there's no need to run amok kicking footballs through windows and writing on the walls. . . . Secondly, I can take a joke as well as any man, but I've noticed a lot of language about the place and if there's one thing I can't stand it's language. I forget what the third point is.[22]

Both these passages have usually been taken to echo a sentence from the first paragraph of Beckett's novel, *The Unnamable*:

> The fact would seem to be, if in my situation one may speak of facts, not only that I shall have to speak of things of which I cannot speak, but also, which is even more interesting, but also that I, which is if possible even more interesting, that I shall have to, I forget, no matter.[23]

But in fact the Stoppard speeches are closer to a remark made (according to Ellmann) by Ettore Schmitz, who was a friend of Joyce's in Trieste: "There are three things I always forget: names, faces, and—the third thing I forget."[24]

It should by now be apparent that the surface of *Travesties* is littered with allusions to Joyce's masterpiece of fiction—and to Ellmann's masterpiece of biography. There is also, I think, a deeper kinship between *Travesties* and *Ulysses*. Act 1 of *Travesties* (Joyce's act) may be an exercise in postmodern carnival, but act 2, which has Lenin at its center, investigates more earnestly the role of the artist in society, and as the complexities of this role become apparent, so do the complexities of the characters undertaking the investigation. Both these preoccupations—with the role of the artist and with the complexity of human nature—are, of course, central to *Ulysses*.

Stoppard has always felt unsure of his ability to plumb the depths of character. His first full-length play, *Enter a Free Man*, took two characters (Linda and Riley) through a process of exhilaration and disillusionment, but Stoppard has subsequently confessed that the whole enterprise was a fraud:

> *Enter a Free man* looks as though it's about people as real ... as the people in *Coronation Street*. But to me the whole thing is a big phoney, because they're only real because I've seen them in other people's plays. I haven't actually met any of them myself.[25]

Recently—in *Professional Foul, Night and Day,* and (more successfully) in *The Real Thing*—Stoppard has revived his attempts to show characters experiencing "self-knowledge through pain."[26] But during the ten years that began with *Rosencrantz and Guildenstern Are Dead* (1967) he generally kept close to "a slightly literate music-hall"[27] and eschewed depths of character. The very urbane nervous breakdown suffered by Dorothy Moore in *Jumpers* illustrates the point very well—especially when one considers the gap that must surely exist between her sufferings and those of Stoppard's first wife, Jose, who experienced a breakdown at about the same time.

The second act of *Travesties* does, however, peer cautiously into the inner recesses of certain characters. Lenin is the first to be unmasked. Perhaps because he did not trust himself to evoke the character in his own words, Stoppard put together a documentary portrait; he concedes in his acknowledgements that "nearly everything spoken by Lenin and Nadezhda Krupskaya herein comes from his Collected Writings and from her *Memories of Lenin*" (15). The documents Lenin is made to quote tend to highlight the absurdities and contradictions inherent in his political strategy and his aesthetic theory. Stoppard comments thus on the latter:

> Lenin keeps convicting himself out of his own mouth. It's absurd. It's full of incredible syllogisms. All the publishing and libraries and bookshops and newspapers must be controlled by the Party. The press will be free. Anybody can write anything they like but anybody who uses the Party press to speak against the Party naturally won't be allowed to do it. And then you go back to the first proposition that everything's controlled by the Party, and you're going round in circles. It's sheer nonsense.[28]

Modernism and Postmodernism in "Travesties" 167

Lenin's logical tangles probably provoke laughter in the first instance, but slowly the audience begins to sense the deep frustrations that underlie the apparent nonsense. In Stoppard's words, "you don't really think that man has contradicted himself throughout and condemned himself out of his own mouth. You think he really had a burden to carry."[29]

Most of the documents quoted by Lenin in *Travesties* date from 1916-17. However, nothing from this period gave an adequate sense of the man's tortured state of mind. To convey this inner agony Stoppard went back to a much earlier conversation in which Lenin spoke frankly with Maxim Gorki about the tension between his love of art and his devotion to politics. This conversation (as reported by Gorki) provides the basis for the moving speech with which Lenin concludes his part in *Travesties*:

> I don't know of anything greater than the Appassionata, Amazing, superhuman music. It always makes me feel, perhaps naively, it makes me feel proud of the miracles that human beings can perform. But I can't listen to music often. It affects my nerves, makes me want to say nice stupid things and pat the heads of those people who while living in this vile hell can create such beauty. Nowadays we can't pat heads or we'll get our hands bitten off. We've got to *hit* heads, hit them without mercy, though ideally we're against doing violence to people. . . . Hm, one's duty is infernally hard. (89)[30]

Once he is gone Nadya wraps up her role in the play with an equally affecting speech, for which Stoppard again had to go to a remote early period of her life (1896):

> Once when Vladimir was in prison—in St. Petersburg—he wrote to me and asked that at certain times of day I should go and stand on a particular square of pavement on the Shpalernaya. When the prisoners were taken out for exercise it was possible through one of the windows in the corridor to catch a momentary glimpse of this spot. I went for several days and stood a long while on the pavement. But he never saw me. Something went wrong. I forget what. (89)[31]

To ensure maximum emotional impact for these speeches Stoppard has them accompanied by dim light and powerful music (Beethoven's *Appassionata* Sonata). All in all, his means may appear gauche when compared with Joyce's, but in its crude way his portrait of the Lenins does evoke a real sense of fumbling, fallible, Bloom-like humanity.

This humanity finally rubs off on Old Carr as well, thanks in part to the fact that his final line ("I forget the third thing") echoes Nadya's

("I forget what"). At the same time, as I have indicated already, Carr echoes a quip of Ettore Schmitz's. There is thus a curious blend of comedy and pathos here. Carr may seem an unlikely candidate for pathos, but his recent humiliation at the hands of Old Cecily has rendered him a touch pathetic even before his last speech begins, and Stoppard reinforces the elegiac mood by resorting to fading light (as he did for the Lenins' farewell). So the tone of the entire epilogue (which is what the final speech amounts to) is curiously ambiguous.

This mood perfectly matches the content of the speech, which acknowledges the equal and opposite claims of Joyce and Lenin. Act 1 has focused on Joyce the artist and his contemptuous dismissal of politics (revolutionary or otherwise); act 2 has concentrated on Lenin the politician and his insistence that art be subjugated to political considerations. Joyce is presented in a way that provokes our admiration; Lenin, in a way that rouses our sympathy. Carr's wonderfully inept epilogue demonstrates both by its style and by its content that there can be no reconciliation between these extremes; "you're either a revolutionary"—he might just as well have said "a politician"—"or you're not, and if you're not you might as well be an artist as anything else," followed by a mirror image of the same observation ("if you can't be an artist, you might as well be a revolutionary").

So the play ends with a well-wrought reconciliation of opposing forces—a synthesis that would please Cleanth Brooks and other modernist critics. Drama critics have on the whole been less impressed. (Modernism and drama were always uncomfortable bedfellows, of course—at least until the advent of Beckett.) Kenneth Tynan, for example, described the play as "a triple-decker bus that isn't going anywhere"[32]—"triple-decker" because Tristan Tzara is nominally a principal character, although he contributes nothing significant to the ideological structure.

It is true that Stoppard—like the Joyce he depicts in act 1—has created "a corpse that will dance for some time yet and *leave the world precisely as it finds it."* But it needs to be stressed that he did not take the easiest road to this inconclusive conclusion. He could have allowed his slick simulacrum of Joyce to preside over two acts of empty carnival; instead he emulated the real Joyce and, in act 2, penetrated deeper—to the inner conflicts, uncertainties, and (*pace* Tynan) the drama that inhibit the greater part of mankind from any determined attempt to change the world. Ultimately, then, modernism and postmodernism do not compete in *Travesties* as they do in *The Tooth of Crime* and *No-Man's Land;* rather they point to the same conclusion, the modernism evoking (in act 2) what the postmodernism demonstrates (in act 1)—that art and politics do not mix, and revolution in the one bears no obvious relation to revolution in the other.

NOTES

1. This interpretation is argued at length by L. I. Wilcox in a forthcoming article in *Modern Drama*.
2. Sam Shepard, *"The Tooth of Crime" and "Geography of a Horse Dreamer"* (London: Faber and Faber, 1974), 59.
3. Ibid., 58.
4. That the character of Joyce does "carry a sinister suggestion of heartlessness" is argued by Richard Corballis in *Stoppard: The Mystery and the Clockwork* (New York: Methuen, 1984), 85.
5. Tom Stoppard, *Travesties* (London: Faber and Faber, 1975), 23. Henceforth, page references to this edition will be given parenthetically in the text.
6. Craig Owens, "The Allegorical Impulse: Toward a Theory of Postmodernism," in *Art After Modernism: Rethinking Representation*, ed. Brian Wallis (New York: New Museum of Contemporary Art, 1984), 205.
7. On page 33, the lines beginning with Carr's "Tell me . . . are you some kind of poet" and ending with Joyce's "No—Dublin, don't tell me you know it!" are not readily reducible to limerick form.
8. Richard Ellmann, *James Joyce*, 2d ed., rev. (Oxford: Oxford University Press, 1982), 397. For the convenience of readers I quote from the revised edition of the late Professor Ellmann's book. All the passages cited are also in the earlier edition, which Stoppard must have used.
9. James Joyce, *Ulysses*, 2d ed., rev. (New York: Random House, 1961), 30.
10. Stoppard, *Travesties*, 62; cf. Joyce, *Ulysses*, 12.
11. Ellmann, *James Joyce*, 416-17.
12. Ronald Hayman, *Tom Stoppard* (London: Heinemann, 1977), 9.
13. Ibid., 3.
14. Mark Amory, "The Joke's the Thing," *Sunday Times Magazine*, 9 June 1974, 74.
15. Samuel Beckett, *Disjecta: Miscellaneous Writings and a Dramatic Fragment*, ed. Ruby Cohn (London: John Calder, 1983), 26–27.
16. See Tom Stoppard's review of *Orghast*, by Ted Hughes, *Times Literary Supplement*, 13 October 1972, 1174.
17. See Ellmann, *James Joyce*, 311.
18. Giles Gordon, "Tom Stoppard" (interview) *Transatlantic Review* 29 (1968): 24.
19. Greene's remarks are quoted in Stephen Jones, ed., *A Flann O'Brien Reader* (New York: Viking Press, 1978), 2.
20. Neil Sammells, "Earning Liberties: *Travesties* and *The Importance of Being Earnest*," *Modern Drama* 29 (1986): 386.
21. Joyce, *Ulysses*, 5. John Harty has privately suggested to me that the first phrase Carr uses to describe the Limmat River ("swiftly-gliding") echoes "both Stephen's use of rich poetical images from such poets as Swinburne and Shakespeare and also Stephen's concern voiced in 'Proteus' about Jonathan Swift's madness."
22. Edward Berman, ed., *Ten of the Best: British Short Plays* (London: Inter-Action, 1979), 94.

23. Samuel Beckett, *The Unnamable* (New York: Grove Press, 1958), 4.
24. Ellmann, *James Joyce,* 272.
25. Hayman, *Tom Stoppard,* 6.
26. The phrase is used by Henry of his own play *(House of Cards)* in Stoppard's *The Real Thing,* 2d. ed., rev. (London: Faber and Faber, 1983), 62.
27. Hayman, *Tom Stoppard,* 5.
28. Ibid., 10.
29. Ibid., 11.
30. For Lenin's original remarks to Gorki see Maxim Gorki, *Days With Lenin* (New York: International Publishers, 1932), 52.
31. The speech is based on N. K. Krupskaya, *Reminiscences of Lenin,* trans. Bernard Isaacs (Moscow: Foreign Languages Publishing House, 1959), 28. Actually, there is an ironic relationship between this speech, with its manifest devotion to Lenin, and the preceding speech by Lenin, which is based on remarks arising out of his infatuation with Inessa Armand.
32. Kenneth Tynan, *Show People: Profiles in Entertainment* (New York: Simon and Schuster, 1979), 109.

10
Joycean Provections

FRITZ SENN

> Is there any thing whereof it may be said, See, this is new?
> —Ecclesiastes 1:10

The purpose of this presentation is not to say anything new but to subsume, under a specific focus, part of what we already know and to suggest how we might describe the graph of a recurrent, basic, Joycean motion and show some of its pervasive actualizations. This motion is, in short, an excessive bias, a tendency to overdo, to break out of norms, to go beyond.

Take the beginning of *A Portrait*. Whether we read it as a novel attempt at imitative form, as psychological realism, or whatever

> he had a hairy face—*O, the green wothe botheth*—When you wet the bed first it is warm then it gets cold—*Pull out his eyes, Apologise (P 7–8)*[1]

these passages, in their abrupt immediacy, without conventional exposition, are surrounded by the invisible broken shells of narrative norms and restrictions. It is a fair guess that *Stephen Hero* did not begin quite like that and that some former version was changed in ways that must have appeared excessive at the time, that must have exceeded some convention. And so, at each turn of the development, something changed in degree and in kind. It is a long way from the early epiphanic sketches to the exuberance of *Finnegans Wake*. This exuberance or excess, an insistent drive out of—beyond—confines that had otherwise been largely taken for granted, will be looked into.

Joyce's own life-style was characterized by constant movement: Dublin—Trieste—Zürich—Paris are the best known stations. Each place involved numerous changes of address. Joyce did not stay put; he kept moving, and not always out of external necessity. The restlessness is obvious. Literary prototypes like Daidalos or Odysseus were on the move as well. In such cases the home life inevitably suffers, but restlessness also provides the stuff epics are made of. More to the point is the way the works transformed themselves, none of them repeating their predecessors; none of them, by the same token, could have been predicted; each one is sui generis. We have no way of guessing what Joyce might have written after *Finnegans Wake*. So Joyce's dynamic development is well in evidence.

It is, by way of illustration, appropriate that Joyce's one central prototype would be named "Bloom." Within that choice—which was certainly overdetermined—*Bloom* is essentially something growing, blossoming, budding to withering, with a whole range of possibilities from an emigrant Virag to a Dongiovannish Henry Flower, via Don Poldo de la Flora, Professor Blumenduft, or L. Boom as a typographical mischance; with arabesques like *bloomers*; derivatives like *blooming* and *booming* and further flourishes. It extends to the lush language of flowers, which is shortened to the "language of flow" or else the "language of flow" (as in *flowing*; both at *U* 11.298)—to name just a few exfoliations.[2] We may appreciate these ramifications when we consider that no such offshoots are derivable from the corresponding name, Dedalus.

ENORMOUS ELABORATION OF THE MATERIAL

> your Cork legs are running away with you
> —Joyce, *Ulysses*

Early critics were outspoken about Joyce's enormities and excesses; among a later generation, S. L. Goldberg was a very perceptive counsel for the prosecution: for him, Joyce was constantly overreaching and had to fail in doing so (fail, of course, according to hidebound norms, tacit or stated). According to Goldberg, it is a critical commonplace that Joyce "laboured some things too much," time and again, for example, "lapsing into mere parody,"[3] and little else, losing a sense of sane proportion. In *The Classical Temper* the lapses are detailed: what Joyce "drifted towards"—and clearly shouldn't have — are "romantic infinities" and "profundities"; "infinities" suggest a surplus and "profundities" seem to be a mere appearance.[4]

What is wrong with *Ulysses* "is obvious: (1) the enormous elaboration of the material, (2) the rather pretentious parade of literary machinery, (3) the encumbering and mortifying boredom."[5] Put more concisely, *Ulysses* (and *Finnegans Wake*, for which Goldberg does not particularly care either) violates some middle-of-the-road (sane, life-enhancing) standard. Joyce, in short, went *too far,* did *too much* of many bad things, was *"e-normous"*—that is, went *outside* of some implied norm. The charge has often been repeated. If put neutrally, it is wholly justified.

If we focus not so much on the results but on the impetus behind them, one way of rephrasing all of the above is that Joyce, man and author, got carried away. The man got carried away when he went to court in wartime Zürich over a pair of trousers; when he appealed to the highest possible authorities; when he went campaigning for the tenor John Sullivan in Paris; when he persevered in a campaign against a Frankfurt newspaper that had erroneously inserted his name.

The author inevitably got carried away in his works. The addition of "The Dead" changed scope, dimension, reverberation of *Dubliners,* a collection of stories that, even without it, was peculiar enough to frighten publishers in two countries—and changed the English short story. A slightly amorphous manuscript, *Stephen Hero,* was abandoned and reshaped into a novel of excessively imitative forms. Edward Garnett thought it, in a famous reader's report, frankly honest, "unconventional," full of "longueurs," without restraint or proportion, very much in need of pruning.[6] Joyce lost admirers all along the rocky way to the publication of *Ulysses,* and more so when he was engaged in his *Work in Progress.* The progress was a way fewer were prepared to go with him. Former friends and supporters, notably his brother Stanislaus, refused to be carried away when he was.

Being *carried away* determines a large part of Joyce. In writing, he seems to have been swept along by what he was doing, as though he were the victim of powerful impulses, which could be seen as an obsession, like making Anna Livia Plurabelle more watery by fluvial accretions. But of course it was his own doing. "Being carried away" looks like a passive description of a very active urge. As it seems in Bloom's musings on marital entanglements:

if he regarded her with affection, carried away by a wave of folly (*U* 16.1387)

Careers, like Parnell's, can be ruined by such excess, whether it consists of acting or being acted on. The theme is one of the oldest in tragedy: Achilles or Othello succumb to some passion; hubris is one of the oldest dramatic forces; in another framework it becomes the subject of comedy, which exaggerates human traits. Naturally some Joycean plots follow the familiar literary pattern, as in *Dubliners*:

—Mrs. Sinico in "A Painful Case" gets carried away, twice, both times with painful results. An inanimate engine almost takes this—"carried away"—literally. Mr. Duffy presents the alternative—of never being carried away—as a principle of life.
—The hero of "Araby" experiences a romantic passion that takes him on a frustrated quest.
—In "Counterparts," Farrington's "felicitous moment" has dire consequences and precipitates the downhill chain reaction.
—Mrs. Kearney, in "A Mother," is evidently going too far (her "conduct was condemned on all hands" [D 149.10]).[7]
—As against this, Eveline is not carried away, at least not by centrifugal forces or a spirit of adventure. But, in some mysterious way, Father Flynn once was.

Much in *Ulysses* hinges on Molly Bloom being carried away, and allowing herself to do so, in what has all the air of being exceptional behavior. Her husband, in contrast, does not take conventionally expected action—does pointedly not go to the stereotype extremes of rage and revenge, or, to use the point of view adopted here, he engages in all sorts of excess deviations. Typically, as Joyce went along, being carried away becomes more and more an act—or passion—of literary form, of salient traits of narrative and technique, a mode of linguistic and stylistic existence.

The prose of the *Portrait*, especially passages of crisis or elation, tends to swell in successive waves, phases that become longer and more elaborate. The moments of rapture on the beach toward the end of chapter 4 are rendered in analogous exaltation. The "fabulous artificer" in the form of "a hawklike man" inspires soaring prose. It may set off in relative sobriety: "His heart trembled"; a parallel clause is added, a slightly longer one: "his breath came faster"; then, without pause, an expansive sentence puts inspiration into image and words: "and a wild spirit passed over his limbs as though he were soaring sunward." He then reverts to an augmented variant of the beginning: "His heart trembled in an ecstasy of fear and his soul was in flight." In the next move the first motives become launching points for tumescent flourishes, in which both "breath" (which is no longer Stephen's own) and "spirit" are taken up and modified: "His *soul* was *soaring* in an *air* beyond the world and the body he knew was purified in a *breath* and delivered of incertitude and made radiant and commingled with the element of the *spirit*." This breathless expansion of "his soul was in flight" has snowballed to thirty-five words, with many repetitions (here italicized for demonstration) and much elaboration. Another tumescent offshoot brings the paragraph to a soaring close:

"An *ecstasy* of *flight* made *radiant* his eyes and *wild his breath* and *tremulous* and *wild* and *radiant* his windswept *limbs*" (P 169). There is elation as well as dilation in the development from "his limbs" to limbs that have become tremulous and wild and radiant as well as windswept. The ecstasy, a movement outside its origin, is not alone in what the words mean but in the intensified energy of their performance.

PROVECTION

> But what do you call it?
>
> —Joyce, *Ulysses*

It becomes necessary to label what we think we perceive. First, however, I will make it quite clear that the terms offered for convenience are emphatically *not gasp terms,* that is, they are to be understood without the respiratory indication of reverence, without that minimal pause and change of voice that accompanies a word being heaved onto an altar. In the old times, we remember, the gasp terms were "Symbol," "Myth," or "Irony." Now they are "TEXT," or allgaspinous "DISCOURSE." We all remember when "silence" acquired its capital S and "absence" its accolade as they soared straight into the realm of chic metaphysics and out of practical usefulness.[8]

This is not how I would like to be understood at all. The terms suggested here are without liturgical radiance and should be plainly descriptive and even helpful, maybe at some stage replaced by more efficient ones. For easier communication, carried-away-ness in all its deportment needs a terminological label. After some searching, and trying out verbal nouns like *ekstasis* (think of the last part of chapter 4 in *Portrait*), *transport, excess, effusion,* the term deemed optimal is that of the title, *provection*. The basic metaphor is Latin *pro-vehere*, a verb: "go beyond limits set"; with a prefix *pro* to indicate a movement forward, and a stem *veh*(-ere)[9] (related to *veh*icles like *wagon* or *wain*): "to convey or carry." *Vehere* seems to be related to our word *way* as well as, fittingly, the German *be-wegen*. The overall topic, of course, is movement. *Proveho* means "I carry forward or proceed" (often to a particular degree, or stage of activity, feeling). It can mean "advance" or "promote" to a higher rank. In the passive or the middle voice (with passive form and active meaning) *provehor* includes "being carried away."

Virgil[10] used the verb in a rhetorical question. When quick action is called for, a speaker asks:

quid ultra provehor / et fando surgentis demoror Austros? (Why should I go on further [literally: be carried on] and by my speech delay the rising winds?) (Aen. 3.481)

Speech, the Romans knew, has a way of carrying us forward. We might even now see much of *Ulysses* as inverting traditional epic action; in Joyce's verbose novel action is partly supplanted by speech and the winds of rhetoric. In the Aeolus chapter Professor MacHugh fittingly advises against provection:

> We mustn't be led away by words, by sounds of words. We think of Rome. . . . (U 7.485)

The chapter's mode is an inflated case in point. *Ulysses*—such my digressive vignette—is very much based on verbal *"ultra provehi"*; the *Wake* seems to be its ultimate incarnation.

EXAGGERATION AND CHANGE

"Mind C.K. does not pile it on" is the advice passed on by the ghost of Paddy Dignam, in a text-generated spiritualist séance, to all those still on the wrong side of Maya (U 12.362). This is good advice at all times and especially so within the episode, the Cyclops chapter, which is one of salient exaggeration. Cyclops does indeed pile it on, gigantically. The very interpolation in which the phrase occurs acts out the notion, jocularly thrown into the preceding talk, that someone has seen a ghost. The idea is not only magnified but transformed—provected—into something else: the machinery and the vocabulary of séances are brought into play. At the same time, the machinery of provection itself becomes manifest in textbook exemplification.

Provection is characterized by a forward motion in a given direction, by a marked increase (a tendency toward hyperbole); and by a change of direction, a departure, a deviation, derailment, whose exact point of origin may not be easy to determine.

The characteristics of provection are, in the first place:

augmentation, intensification, hypertrophy, amplification,

and then, secondly,

some divergence, a turn, a change, some divarication, shunting (this diversion is naturally, again, in relation to some *implied norm* or *expectation*).

In other words, whatever new element will surface, there is going to be more of it, and it is going to become something—at least slightly—different. Progression slides into digression. Too much more makes a qualitative difference: "Où le trop d'une qualité commence, la qualité finit et prend un autre nom."[11] Hypertrophy results in a different turn, a change in kind. (Misusing a well-known Jakobsonian distinction, one might bring the contiguous forward movement close to metonymous augmentation and align the change in kind more to metaphor.)

In fact, the graphic equivalent of provection is a vector, usually an iconic sign in the shape of an arrow, with a certain direction. The appropriate pictorial shape might be an arrow of increasing width, probably bent, or even bifurcated, to indicate the gathering of momentum and its deflection. Notice how Stephen's progress in *Portrait* might be diagramed in terms of vectors: perhaps toward learning, or justice (in the first chapter); then toward sin (chapter 2); again in contrast, toward Christian purity and order (chapter 3); or (in chapter 4)[12] toward creation, flying and falling; and toward exile in the final chapter. Vectorial descriptions would of course vary with the observer; the graphic possibilities themselves, however, are evident: the novel *could* be charted.

Take an instance in *Ulysses,* as we find Stephen, early on and throughout, theologically—also psychologically—obsessed with paternal substances. "Arius," he tells himself, was

> warring his life long upon the consubstantiality of the Son with the Father. (*U* 1.657)

This, by the by, is already an exaggeration for emphasis; Arius, according to the documents, was hardly "warring his life long" (but his name is derived from the heathen war god, Ares). Whatever the origin of the phrase, it will soon be self-parodistically exaggerated in a protean change: the same idea, but more of it, and with a difference:

> Warring his life long upon the contransmagnificandjewbangtantiality. (*U* 3.51)

A weight has been added to create the longest word so far in the whole book, a difficult one to articulate, an oddity and ostensible microprovection. And, almost self-reflexively, a characterization is included: Augmentation is signaled by "magnificand"—something that is to be made bigger. The derailment finds expression in "bang"—a highly effective, flagrant ingredient that is not part of the theological expectation.

MAGNIFICATION AND *BANG* CAN SERVE AS PRACTICAL SHORTHAND FOR JOYCEAN DEVELOPMENTS AND TECHNIQUES

Mulligan, Ulyssean herald, foreshadows many provective techniques; as soon as he appears, he ceremoniously intones dislocated words from the Mass, and is noticeable for perpetual histrionic excess. Typically, he mimics Stephen's theorizing on Shakespeare. His exaggeration, moreover, precedes the original; we are given the mock echo several chapters before we hear the original sound.

He proves by algebra . . .

Proof and "algebra" promise to be exact and demonstrable

. . . that Hamlet's grandson is Shakespeare's grandfather . . .

The two *grand*s magnify and they turn the proposition into something grotesque, absurd:

. . . that he himself is the ghost of his own father. (*U* 1.555)

One way of saying all this is that the Joycean text often deviates almost instantly into parody, which is often more of the same, piled up, with an additional twist. Correspondingly, Mulligan drifts from a "snotgreen sea," based on Homeric patterns, right away to an augmented and diverted "scrotumtightening sea"—an epithet no contemporary reader was prepared for—as well as from Swinburne an English into Homeric Greek (*"Epi oinopa ponton"*) and an Attic quotation (*"Thalatta! Thalatta!"* [*U* 1.78–80]). If we enter into the spirit of the thing and, in our turn, Hellenize the book in which Mulligan wants to "Hellenize" the island (1.158), we are provecting it close toward an ancient epic, and everything in the novel becomes—potentially—something different, more grandiose and, at the same time, far away.[13]

On a more subdued note, Bloom is introduced to us by his taste preference,

Mr Leopold Bloom ate with relish . . . (*U* 4.1)

Then we are carried into an extended catalogue of five detailed items, from "thick giblet soup" to "fried hencods' roes." The third sentence offers more of the same, "grilled mutton kidney" as a superlative choice; diversion then is provided, not by a bang, but a "tang" of—of all things—urine, urine affecting, mind you, Bloom's palate. Somehow, the direction has taken an odd turn. Early readers had not yet developed a taste for such a faintly scented gustatory provection.

Being carried away is signaled, for example, in what turns out to be Mulligan's longest early speech in the first chapter, his What-is-death? justification to Stephen. It moves from idiomatic depiction of death as a medical experience to literary embroideries like "sir Peter Teazle," and on toward uneasily jocular hyperbole:

I don't whinge like some hired mute from Lalouette's. (1.213)

(There is, as we note in passing, an interesting touch in Mulligan comporting himself like someone who is "mute.") The process of escalation is signaled in a narrative comment (which implies Stephen's awareness of it as an observable process):

He had spoken himself into boldness. (1.216)

Mulligan has been carried away—has provected himself—*somewhere else*: into boldness. A similar escalation takes place when, at the end of Eumaeus, Stephen begins to sing "an old German song" and then, moments later, is heard singing "more boldly" (*U* 16.1812, 1883). These are common, everyday occurrences. They would hardly be worth pointing out if the whole novel did not speak itself—write itself—into a boldness that took decades to assimilate. *Bold* (as in "bold hand") in *Ulysses* can cause a shock; in typography it is used for emphasis or an increase in volume. When we next come across "boldness" it is in one of those inserts of the Cyclops chapter, where Bob Doran is made to say, in exaggerated, stylized courtesy:

But, should I have overstepped the limits of reserve let the sincerity of my feelings be the excuse for my boldness. (12.789)

Whether we call this parody or hyperbole, the form itself consists in overstepping limits of reserve, which in actuality might be due to sincerity of feelings, but in its verbal excess points to the opposite. The Cyclopean inserts (in one of which the passage occurs) are in themselves crassly provective. They pick up a trait in the conversation or action and take it to absurd lengths; within themselves they contain subinserts; at each point they are expandable into regressive sidespins.

Any vector analysis of a Joycean strandentwining passage would be highly intricate, if it could be ever complete. For demonstration, only a few features are singled out in a Cyclopean interpolation, the one in which the not intrinsically alluring Dublin markets are upgraded into the romance of Irish legends:

> A pleasant land it is in sooth of murmuring waters, fishful streams . . .

This leads to an elaboration of fishful streams: the epithet is implemented; specified fish are listed:

> where sport the gurnard, the plaice, the roach, the halibut, the gibbed haddock, the grilse, the dab, the brill, the flounder, the pollock . . . (*U* 12.70)

At a certain point we may realize that, independent of the point of origin, fishiness has become its own goal and satisfaction. Most of the specimens listed are not to be found in Irish fishful streams and murmuring sweet waters at all, but in the open sea. In the Cyclopean spirit of incongruous enthusiasm, the list has written itself into unnoticed saltiness, or perhaps carelessness. Then, in yet another turn, the catalog trails off into bathetic generality and awkward repetition, not at all in keeping with the initial note of picturesque stereotypes:

> and other denizens of the aqueous kingdom too numerous to be enumerated. (*U* 12.70)

With a marked change of tone, enumeration itself imposes itself on the pattern. We have moved from water, streams, and murmurs to numbers. The expansive technique is not a modernist Joycean invention. In this case it was already used by one of Joyce's forerunners, Ovid, who in *Metamorphoses* has *his* giant Polyphemus make verbal and vapid love to the nymph Galatea in precisely such provective bursts of piled-up enumeration and self-perpetuation.[14] The practice is as old as the epic itself; Joyce found new ways of foregrounding it.

"PROLONGED, PROVOCATIVE"

In the central chapters of *Ulysses* the provections of artifice are matched by carried-away-ness on the level of events. In Sirens,

Cyclops, or Nausicaa, the protagonists can be carried away, each in his or her own fashion. Cyclopean narrow-mindedness, fanaticism, and prejudice make it all the more easy to escalate from mere words to arguments and the menace of actual ballistics. Typically, the Citizen is first seen "having a great confab with himself," passes on to more and more haranguing and sermonizing, and ends up with "Did I kill him or what?" and a "volley of oaths" (*U* 12.119, 1901). In tumescent excess, fatuous words become an empty biscuit tin. The chapter's mode enlarges this intensification into a seismic catastrophe (or quasi-scientific dislocution of the power of Poseidon, the shaker of the earth).

But, more surprisingly, Bloom, apostrophized as "prudent" in this episode, is extremely *in*cautious; is being carried away, too, forgets his usual social reserve, becomes argumentative—in fact a voluminous talker—and is, atypically, going out of his silent way to ask for trouble. He, too, ascends toward rhetorical climaxes with precipitate exits. We know why he is worked up and why his aggressions are displaced. This is the moment when a painful provection that his mind does not want to dwell upon is likely to take place in his home, too.

Getting worked up is natural, often of great human interest, and therefore a prime topic for all literature. There is nothing new in the various emotional climaxes that *Ulysses* still contains. Of concern here is that, once more, the emotion, in textual empathy, moves the style. The Hyperbolic Asides, the nonrealistic insertions, act like a provective chorus that comments on what is going on, a further remove from the narrator's internal and already hyperbolic remarks. Overstatement and intensification are the order of the day. The chapter sets off with a harmless encounter that is magnified into a near accident—"he near drove his gear into my eye" (12.3)—and fittingly ends with the superlative human achievement of transfiguration, in accordance with classical and biblical precedent. One of the Latin meanings of *provehere* is to "promote in rank": apotheosis is the highest conceivable promotion.

The instances given have already proved it to be almost impossible to separate miniexamples neatly from the larger issues. It may well be that the impulse from the microcosmic particle to the universal application is the most central of all provections that characterize the reading of Joyce. Synecdochically, we move from the discussion of small particles to more comprehensive entanglement.

The Ithaca chapter magnifies a scientific approach into a disorienting accumulation of facts and relations. In one instance an imaginary route leads from "the cliffs of Moher," Irish and terrestrial, to "the delta in the constellation of Cassiopeia" and into "incalculable eons of peregrinations" (*U* 17.1974, 2019); meditations may lead into imaginary, absurd (and faulty) numbers. Or else we may find deviations from the deadpan, scientific diction into one that is incompatible; take Bloom's doings on entering his bed:

> He kissed the plump mellow yellow smellow melons of her rump, on each plump melonous hemisphere, in their mellow yellow furrow, with obscure prolonged provocative melonsmellonous osculation. (17.2241)

Here a sudden burst of sensuality provects itself in a flutter of fruit and smells and physical impressions, *or else*—to change the angle of observation—a choreography of signifiers that clamor for attention. In this sensuous whirl, abstractions are momentarily suspended. We may experience *mellow* as touching *yellow* and generating *smellow* and squinting at *furrow*. Or we notice how *plump* kisses the distant word *rump,* and *obscure* strives to mate with *osculation*. The sounds and shapes of words seem to match the bodily shapes and sensations.

All of this de-Ithacizes Ithaca for an inspired, digressive moment. Yet it also magnifies Ithacan contrastive symmetries and adds an ultra-Ithacan coinage like "provocative melonsmellonous osculation" with a compound adjective posing as a scientific one. Language as an orchestration of acoustic, echoing and mating sounds, is what we might expect to find in a chapter like Sirens (where, chances are, we would assimilate the melons to Greek *melos*).

There is no need to articulate—at this late hour in Joyce exegesis—how the Sirens chapter is provected, how its raptures are put into sound effects. Music can serve as a welcome, though intermittent, anodyne to stave off perturbances. Father Cowley, Ben Dollard, Simon Dedalus are enraptured by music, "a kind of drunkenness," Bloom muses, "enthusiasts" (11.1192). Enthusiasm is a particularly inspired variety of being carried away, originally by intervention from above.

Stylistic correspondences to theme and subject matter are now taken for granted. But even sympathetic first readers had not yet been conditioned the same way. One staunch supporter in 1919 showed himself highly allergic to the chapter's then radically novel features: "You have gone too far," he wrote; "you have once again gone 'down where the asparagus grows' "—a direction not desired. The writer who turned out metaphorical illustrations for what I call provection was Ezra Pound, who not only commented on the chapter, but imitated it.

> The peri-o-perip-o-periodico-parapatetico-periodopathetico-I dont-off-the markgetical structure of yr. first or peremier para-petitec graph.[15]

He parodied the mode, singing the Sirens into absurdity, exaggerating Joyce's excesses. He provected the provections, and in the process was carried away himself. His vivid implication is not only that Joyce went too far—the wrong way—but that he deviated into the "off-the markgetical." Sirens, Pound remarked,

> —will cause all but your most pig-o-peripatec-headed readers to think you have gone marteau-dingo-maboule-

We don't have to know what "gone marteau-dingo-maboule" precisely calls up, but we recognize charges that were often to be leveled, in less imaginative wording, against the author. Joyce's answer was typical and curt in terms of being carried away, that there was no other way open to him, and of negative justification:

> [it] is not capricious.[16]

What may look like excessive capering, in other words, may have its intricate justification. To show new angles of the noncapriciousness of Joyce's ways has now become a mainstream scholarly occupation. The tendency nowadays is to characterize the *Ulysses* chapters precisely in terms *of their provections*. Many of the entries in Joyce's schema, or schemas, consist in labels for their excessive programs. Carried away in my turn, I add to them in blissful contagion.

CIRCE

In a different sense, Circe by its very nature is predisposed for provection. A change into animals, not just swine, by metaphorical convention, suggests the exaggeration of certain traits to the exclusion of others.[17] Psychologically, the chapter is codetermined by a seeming lack of conscious restraints. Lust, fear, wishfulfillment are blatantly brought forward, magnified, staged with phantasmagoric bangs. In perspective, we are not confined by the circumferences of any one mind—or the sum total of the minds of the figures in it.

Circe is egressive: it frankly steps outside of limits that were, so far, still observed. In Circe, *Ulysses* is getting beyond, or beside, itself. Changes of voices and roles, as they abounded in the first chapter, where they were still restricted by everyday verisimilitude, have taken on a life of their own; what used to be Mulligan's conspicuous role adverbs at the beginning are now blown up into spectacular masquerades. By design the chapter is expansive and distortive (its opening already mentions *stretches* and—conversely—*stunted*). The design itself was further expanded and distorted. Joyce reported on its progress and setbacks: "It gets wilder and worse and more involved."[18] We can study its expansion and elaboration as almost step-by-step provection.

Michael Groden, in his study of the genesis of *Ulysses*, distinguishes three stages; the third one, a turning point for the whole book, was the ebullient Circe chapter, whose continual excrescences affected the rest of the novel, including what had already been written. Revising Circe, Joyce once more changed gear, and decisively so.[19]

Typically, a scene that most readers would now consider central, the messianic scene, was a later addition. Groden reports that it "results from Bloom's tendency to correct other people and to lecture them."[20] Joyce inserted the whole extended scene after Zoe's request for "a swaggerroot" and Bloom's lewd remark that "the mouth can be better engaged than with a cylinder of rank weed" (15.1347). The mouth then instantly does become better engaged. The "stump speech" that grows out of such a triviality will promote Bloom to imperial heights and again *de*mote him to carbonization. At the end the mouth will be magnified into "six hundred voices," while, anticlimactically, Bloom becomes "mute, shrunken" (15.1953). In reality, the whole, elongated episode takes up next to no time. It may be appropriate that the entire swaggering and rank arabesque sprouts from vegetable cues like "swaggerroot" and "rank weed."

The medical testimony that is given at Bloom's trial features biological excesses, exaggerations: Bloom is "bisexually abnormal"—"born out of bedlock"—"there is unbridled lust . . . traces of elephantiasis" (15.1777). This "womanly man" (15.1798) deviates into the other sex, with instant pregnancy and the birth of eight children, whose names in themselves form a minor provective list patterned on gold and silver. Of course, by the time we come upon these passages we have become used to the chapter's hallucinatory enormities and are no longer surprised. Homer's Kirke with her charms, I might add, was herself a great and magical provector, the only one, moreover, who managed to hold back Odysseus for a whole year.

We may turn to the whole chapter, the messianic scene, the notesheets, the galleys, or individual passages, or words, to find, at each level, minuscule or larger samples of what is here being exemplified. At this stage there is no reader of this essay—unless it has failed grievously—who could not, off the cuff, think of numerous further instances and applications.

VECTORIOUS READYEYES

As always, there is a certain pointlessness in applying some earlier, evolving principle to *Finnegans Wake,* and this is not just because of our abysmal ignorance about it, which turns each utterance into a scholarly imposture. But also because of its own, extreme, culminative nature. How to show provection in what is already provection per se? A work that looks, at first and most subsequent glances, to be based, manifestly, on excess, carried-away-ness, on exuberance, on effusion (*riverrun* sets it off); that sports its "toomuchness, the fartoomanyness" (*FW* 122.36) throughout? Each single word seems made up of magnification and of bangs. Reading the *Wake* is mainly a matter of hermeneutic provection. Its phrases are (but we use other synonyms) multivective. Something like

Jungfraud's Messongebook (460.20)

(even without any context) piles a manifest *Jung* on a latent *Freud* (and inverts their traditional causal sequence); it suggests a German virgin *(Jungfrau)* and, perhaps, a book of *messages,* or a book to be taken to Mass (Ger. *Messe*)—in which case *virgin* would more likely become *the* Virgin. Psychoanalysis commented on virginity and on mariolatry. Old men (as the two analysts are generally envisaged and were so in times of *Work in Progress*) are pitted against young *(jung)* women *(Frau).* Old and young men and women have dreams *(songe);* Jung and Freud interpreted them—differently. And it may be all *fraud* and lies *(mensonge);* if so, the French ghost word introduces *men* and couples them with *dream*: when men and women and analysts get together, there may be messages or lies (and what about *song* and *songbook?*). All of these readings have been done many times over; my phrasings are old wine in appropriately labeled new bottles to show nothing more than that Wakean provection need not be proved in detail; on its very surface it has always intrigued us.

If anything, it might be observed that provection can turn into revection. The vehicularity is spelled out, say, in a return from

Carry me along

on the last page, to

brings us . . . back

on the first. The text, at one point, displays an iconic

greater TH<small>a</small>N or less <small>T H</small> a N

with diminishing and then increasing size of the letters; and follows it by

> vectorious readyeyes (298.14)

which is, geometrically, some vector radius, but no doubt also one of those numerous self-descriptive confessions. The ready eyes are also ours.

But then, what would we *not* find in *Finnegans Wake*? Looking at it with vectorious ready eyes, however, we might come up with a few specifically Wakean provections. One characteristic variant is its kaleidoscopic splurges—multiple displays of its verbal material. They may look, but are not, "whorled without aimed" (272.4). They are small-scale replicas of the whole, which reprocesses its themes and elements. Typical for such autodinetic (from *dinê*, or *dinos*, "whirl") runs is the one example, certainly representative:

> Totalled in toldteld and teldtold in tittletell tattle. (597.8)

This is vertiginous, tongue-twisting same-anew-ness in phonemic permutation; or else self-generative variety; or elaborative dilation. A pattern is extended in apparent self-complacency. Here I merely rephrase, in the chosen terminology, what every reader can observe—duplication and reprocessing. We find a symmetry that is askew, with an increase toward the end: *toldteld* mirrors *teldtold*, but *totalled* is magnified into two words—with a change of syllabic elements: *tittletell tattle*.

Semantically there is also decrease from *Total*, or *all told*, to what is very small: *tittle*. Or else: the whole—*Totalled* (*total* plus *all*, and something big, *tall*, as well)—is split up into various *tellings*, past and present, tellings obviously not all reliable. So the *Wake*—again nothing new—is variably retelling what it has been saying; and I am again doing what the quote says, concentrating on the energies of the whole process—amplification and minuscule bangs.

Finnegans Wake often drifts into what I would call *par(a)echoes* of itself, which merely describes an acoustic feature of "the same anew." Our sentence tells us "the same anew" and *does* it visibly and audibly. The Greeks actually did use the term *para-echo: parêchêma* was a succession of similar sounds, alliteration. *Finnegans Wake* tends to become parechetic. Parechetically, I am here making similar sounds for similar features.

The *Wake*'s opening alerts us to the processes that will follow. When a bit of the story gets underway, we have a rearrival that has not yet occurred, and then—the second movement in the second paragraph—we come to a programmatic:

nor had topsawyer's rocks by the stream Oconee exaggerated themselse

We begin with exaggeration, but in the original sense of piling up heaps *(agger)* of rocks, needed for building and civilization ("buildung upon buildung," we will soon hear). Something is piled on. Conveniently, *agger* derives from a vehicular action: *ad-gerere* (carry to). But already the implication is of *too much,* at least too much verbiage, of disproportional augmentation. What is heaped up, or exaggerated, is, *reciprocally, oneself,* and in the same sweep—*transitively*—something *else*. If we expect "selves," we have been sidetracked into "else"—again, increase and difference. Exaggerations change the nature of what they exaggerate. The reproduction called up is human and cultural but reminds us, epiphenomenally, of the textual autogenesis so typical for the book where the phrase occurs. This sentence takes us to another Dublin, beyond the Atlantic,

to Laurens County's gorgios

the country of topsawyers and different Finns. Relevant for the present purposes is that such a Dublin in Georgia may not be the same as the one many Irishmen left behind. Something changes in transit. We also come across a strong female (and riverine) element that has been absent from the first movement: the stream Oconee. It reinforces birth (as in *née*) and perhaps the place of birth (if *con* is taken to be French): the first letter, O—round and open and gaping—will acquire iconic significance later in the book. All the while, the text goes on, those rocks exaggerating themselves were also

doublin their mumper

Doubling a number all the time is one of the oldest tricks of increases that exceed our imagination. In this case the reduplication is not quite the same. *Dublin* becomes *doublin, number* turns into *mumper*. At certain times the variations matter more than the points of origin. Leaving oedipal *mums* aside, as well as *member,* note that to *mump* can mean "deceive, overeach, to beg." A *mumper* is also an imposter or a beggar. And in part, the most effective part, the word still remains opaque.

The rocks on the stream Oconee in the next phrase—"thuartpeatrick"—transform themselves into the rock on which the Church was founded. That, too, from the humble beginnings to the establishment of a mighty Catholic church, was quite a provection. If, however, we draw *gorgios* into the orbit of stone and rock and Greek *Gorgo*, we get a metamorphosis of different, and grim, consequences (Greek *gorgos* means "grim, terrible"). So we, affected readers, pile meanings upon meanings in extrapolative excess. After decades of *Wake* exegesis, our multivectorial urge has been well attested.

COUNTERCURRENTS

My tautological ramifications must not obliterate the correlative counterprocesses. In true paradoxical confirmation, a devective reading should supplement the ones given here. As always, it would be possible to phrase all the foregoing descriptions in exactly the opposite way. The *Wake*, sure enough, exaggerates itself, but it also seems to return to a nearly simple, low key, fade out at its end, just as *Ulysses* regresses to the semblance of an earlier mode. In one way the Penelope chapter is also the simplest one, the most homogeneous in the whole book.

It is the Cyclops episode, with its blatant egressive insertions, that has been used as a showpiece. Naturally and truistically, it is also characterized by *de*vection, *de*flation—by bathetic drops, anti-climaxes. In the end, the Citizen, waddling and "puffing and blowing with the dropsy" (*U* 12.1785), is less of an athletic giant than the words expended on him might have indicated. But, of course, no reader ever trusted those descriptions of "a broadshouldered deep-chested stronglimbed" hero (12.152) in the first place. We subtract what the exaggerating agencies pile on. Obviously, Bloom's vehicular elevation to heaven, an Elijah "at an angle of fortyfive degrees," is at the same time a descent into the ludicrous. Before that, he rhetorically and emotionally stands up "to it then with force like men" but collapses, all of a sudden, "as limp as a wet rag" (12.1475–79), a movement that the subsequent chapter, Nausicaa, will magnify in its own curve of swelling and deflation; Joyce termed them "tumescence-detumescence."

In general we move from realistic events to more and more imaginative flights, move—a trait of *Ulysses*—from indicative modes, as things are, more and more toward *what if* or *imagine that*, which is to say, subjunctive ones, events doubly fictitious. The parallactic interpolations in Cyclops tend to be conjunctival.

On the level of content, devection is a theme of *Dubliners,* the shorthand for which has conventionally been "paralysis": reality lags behind expectation. Joyce's first prose sentence deprives someone of hope before we know who the someone is. In some essential sense, the stories trail off devectively. Goals are not reached; escapes not made; lives not changed; desires not satisfied; poetry remains unwritten.

If the implications of the title *Ulysses* guided our expectations, then the drop from antique heroic exploits to domestic quotidian fumblings is felt to be, at first glance, a devective letdown. *Ulysses* was considered lacking in momentous events. Conventional heroism is not achieved; Bloom does not seem to jerk himself up to assume command and reestablish disrupted orders (though this is debatable, dependent on interpretation). When Stephen is ejected out of *Ulysses*—and out of the Joycean canon—into the wilderness behind Bloom's garden, nobody (except a few critics) knows if he is also provected into authorship and creativity; most of us doubt that he will be launched into a musical career managed by Leopold Bloom, man of many counsels, or into a liaison with Marion Bloom. We cannot tell how Molly will act next morning, only a few hours away—who will be master and who servant. In view of predominantly devective cues, it is remarkable that an interpretative and habitual bias leads us to provect meaning, often in "symbolic" expansion.[21] Conversely, one commonplace view of Joyce's later works is that the paucity of events has been compensated by the well-known provective artifices.

Secondly, the provective exuberance is caught up by schematic devices, by repetitions, cross-references, by structural reinforcement, architectural bracketings. Repetitions, kaleidoscopic permutations—the sort of motives we like to tabulate—are cognitive supports in what might become a chaotic whirl (as early readers testified).

All of Joyce's works had a way of getting out of hand. It is characteristic of *Ulysses* that its episodes tend to get longer and more involved and more pointedly arabesquable. The later works often resemble a sentence underway, in which (as in Eumaeus) more and more subordination can be added. Against such increase in length and complexity, there are structural checks, coordinates. Once we can look at *Portrait* or *Ulysses* panoramically, spread out in space before us, not as ways to traverse in time, they appear symmetrical, contrived, dovetailed, with balances that may even appear too neat, too carefully elaborated.

The schemas are such checks. With their fastenings, clamps, braces, correspondences, they make the supporting devices visible: they also reveal a ground plan, order, arrangement. A schema is essentially, originally, something that "holds." Joyce's schematic symmetries, however, are lopsided, conceptual, and abstractive. It may take an effort to discover them (which does not make them less functional). Schematically, Nestor balances Ithaca. There is positional symmetry; we have catechism, personal or impersonal; further analogies can be uncovered. Nestor suggests a way to come to terms with the later episode, and vice versa. But the differences are overwhelming as well. There is considerable provective development from Nestor, the shortest chapter of the book, to Ithaca, the second longest, most fragmented one, expandable ad libitum. Spatial relationships help us to get our bearings and to make additional sense in retrospect.

Dynamic drives have to be balanced by static checks; we need both, and at certain times in our critical understanding we may have to give more prominence to one over the other. In a first phase of bewilderment readers needed a Stuart Gilbert tabulation to chart the chaos into the surety of order and schema. Once we have been systematizing too long, it becomes necessary to stress the counterforces.

Joyce's works came into being in a tension between luxuriating urges and a need for control. The dynamic drives had to be caught by systematization. But then, in the workshop, the material got out of schema again and had to be recaptured in a continuous process of (as the *Wake* has it)

a sot of a swigswag, systomy dystomy (*FW* 597.21)

In motive paradox Joyce reintegrated what is in essence an egressive feature, one that pushes beyond confines. The graph might be seen as a vicious circle of emergent *patterns,* then a *pattern extension,* which leads to a *pattern eruption* (the recurrent two stages of provection as they have been reiterated here extensively), and finally the *repatterning of pattern eruption* in contradictory reintegration. This essay has naturally put its stress on *dy*stomy, the *ex*-cess, whatever transgresses the current system.

A WINGED FORM FLYING ABOVE THE WAVES

Both dynamic drives and the static checks are present in the myth of the artificer Daedalus, whose deeds were of excess. His mind took him to reaches not explored before. Out of exaggerated envy he killed a rival (who had outdone him in artistry). He fled to Crete, created the likeness of an animal to gratify the lust of a no doubt greatly provected queen. The resulting hybrid, Minotauros, was too much of a bull for comfort or prestige—something monstrous, a being sui generis (he occurs, rightly, in the *Ulysses* chapter of the most monstrous births, U 14.994). Daedalus built a maze that forced intruders to go forward and to deviate constantly. He was the first human to fly above nets. In contrast, his son's exuberance turned out to be disastrous; he aimed too high and fell too low. The family biography is one of overreaching, as myths always are. But Daedalus was also a structurer, contriver; the labyrinth was an engineering feat, carefully planned and laid out. The fabulous artificer was in artistic control of his material (he systematically arranged the feathers for his wings),[22] someone looking ahead. He cautioned his son to a middle course of sane restraint.

The other prevalent Greek myth was in one sense a lesson *against* unbridled provection. Odysseus of many resources and counsels kept a tight rein on his emotions, was in control, did—with a few consequential exceptions—*not* allow himself to be carried away. Nor, on the whole, does Bloom (except in the encounter with the Citizen). But the novel's exuberant modes carry him away, allow, for example, the urges of his psyche to take over. In contrast to the *Odyssey*—with its relatively even hexametrical flow and conventional diction—its Irish dislocution keeps changing the venue almost as an end in itself.[23]

Many stories set off with a deflection from an expected or prescribed course of events. The *Odyssey* is such a story. Odysseus wanted to return, but was deviated, geographically, at the fateful Cap of Malea (*Od.* 9.80), at times by divine interference, occasionally by the folly of his comrades, sometimes by his own nature—so an epic came into being. Stories worth telling are often based on provective disturbances. Once exposed to a series of adventures, Odysseus was prudent and purposeful, in other words, less at the mercy of distractive forces than most humans or one-track monsters, which gave him an advantage. Above all, he was able to use provection strategically in opportunist manipulation: by eloquence, strength, perseverance, disguise, equivocation, or the use of potent Greek wine—by what can be called his polytropy. But there *is* a restless strain in him (his final reconciliation with Poseidon is still far away and conditional). Later writers magnified the Faustian streak, an unsatisfiable curiosity and lust for adventure. Dante's Ulisse confesses that "desire to gain experience of the world"

> l'ardore . . . a divenir del mondo esperto. (*Inf.* 26. 97–98)

This Odysseus is provected past the straits of Gibraltar to flounder on the high seas. Leopold Bloom inherited some of that quality, too.

"EXSOGGERRAIDER!"

Simplifications like all the above are permissible at the stage of initiation to introduce a notion like the provective urge. As we go on, we would have to acknowledge—without much surprise—the multivectorial nature of Joyce's work, especially and self-evidently *Finnegans Wake*. There are, naturally, several provectors at work at all times, in perpetual concert. It is up to us to recognize and to describe them as adequately as our perceptions let us.

Imagine a vectoral disentanglement of, say, "The Dead"—in how many ways we might characterize the movements of increase/decrease and the swervings. There is an increase of emotion, a concentration backward in time, then inward, away from the extensive world of surface without. There is a narrowing of scope, less and less action. (One action ardently anticipated does not take place.) The cast diminishes, with fewer and fewer people on the scene, and more and more isolation. There is also, at the end, a cosmic widening. The language escalates to supreme cadences—or else it degenerates into purplish kitsch. As readers, we take and bundle our vectoral choices and call them interpretation.

Separating and perhaps characterizing provective features may help to sharpen our observation and to articulate what we notice. It is arguable, for example, that the comparative neglect of Joyce's poetry or of his one play, *Exiles,* may be due, in part, to the lack of artistic provection in those works, which emphatically need not thereby make them less valuable. Provection does not automatically confer significance. But it has to be admitted that a certain provective conditioning seems to be a trademark of the Joycean reader who is likely to become spoiled, in the process, beyond retrieval.

For, of course, in the ultimate act that every reading is, *we* are the provectors, the exaggerators. We rise to the challenge. We get carried away, physically, from many parts of the world to attend a few days of conferential excess in Dublin, Trieste, Seville, Cesena, Leeds, Frankfurt, Philadelphia, Honolulu, or Dubrovnik, in our characteristic elation or symposiasm. To fly, sail, drive, all the way from Amsterdam, Kuwait, New Zealand, or Zürich to distant Milwaukee is what the Romans originally meant by *provehi*. Our publications are prolific, immense in size, and some very odd in kind. In our lectures and essays and workshops or, in particular, *Wake* reading groups we exceed, we keep piling it on, we deviate, we go beyond the boundaries and sometimes have to be called back by Bloomian common sense. Joyceans are provectors par excellence—which does not always translate as "by excellence." On the whole, unlike the old Daedalian provector, we excel more by quantitative magnification than by inspired bangs.

NOTES

1. James Joyce, *"A Portrait of the Artist as a Young Man": Text, Criticism, and Notes*, ed. Chester Anderson (New York: Viking Press, 1968). Hereafter cited as *P*.

2. *Ulysses*, ed. Hans Gabler, et al. (New York and London: Garland, 1986). Hereafter cited as *U*.

3. S. L. Goldberg, *James Joyce* (Edinburgh and London: Oliver and Boyd, 1962), 95.

4. "And in the expression of that [classical] temper—despite the romantic infinities and 'profundities' towards which he drifted himself and, even more, those saddled upon him since—lies all that is most fundamental, free and vital in his work." S. L. Goldberg, *The Classical Temper* (London: Chatto and Windus, 1961), 314-15.

5. Ibid., 21-22.

6. "It is too discursive, formless, unrestrained, and ugly things, ugly words, are too prominent; indeed at times they seem to be shoved in one's face, on purpose, unnecessarily.... His pen and his thoughts seem to have run away with him sometimes." The strictures are that there is too much and that something got out of hand. Garnett's report is commonly available in The Viking Critical Library edition of *A Portrait of the Artist as a Young Man* (New York: Viking Press, 1968), 319-20.

7. *"Dubliners": Text, Criticism, and Notes*, ed. Robert Scholes and A. Walton Litz (New York: Viking Press, 1969). Hereafter cited as *D*.

8. It would be easy to establish a kind of weather forecast to predict the next gasp term in line. One of the up and coming havoc words is *desire*.

9. Its Sanskrit relative *vah* obligingly begins a paragraph in part 4 of *Finnegans Wake*: "Vah!" (594.1).

10. Quintilian gives examples of the verb's usage, as in *audacia provecti* ("carried away by daring" or "emboldened"; *Institutio Oratoria* 1.3.4); or when he writes: "Grammar must know its own limits":

> "Et grammatice ... fines suos norit, praesertim tantum ab hac appellationis suae paupertate, intra quam primi illi constitere, provecta" (especially as it has *encroached so far beyond the boundaries* to which its unpretentious name should restrict it and to which its early professors actually confined themselves); *Institutio Oratoria of Quintilian*, 2.1.4), trans. H. E. Butler (Cambridge: Harvard University Press, Loeb Classical Library, 1979), 1:206-7.

The term *provection*—still to be seen as provisional (occurring so to speak still on the synoptic, left-hand page, and not part of the clear reading text)—also easily lends itself to convenient derivative forms (as they will be used), including antonyms (it would be possible to characterize S. L. Goldberg's views on Joyce descriptively as "invective" ones).

11. Pierre Marivaux, *Réflexions, Journaux et Œuvres diverses* (Paris: Garnier, 1916), 501.

12. The first section of chapter 4 clearly shows Stephen in excessive dedication to a laborious Christian life, but it also shows how the accumulated devotion gradually slides into something else (*P* 147-53).

13. Stuart Gilbert's charting of Homeric analogies and Buddhist-theosophist cor-

respondences (*James Joyce's "Ulysses,"* 1930) has frequently been considered excessive.

14. The echoes and the literary manner are developed in "Ovidian Roots of Gigantism in Joyce's *Ulysses,*" to appear in a forthcoming issue of the *Journal of Modern Literature.*

15. Letter of 10 June 1919. Forrest Read, ed., *Pound/Joyce* (New York: New Directions, 1967), 157 ff.

16. Letter of 6 August 1919 to Harriet Shaw Weaver. Joyce, *Letters,* ed. Stuart Gilbert (New York: The Viking Press, 1957, 1966), 1:129.

17. "The essence of the animal into man metamorphosis seems to be that man becomes an animal when he loses his many-sided human wholeness. One of his functions gets out of hand and usurps the powers belonging to the governing authority of his virtuous republic." Frank Budgen, *James Joyce and the Making of "Ulysses"* (1934; reprint, Bloomington: Indiana University Press, 1960), 229.

18. *Letters of James Joyce,* 1:147.

19. Michael Groden, *"Ulysses" in Progress* (Princeton: Princeton University Press, 1977), 166 ff.

20. Ibid., 173.

21. From this point of view, *symbol* is considered nearly synonymous with provection: *symballein* also meant a move in a certain direction.

22. *"nam ponit in ordine pennas"* ("he lays feathers in order") (*Metamorphoses* 8. 189).

23. Both statements are valid and untrue: of course the *Odyssey* is also provectively diversified, and *Ulysses* is much more coherent than it once seemed.

11
"The Veripatetic Imago"

SIDNEY FESHBACH

(for Zack Bowen)

Many critics have written about Stephen Dedalus's handling, or distorting, of Thomas Aquinas in the fifth chapter of *A Portrait*; but, in my opinion, because they did not deal directly or thoroughly enough with the source and context in the *Summa Theologiae* or with Stephen's rhetorical strategies, they missed much of the intellectual drama in his academic discourse.[1] This scene of his walking and talking with Lynch, which some have found dull and the hero boring and priggish and properly deflated by the grosser collegian, has as much drama of intense intellectual synthesis as, for example, the divisive, emotional Christmas-dinner scene. To highlight this drama, my essay focuses narrowly on Stephen's few paragraphs on the triplet of terms, *integritas, consonantia,* and *claritas,* comparing them with their corresponding source in Aquinas's *Summa Theologiae, Prima Pars, Quaestio* 39, *Articulus* 8. The essay adopts two approaches. The first is to make a more thorough comparison of the two passages than has been done. So many have written on some relationships of these two passages, yet no one, to my knowledge, has analyzed how the story's drama is expressed not only in Stephen's motives and intellectual strategies but in direct correspondence with the original context in Aquinas's question 39 and, as everywhere else in the novel, in the style, the syntax, of his discourse. There is much to learn from such an intense examination, especially if the findings are related to the entire novel.

The most complete comparison to date, in William Noon's *Joyce and Aquinas,* was very important as the first extensive treatment, but I believe its judgments regarding where Stephen stands in regard to "objectivity" and "subjectivity" mislead our judgments. It accuses him of a subjectivity that deviates essentially from the objectivity of

Aquinas; yet, Noon knew that Aquinas had himself begun to include along with his profound sensitivity and appreciation for the existence of the created world a greater amount of subjectivity.[2] Such subjectivity had begun before Aquinas, as Umberto Eco, in *Art and Beauty in the Middle Ages,* summarizes:

> The *Summa* of Alexander contained the seeds of even more radical, if less obvious, innovations than [those of Bonaventure]. The two theses . . . — that beauty is grounded in the form of the object, and that beauty is defined in relation to the knowing subject—were subsequently developed, the first by Albertus Magnus. . . . But what Albertus did not concede was that the relation of an object to the knowing subject might be a constitutive element in its beauty. His aesthetics, unlike that of the *Summa* of Alexander, was rigorously objectivist. . . . For Albertus, beauty is objectively present in things without the help or hindrance of men. The other kind of objectivism considers beauty to be a transcendental property also, but a property which is disclosed in relation to a knowing subject. This is St. Thomas Aquinas's kind of objectivism.[3]

I believe it true that Stephen, too, has profound appreciation for the activity of the senses and the created world, and that perhaps he has carried forward Aquinas's "objectivism" with a "knowing subject" in relation to apprehension and aesthetics in a secular mode. Noon, Eco, or, earlier, Kenner,[4] writing in the Age of Academic Irony, were satisfied to describe Stephen pejoratively as Sabellian, aesthete, and angelic, respectively. Ironies of many sorts are, of course, at work in the novel, but they are not its universal subtext; I believe these critics dug beneath the story too easily and casually, undermining a more complex and solid character, while the data closer to the surface were more vital and more important for reading, enjoying, and understanding him.

Stephen's statements about the active processing of mental images have significant resemblances to work by Franz Brentano, who, building a theory of phenomenology and intentionality derived from Aristotle and Aquinas, initiated the modern phase of phenomenological studies.[5] Because of the resemblance of Stephen's ideas to Brentano's work, I have used in this essay some terms from phenomenology, but I have not stressed their origins or implications or used a phenomenological method of analysis. Too often Stephen's theories have been analyzed in vitro, and so the second approach of this essay is to indicate how this source study affects our understanding of Stephen's motivations and the drama within the dramatic curve of the novel. When Stephen lectures Lynch on his theories of apprehension and aesthetics, he is at a precise moment in his spiritual development, his artistic career, and his social relationships. Analysis of the topics and the mechanics of the language and syntax of his adaptations of Aquinas shows that they figure directly in various dramatic lines of the novel as well as in a crucial nexus of motifs in *Ulysses*. In conclusion, I speculate about Stephen as an artist and his future as a young man. Because I decry several ahistorical efforts or peculiar redefinitions of history in recent literary criticism, I add that due to the spatial limits of this essay I have not tried to justify my analyses of these sections of the *Summa Theologiae* or *A Portrait,* but I believe they have a strong historical basis (in nineteenth century models of history, historical narrative, evidence, and causality), and, though unfortunately fallible, they seek, finally, to be historically fair to these texts. For example, within the limits of my understanding, I try not to separate Aquinas's aesthetics from his religion and theology; indeed, Joyce knew that respecting his theological position was necessary in order to understand Stephen's deliberate literary secularism and a strategic error in his discourse.

In his analytic polarizations and synthetic totalities, Aquinas progresses profoundly and admirably toward a "Daedalian" unified theory of world and mind, matter and idea, apprephension of objects and perception of beauty, Aristotle and Plato, and so forth; as just noted, his "kind of objectivism" includes importantly "a knowing subject." While Aquinas's theories are ultimately inseparable from his theology, his particular balance of the objective and the subjective "represents a substantial move in the direction of humanism."[6] The "Platonic idealist heavenly" tilt of "Daedalian" Aquinas was emphasized by the Thomistic Neoplatonists Marcilo Ficino and Pico della Mirandola and the "Aristotelian materialist worldly" tilt by the Cusanic Giordano Bruno.

Continuing Aquinas's humanistic potential, Pico's theories intensify the subjective by indicating the passage of the human soul from the vegetal to the divine. In "A Slow and Dark Birth," I showed that to organize his novel, Joyce used a Platonic tradition, going backward from Walter Pater's description in *The Renaissance* of Pico's theories of the progression of the soul through the five stages, through Aquinas's dating of the prenatal sequence of the soul, to Augustine's spiritual dialectics, Aristotle's analysis of the biological stages of human form, and Plato's progress of the soul on the chariot pulled by the horse of reason and the horse of flesh.[7] The progression—vegetal, animal, rational, angelic, and divine—is marked in the novel by five major "cries." The "cry" most relevant to that portion of chapter 5 being analyzed here occurs near the end of chapter 4, when Stephen sees the young woman standing in the water. "*—Heavenly God! cried Stephen's soul*, in an outburst of profane joy. . . . A wild *angel* had appeared to him, the *angel* of mortal youth and beauty, an envoy from the fair courts of life, to throw open before him in an instant of ecstasy the gates of all the ways of error and glory" (*P* 171–172, my emphasis). Similarly, continuing Aquinas's naturalistic potential, Bruno's theories form a significant stage in the naturalization of theology, to correlating the discovery of multiple worlds with the expression of multiple perspectives. By contrast with Pico, he is Brunian when Joyce transfers a description of Bruno to Stephen's list of the doings of Simon. Of Bruno, Joyce wrote, "That life reads like a heroic fable in these days of millionaires. A Dominican monk, a gipsy professor, a commentator of old philosophies and a deviser of new ones, a playwright, a polemist, a counsel for his own defence, and, finally, a martyr burned at the stake in the Campo dei Fiori—Bruno, through all these modes and accidents (as he would have called them) of being, remains a consistent spirtual unity" (*CW* 133), and of Simon, Stephen says that he was,

> —A medical student, an oarsman, a tenor, an amateur actor, a shouting politician, a small landlord, a small investor, a drinker, a good fellow, a storyteller, somebody's secretary, something in a distillery, a taxgatherer, a bankrupt and at present a praiser of his own past.
> Cranly laughed, tightening his grip on Stephen's arm, and said:
> —The distillery is damn good. (*P* 241)

Simon has been "a consistent spiritual unity" in the "being" of the marketplace. Both Pico and Bruno help Joyce, and Stephen, to humanize, to naturalize, to secularize Aquinas; Joyce (and Stephen) retains his structures of transcendence and immanence and, at the same time, brackets off his theology. Stephen answers Cranly with, "I fear more than that [the God of the Roman Catholics would strike me down] the chemical action which would be set up in my soul by a false homage to a symbol behind which are massed twenty centuries of authority and veneration" (*P* 243). However, Stephen's not looking a second or third time at, not respecting sufficiently, the power and care of Aquinas's intellect allows a strategic error to slip into his thinking and, indeed, to start a "chemical reaction" in his "soul" of great consequence to his intentions for himself as an artist.

THE QUESTIONS OF AQUINAS AND DEDALUS

AQUINAS'S QUESTIONS

Moving magisterially in the *Prima Pars* of the *Summa Theologiae* through "Christian theology" (Q. 1), "existence and the nature of God" (Q. 2–11), "knowledge in God" (Q. 12–13), "God's will and providence" (Q. 19–26), and "the Trinity" (Q. 27–32), Aquinas considers the three Persons, "the Father, Son, and Holy Ghost" (Q. 33–43); in questions 39–42, he reviews the "Trinitarian formulas inherited or developed by medieval theology. . . ."[8] The design of each question in general follows a form of stating a topic, the authorities on this topic, its problems, its proper or adequate methods, and its logical replies. It happens that the structure of 1a.39.8, on which we focus most of our attention, is different: "The structure of this article is unusual. . . ; there is no distinct Reply, but an immediate handling of the authorities in arguments 1–5; the Reply can be read by referring back to each argument in turn."[9] Stephen's discourse has some overall resemblances to Aquinas's ordering, but, to my eye, they are superficial: this needs further study.

QUESTION 39

Because it is not possible to repeat here the entire question 39, it should be noted that Aquinas has already considered the Trinity and the three different Persons and is now, in considering the relationships of "persons" and "essence," questioning whether and to what extent the language used by earlier theologians for a characteristic act may be attributed to the Person and the Person's names. All of this question is relevant to Stephen because, as can be found throughout his life in *A Portrait* and most emphatically in the beach scene in which his own names are confirmed (chapter 4), he is concerned with the relationship of names to objects and qualities to names and to objects. On the strand, this is presented in a crescendo when his name gives the attributes of his destiny, as, for example, "Stephen" refers to his becoming "crowned," or *"stephaneforos"* and *"stephanoumenos,"* and "Dedalus" to becoming an "artificer." I am startled by Joyce's brilliance, to have seen the connection between these "theolologicophilolological" (*U* 168) problems and the nature of his fiction in which his main character is made of words and, as words, feels in his soul and complete being the actions, passions, dynamic implications, strengths, and problems of words. With Augustine, the rhetorician who turned to the Christian Logos, Joyce saw that the play of words in linguistic reflexivity could express and be for the readers palpable drama.

Every one of the eight points of question 39 hints at profound mystery and drama:

> the persons [of the Trinity] compared to the essence [has] eight points [articles] of inquiry: 1. whether in the godhead essence is the same as person; 2. whether it is all right to say, "Three persons are one essence";

3. whether we should predicate essential names of the persons in the plural or in the singular; 4. whether the adjectives, verbs, or participles for characteristic acts may be predicated of essential, concrete names; 5. and of essential, abstract names; 6. whether the names of the persons may be predicated of concrete, essential names; 7. whether the appropriation of essential attributes to persons is allowable; and 8. which are the right appropriations.[10]

I cannot deal here with the secular restatements of this whole question in the novel, no less take into account these in *Ulysses*, but can consider some from article 8 and especially its analysis of the triplet of terms that Stephen takes for his discourse, *integritas, consonantia,* and *claritas*. (In the following analysis, the lettering, Lts. a–n, of Aquinas's statements is mine: I found it necessary in order to indicate briefly consecutive propositions and jumps between two different sections. Some terms I have used in uppercase for Aquinas and these terms in lowercase for Stephen.)

Aquinas's reply to article 8, "whether the holy doctors have correctly assigned [appropriated] essential attributes to the persons," may be divided into two major thematic sections. Stephen says, "[In the second section (Lts. i–n)] Aquinas says: *ad pulcritudinem tria requiruntur, integritas, consonantia, claritas.* . . . Do these correspond to the phases of apprehension [found in the first section (Lts. a–h)]?" (*P* 212). The first thematic section (Lts. a–h) assumes Being and it emphasizes phases of apprehension; the second section (Lts. i–n) assumes divinity, the Procession of the Trinity, and attributions to the Persons, and it notes in a profound aside the qualities of Beauty. The two thematic sections have different methods or, more accurately, they work with different traditions of assumptions and analyses, namely, Aristotelian for Being and sequential phases of apprehension and Platonic for the Procession and simultaneous qualities of Beauty. Stephen seeks to match two "stages" or "phases of apprehension" in the Aristotelian section (Lts. c and d) with the terms for Beauty in the Platonic section (Lts. i–l).

Aquinas begins, (c) "For we examine it first in itself, as it is a certain being"; (d) "next, as it is one"; (e) "thirdly, as it has in it a power to act and to cause"; (f) "fourthly, as it stands in its relationship to its effects." Having advanced our understanding by means appropriate to the creature, Aquinas then makes a transition to considering "God absolutely in His being" as such is described in "Trinitarian formulas inherited or developed by medieval theology." I do not pretend to understand these mysteries as a "believer" must, but their tradition and their logic as used by Aquinas have been well revealed by him and well charted by historians of religion. Aquinas approached the Procession of the Trinity as actualities in a manner associated with the traditional arguments of Augustine, Platonists, and Plato as well as the credenda, of course, of the Christian Bible. The aspect of the Platonic tradition I want to emphasize describes the nature of words, including names and essences, such, for example, that the "many" can spring instantly or in time from the "one," or the "one" can collect the "many," or the two can fuse, or separate, or exist simultaneously, or exist separately, can function as simultaneously and separately in a single coherent symbolic system, and so forth. With words and names, everything can be identified with everything else, differentiated into the largest dictionary or reduced into one word. In *Ulysses*, *Bloom* and *Stephen* are rewritten as *Blephen* and *Stoom*, which may be interpreted to mean the persons of the *father* and the *son*, biologically or not biologically related, can be thought of linguistically as one person, *fatherson*, and another person, *sonfather*. This makes use of the logic of tautology, the poetics of absolute metaphor and identity, and the equivocity of names and terms.

As I interpret Aquinas's methods and traditions, he approached article 8 using the assumptions of Aristotle's "materialis," hylemorphic analysis, and four causes. Where the first portion of article 8 (Lts. a–h) is Aristotelian, the second (Lts. i–n), being based on ideas of "essence" and "essential attributes," is Platonic, that is, the discussion of the Procession is not from creature to creator, but creator in the instant of being Father, Son, and Holy Ghost, from eternity to eternity (and, elsewhere, in a cosmogony, from eternity to here). After establishing the phases of apprehension relevant to Being and God (Lts. a–i), Aquinas shifts to discussing whether the descriptions by the earlier theologians may be discussed in terms of "appropriation." "Simply as a term 'appropriation' is roughly equivalent to the turning of a common into a proper noun. . . . In Trinitarian theology, however, appropriation is the ascription of common, therefore essential, names to one of the persons; in its concrete sense, an 'appropriation' is a name midway between a common and a proper or personal name. . . . Appropriation involves two presumptions: that some names, especially because of Scripture, are indeed proper and personal; that some are common, by reason of the consubstantiality and co-equality of the persons."[11] It is important to stress that these appropriations are achieved through resemblance (similitude) and, equally importantly, not through identity. Aquinas speaks of Hilary's appropriations of how "eternity" defined as "nonderived existence" is appropriate to the Father as "principle not from a principle," "comeliness" or "Beauty" is appropriate to the Son because Beauty "bears a *resemblance* to the properties of the Son" (my emphasis). Stephen shows he is aware of Aquinas's move from the Aristotelian to the Platonic when he says, as an Aristotelian, that "Aristotle's entire system of philosophy rests upon his book of psychology and that, I think, rests on his statement that the same attribute cannot at the same time and in the same connection belong to and not belong to the same subject" (P 208). Note the differentiation into "attributes." He will be appealing to the Platonic in a moment, "When we come to the phenomena of artistic conception, artistic gestation and artistic reproduction I require a new terminology and a new personal experience" (P 208, 209). That is, he requires a terminology in which "attributes" *can belong and not belong simultaneously to the same subject*: this is a good warning to readers that in the Villanelle section language will be handled very differently, that is, Platonically. For Stephen, the Aristotelian is appropriate to the phases of apprehension, and the Platonic is appropriate to the instantaneous, yet divisible in discussion, operations of the mind experiencing the beautiful, leading to writing a poem. Thus, Stephen's approach is to join what Aquinas has carefully kept apart.

Aquinas begins article 8 with a statement about his method; it is important because Stephen does not treat this as merely an introductory statement. It corresponds to his post-Pico and post-Bruno secular humanism. Aquinas's Aristotelian approach to analysis goes from the creature to the creator. (a) "Since our mind is led along from creatures to a knowledge of God, its way of thinking about him has to follow a pattern deriving from them." (b) "Now in our study of any creature there are four orderly stages." Going from creature to creator, from here to eternity, within the mode of "Aristotelian materialism" means using the syllogism, the law of noncontradiction, and the univocity of names, and, supposedly, Aristotelian attitudes dominate this article. An Aristotelian interpretation of *A Portrait* reads both from left to right, that is, the past determining the present, where each event of the life of Stephen forms a diachronic, causal, aggregate sequence, and from right to left, that is, the future determining the present, where each event causes teleologically its prior conditions. These two Aristotelian directions are evidenced in "I was someone else then. . . . I mean, said Stephen, that I was not myself as I am now, as I had to become" (P 240).

Because of the extraordinary powers, the evocative strengths and fluidity, of Platonic words, Aquinas's question is about the functions of language as found in the writings of earlier theologians, how they may extend the meanings of the names of the Persons of the Trinity. He has arrived at this section having already established the transcendent unity of the Trinity, the individuality of the Three Persons, and the Procession of the Trinity. Importantly, within this discussion of the Procession occurs the idea of Beauty (Lts. i–n): (i) "The first level, namely about God in himself in terms of his own being, appears in Hilary's appropriation—of eternity *[aeternitas]* to the Father, beauty *[species]* to the Son, joy *[usus]* to the Holy Spirit." (j) "For eternity, as meaning a non-derived existence, has affinity with the property of the Father, who is principle not from a principle." (k) "Comeliness or beauty bears a resemblance to the properties of the Son." (l) "Beauty *[ad pulcritudinem]* must include three qualities: integrity *[integritas]* or completeness—since things that lack something are thereby ugly"; (m) "right proportion *[consonantia]* or harmony"; (n) "and brightness *[claritas]*—we call things bright in colour beautiful" (*ST.* 1a.39.8).

STEPHEN'S QUESTION

"Aquinas says: *ad pulcritudinem tria requiruntur, integritas, consonantia, claritas.* I translate it so: *Three things are needed for beauty, wholeness, harmony and radiance.* Do these correspond to the phases of apprehension?" (*P* 212). Stephen's question is whether the attributes found in the Platonic section correspond with the phases of apprehension found in the Aristotelian. In working out the correspondence of the simultaneous three terms, he is also tracing a hierarchical sequence occurring in the mind, from the physical "look at" through levels of abstraction to a final aesthetic image, that is, from perceiving the world to feeling beauty.

INTEGRITAS

I begin with Stephen's nonverbal action and command: "Stephen pointed to a basket which a butcher's boy had slung inverted on his head. —Look at that basket. . . ." First, Stephen commands Lynch to direct his visual sense, "look at," at an object in the world, "that basket." Whatever becomes of the references to the objective world in Stephen's process of writing of poetry, he always practices the Scholastic-empiricist's rule of "first in the senses, then in the mind." In this question, Aquinas states the rule this way: "Now among things perceptible to sense, and from these the mind derives its knowledge" (1a. 39.2. Reply). "Emma Clery" may become "E.C." to become "BVM," or the "basket" covering the head of the butcher's boy may eventually imply the platter holding the decollated head of "Cranly" to become "John the Baptist"—but for Stephen's kind of objectivism, as well as, I believe, for Aquinas's, the process must always begin with "look at."

"—I want to see Rosie first, said Stephen" (*P* 245). "In order to see that basket . . . your mind first of all separates the basket from the rest of the visible universe which is not the basket. The first phase of apprehension is a bounding line drawn about the object to be apprehended. An esthetic image is presented to us either in space or in time. You see it as one whole. That is *integritas*" (*P* 212). "The first phase of apprehension" is the act of the mind, that of the "knowing subject," separating what is seen "from the rest of the visible universe." In his next sentence, "An *esthetic* image is presented to us either in space or in time" (emphasis mine), Stephen's introducing an assertion about aesthetics has jumped to Aquinas's Platonic section (Beauty, aesthetics) because he assumes at this point in his discourse the mental processing of an *aesthetic* image. He retains a category of the physical world, space or time, to recall the sensational side of apprehension. By the way, an example in *Ulysses* of the mind's processing a more complex image like this aesthetic one may be where this mental image of the worldly object (the inverted basket) floating in boundless space or time continues in the image of the incertitude of fatherhood, church, and the world itself "founded . . . upon the void" (*U* 170). The similitude of the spherical head and the spherical universe is found, of course, in Plato presenting spatial perfections.

The remainder of this first paragraph shows Stephen's moving back and forth between the Being and Beauty sections until he has constructed an arching bridge between the two. Being: "What is audible is presented in time, what is visible is presented in space." Beauty: "But, temporal, or spatial, the esthetic image is first luminously apprehended as selfbounded and selfcontained upon the immeasurable background of space or time which is not it." In holding the temporal and spatial modes against immeasurable backgrounds, Stephen has drawn out some potentials of Aquinas's next Aristotelian assertions about its "being" and its "oneness." Remember that Aquinas and Stephen are describing a process occurring in and of the mind of a knowing subject. An "esthetic image" is "luminous" in the mind and it is "selfbounded and selfcontained" in the mind: for example, in Aquinas: (Lt. b) "For we examine it first in itself, as it is a certain being" and in Stephen: "the esthetic image is first luminously apprehended." Then, in four separate sentences, Stephen makes increasingly abstract statements by moving between the verbs for the mental "to apprehend" and the mental, but seemingly physical, "to see." "You apprehend it as *one* thing. You see it as one whole. You apprehend its wholeness. That is *integritas*." Stephen uses the two verbs, *apprehend* and *see*, to join both the abstract and the echo of physical experiences while describing only a mental process, as if the mind's activity is still very close to the sensory act in the act of perceiving the physical object. It goes from Aquinas's (c) Being: "next [secondly], as it is one" to his (j) Beauty: "Beauty must include three qualities: integrity *[integritas]* or completeness—since things that lack something are thereby ugly."

In sum, Stephen's *integritas,* the first keystone of the first arch of the bridge, is a Daedalian double point, uniting in a single concept both the operation of the first phase of the four sequential phases of apprehension, based on the act of sensory perception, and the first quality of the three simultaneous mental qualities of an aesthetic image. Perceptual synthesis is followed by mental analysis (to be followed later by mental synthesis), and Being by Beauty.

Stephen's discourse receives a response: "—Bull's eye! said Lynch, laughing. Go on." Lynch's two words convey several things: the *bull* and the *bull's eye* express the condition of Lynch's soul, which seems to think consistently in terms of its earlier "animal" stage, recalling, for example, that when younger he "ate pieces of dried cowdung" (*P* 205); it is playful and, in that, perhaps deflating, the discourse as both a sideshow act and as a "papal bull" on aesthetics; it is direct praise and encouragement of Stephen; it is, appropriate to this section of chapter 5, indirect recall of Aquinas, whose nickname when a student at the university, "Dumb Ox," fits with Stephen's *"bous,"* as well as the cow-bull-minotaur motifs in *A Portrait* and *Ulysses*; and as he was "dumb," it anticipates the first of Stephen's three defensive arms, "silence" (*P* 247). In sum, "Bull's eye" may be interpreted as praise of Stephen's physical eye in seeing the basket and his mental capacity in firing the first definition, his action being as accurate as Aquinas's, the Ox's, eye in hitting the first intellectual target.

CONSONANTIA

For Aquinas's second term, (j) "Beauty must include three qualities," the second of which is (k) "right proportion *[consonantia]* or harmony," Stephen continues to elaborate and reinforce his bridge, this time beginning from Aquinas's Platonic section. Still, he repeats the earlier strategy of moving back and forth between the more abstract and the more physical verbs *to apprehend* and, instead of *to see, to feel*:

> —Then, said Stephen, you *pass* from point to point, led by its formal lines; you *apprehend* it as balanced part against part within its limits; you *feel* the rhythm of its structure. In other words the *synthesis of immediate perception* is followed by the *analysis of apprehension*. Having first *felt*

that it is *one* thing you *feel* now that it is a *thing*. You *apprehend* it as complex, multiple, divisible, separable, made up of its parts, the result of its parts and their sum, harmonious. That is *consonantia*. [Added to the emphasis of *one, thing,* and *consonantia*, my emphasis.]

—Bull's eye again! said Lynch wittily. Tell me now what is *claritas* and you win the cigar.

It is "witty" because, probably, it is approved by Stephen. The "cigar," for a third direct hit, continues the sharpshooter sideshow joke.

CLARITAS

Stephen's discussion of the third term, *claritas*, is longer, for one of the problems he must confront is its historical connection with medieval mysticism of otherworldly light: "It would lead you to believe that he had in mind symbolism or idealism, the supreme quality of beauty being a light from some other world, the idea of which the matter is but the shadow, the reality of which it is but the symbol" (*P* 213). It has been stated that Stephen seeks to secularize by bracketing off Aquinas's theology; he also seeks to individualize and to maintain the individual's experiential integrity by bracketing off a nontheological Kantian philosophy of universalism. That is, he seeks to reject or bracket off the combined idea that "*claritas* is the artistic discovery and representation of the divine purpose in anything or a force of generalisation which would make the esthetic image a universal one, make it outshine its proper conditions." He brackets off both the theological and philosophical as implicitly two kinds of detached or cloistered abstractions, perhaps *mere idealisms*, or perhaps not: "But that is literary talk. I understand it so." His "literary" is contrasted with "marketplace," where can be seen the basket inverted over the head of the butcher's boy, which anticipates Stephen's walk along the strand in Proteus with his eyes shut, then his ears, testing the ineluctable modalities of the audible and the visual. For Stephen (and Joyce), the "being of the marketplace" is the proper domain for testing theories of apprehension and aesthetics, for translating the terms of theology into the practical secular experiences of the everyday world, and for discovering the *quidditas* in the quotidian, for hearing clearly the shout in the street—and the thunder.

In his interpretation of Aquinas's third quality of (l) "brightness, [*claritas*]," that is, "we call things bright in colour beautiful."—Stephen repeats the same terms as before, only he gives greater stress to the more abstract terms: "When you have *apprehended* that basket as one thing and have then *analysed* it according to its form and *apprehended* it as a thing you make the only *synthesis* which is logically and esthetically permissible. You see that it is that thing which it is and no other thing" (*P* 213, my emphasis). That "seeing" is done in the mind of the knowing subject.

CLARITAS: QUIDDITAS

Stephen's peroration for his lecture on this triplet repeats and gathers all his earlier verbs for acts of perception and analysis and synthesis. His discourse began with the question whether the "phases of apprehension" of Being corresponded with the "qualities" of Beauty. He held each idea of the "phases" and the "qualities" first in a correspondence, then as a double point asserting the beginning of an identity: "That is this": first That is *integritas,* then *consonantia,* and then *claritas.* Now he synthesizes them at a higher level of abstraction. Between Aquinas's *speaks* and Galvani's *called* are the verbs for the acts of the mind: *felt, conceived, apprehended, arrested,* and *fascinated.* (*Conceived* recalls its earlier use in "artistic conception.") The peroration is in the service of a new concept, the *quidditas,* and, most importantly, a new person, the artist, as its telos. The pressure of Stephen's assertions has shifted from pushing toward its conclusion to tugging by its future.

At its start is a new identification, that *claritas* is *quidditas,* that radiance is the whatness of a thing; in its middle, as its proper angelic element, is fire, "a fading coal"; and at its end is a return to the earth with a comparison of an intensely interior mental moment with the physiological heart, in the "enchantment of the heart." The previous ideas that began as correspondences are repeated as identities, his speech soaring swiftly and densely and abstractly in a sequence of phrases containing the units of identity, while the phrasal rhythm moves with increasing exaltation, as if to embody as well as to indicate this discourse as an achievement of the angelic intellect.

The radiance of which he speaks is the scholastic *quidditas,* the *whatness* of a thing.

> This supreme quality is felt by the artist when the esthetic image is first conceived in his imagination. The mind in that mysterious instant Shelley likened beautifully to a fading coal. The instant wherein that supreme quality of beauty, the clear radiance of the esthetic image, is apprehended luminously by the mind which has been arrested by its wholeness and fascinated by its harmony is the luminous silent stasis of esthetic pleasure, a spiritual state very like to that cardiac condition which the Italian physiologist Luigi Galvani, using a phrase almost as beautiful as Shelley's, called the enchantment of the heart. (*P* 213)

This portion of the discourse has ended with the expression of the angelic intellect comparable to and completing Stephen's earlier experience along the strand, when his eyes saw the young woman in the water and his soul flamed and, winged as a phoenix, soared, and returned to earth. It differs from the exaltation on the beach in being given without musical repetitions and with an extreme density of new information in each phrase and verb. Indeed, by not letting the accretion become musical, Stephen maintains the prosaic quality of his discourse, imitates the dense discursive styles of Aristotle and Aquinas, and has denied any impulse to transcend the circumstance of his discourse into, for example, religious metaphysics. The style on the beach overflows with Platonic images; this style on the streets hardens with Aristotelian and Thomistic conceptualizing.

After securing this identity of *claritas, quidditas,* and enchantment, "Stephen paused and, though his companion did not speak, felt that his words had called up around them a thoughtenchanted silence" (*P* 213).

We might recall here two phrases by Gabriel Conroy, who, by reason of his first name and his imaginings when falling asleep, is quasi-angelic. His phrases, "thought-tormented music" and "thought-tormented age" (*D* 192, 203), are related to Stephen's "thoughtenchanted silence" because soon, already angelicized and in the instant about to be divinized, Stephen will be dreaming of the voice that comes out of "the enchantment of the heart" and "thought-enchanted silence," the angel Gabriel's voice in the poetic annunciation of the "heart's cry" that begins the next, the Villanelle, section.

But, for now, in this section, after this pause in silence, Stephen begins another "question," regarding the generic qualities of lyric, epic, and dramatic. That is, he returns to Aquinas's next Aristotelian ideas in article 8, in which Stephen sees the power of beauty: (d) "thirdly, as it has in it a power to act and to cause" and (e) "fourthly, as it stands in its relationship to its effects." Stephen says of beauty that "our judgment is influenced . . . by the art itself and by the form of that art" (*P* 213). It is enough to note that Stephen organizes the three generic relationships occasioned by the additional powers of beauty, the lyric, epic, and dramatic, which has been much discussed by post-Kantian German romantic philosophy, in a dialectical sequence common to the Daedalian drama. But analysis of this triplet will draw us away from a central problem in the drama of Stephen's Daedalian discourse in which *he synthesized Being and Beauty without reference to Aquinas's theology.* First, let me sum up Stephen's motives and strategies.

STEPHEN'S MOTIVES AND STRATEGIES

Joyce emphasizes that Stephen's most obvious motive in using Aquinas is to demonstrate his self-chosen isolation in thought, yet it also shows his dependence, for he appears to want to impress his friends and teachers with his knowledge and with his independence from publicizing his knowledge. The dean of studies asks about Stephen's making a statement and disputes quietly with him, including warning him of intellectual dangers. The dean's attitude is repeated by Cranly with more overt worries, disdain, and warnings. Stephen rejects them. His classmate Donovan responds with respect for his ideas, Lynch with temporary attention, and Mulligan in *Ulysses* with exploitation and parody. Before all, and most importantly, his intellectual motive is to use the *Summa* for itself, because this text in Aquinas (*ST* 1a.39.8) is indeed remarkable in its intellectual power to suggest a serious aesthetic in so few words.

Another motive: As mentioned before, chapter 5 begins with his angelic status actualized: hence, studying Aquinas and synthesizing apprehension and aesthetic manifest their own spiritual power and help develop his potential for the divine. That is, appropriate to this moment in his development, Stephen is like Aquinas, who is called by the Roman Catholic Church the *Doctor Angelicus,* and he is exercising his angelic cunning in his construction of his secular *summa poeticae* as well as preparing his soul for its next development. By thinking "higher thoughts," he carries the discourse to the higher transitional transformation, where the potential artist following the experience of "*claritas* is *quidditas*" becomes the "godlike-artist." For *this* essay, I want to stress that his motive is consistently to be Daedalian, to negotiate his flight between the material sea and the ideal sun, to join two different, opposing systems—the perception of actual objects *with* the apprehension by the knowing subject of their beauty; the apprehension of the immanent being of the world *with* the imagination and transcendent Trinitarian theology secularized; the marketplace apprehension of the aesthetic image and the artistic use of it; and more.

There is not enough space here to compare *A Portrait* and *Stephen Hero,* but the manuscript's ideas of "the mechanism of esthetic apprehension" (*SH* 212) and the "gropings of a spiritual eye" (*SH* 211) correspond to *A Portrait*'s "phases of apprehension" and "qualities of beauty." However, the style of the "heaven-ascending essayist," as he is called in *Stephen Hero,* has much the same style as in any other passage of the manuscript, whereas the style in *A Portrait* is made adequate to the tasks of synthesizing Aquinas's Aristotelian and Platonic sections, of transforming that synthesis into the concept of the *quidditas* and activities of the person of the artist, and, dominating all other reasons, of presenting this particular moment in the structure of the novel, the passage of the soul from the angelic to the divine. Or, to use Joyce's terms for Bruno (quoted earlier), the style is adjusted to "all these modes and accidents (as he would have called them) of being" and yet he must "remain a consistent spiritual unity."

STEPHEN'S PREDICAMENT: HIS FUTURE AS A YOUNG MAN

QUESTION 39 AGAIN

The organization of *A Portrait* is such that chapter 5 emphasizes the movement of the soul from the angelic to the divine. Stephen is on the way to becoming the "godlike artist," but not exactly with the qualities he thought. Many passages in all eight articles of question 39 can help underscore, even explain, his predicament; I can mention here only a few.

At one level of the narrative, it is clear that Stephen's soul is in constant developmental motion. Indeed, nowhere in the novel, including, although in a different mode, the Villanelle section, is it stationary. Also, the soul is spherical. Perfectly spherical and in constant motion are two traditional descriptions, congruent with Plato's perfect head, earth, and universe. For example, priestly, and in collegial Latin, Cranly threatens Stephen's soul: Cranly puts forward his handball "by way of a peaceoffering, saying:—*Pax super totum sanguinarium globum.*" He sets off to play, saying "*Nos ad manum ballum jocabimus*" (P 198). Later, he insists "that his ball should be used. He let it rebound twice or thrice to his hand and struck it strongly and swiftly towards the base of the alley, exclaiming in answer to its thud:—Your soul!" (P 204). Finishing this preparation, he throws a fig "rudely into the gutter. Addressing it as it lay, he said:—Depart from me, ye cursed, into everlasting fire!" And to Stephen, he says, "—Do you not fear that those words may be spoken to you on the day of judgment?" (P 239–240). Cranly seeks to prevent the physical sailing and the spiritual ascent and flight of his companion.

The excited motion and ecstatic development of Stephen's soul are apparent in some episodes, especially on the strand, where its progress is heavily marked by both the description of his soul as if emerging from a sepulchre, chrysalis, and ashes, spreading its phoenix wings, and flying, as well as by the passage's syntax, its repetitions and reversals of words and phrases, and its different kinds of strongly stressed rhythms. The experience of his soul's transformation from "rational" ("Stephen Dedalus, S.J.") to "angelic ox" *("bous stephanoumenos")* and "angelic artisan" ("hawklike man") occurs in a style suitable, or adequate, to the experience. But the movement and style of the development of his soul are found even in the short passage on apprehension and aesthetics. As was pointed out before, when Stephen modulated the terms, both nouns and verbs, from correspondence, through identity, to transformed identity as *quidditas*, his soul was also moving from the angelic toward, but not arriving at, the divine.

By analogy with esoteric alchemy, where the effort to make the philosopher's stone is directed as well to the alchemical transformation of the alchemist's soul, this "esoteric style" is also the transformation of the stylist's soul. In the next section of *A Portrait,* the writing of the Villanelle, he reintegrates the metaphors of "biological" artistic conception, gestation, and reproduction with traditional spiritual imagery. Containing references to the terms of the previous section, such as the medical students' talking about "midwifery" and his own about artistic conception and birth, he begins with the idea of the *spermatologos* and then Gabriel's Annunciation. We learn that for him in this moment the divine means that "artistic conception" is felt as angelic Annunciation, "O! In the virgin womb of the imagination the word was made flesh. Gabriel the seraph had come to the virgin's chamber"; that "artistic gestation," in the several stages of writing down the poem, is a spiritual evolution that reverses the formula of "ontogeny recapitulates phylogeny," for in the imagination, the poem's ontogeny recapitulates the phylogenetic "slow and dark birth of the soul" of Stephen; and that in "artistic reproduction," the completed poem is a transubstantiation of Stephen's experiences in and of the world and of himself as an artist. While it is true that Stephen's "artistic" triplet is about creating the poem as object, it is also about his creating himself, not in his physical body, not as Stephen in the everyday marketplace, but as Stephen in the person of the artist: "artistic conception" intends without his announcing such to Lynch, or even without his having full awareness, that his words about aesthetics have just initiated a new quality to the development of his soul. In his imagination, "artistic conception" is the reflexive "conception" of Stephen as artist, "artistic gestation" the "gestation" of Stephen as artist, and "artistic reproduction" the "reproduction" of Stephen as artist. A potential in Stephen's words, thought out and spoken to Lynch, is actualized in the next section.

Earlier, the dean of studies warned Stephen of "Icarian" dangers for the "barnacle goose" (of *Ulysses*):

> —These questions are very profound, Mr Dedalus, said the dean. It is like looking down from the cliffs of Moher into the depths. Many go down into the depths and never come up. Only the trained diver can go down into those depths and explore them and come to the surface again.
> —If you mean speculation, sir, said Stephen, I also am sure that there is no such thing as free thinking inasmuch as all thinking must be bound by its own laws. (P 187)

Whatever the dean's reasons for his warning (and the academic discourse that follows with Lynch is, indeed, Stephen's taking the plunge), the dangers and consequences of speculation are different from what Stephen expected. Beauty, writes Aquinas, following Hilary, finds resemblance *(similitudo)* to the Second Person of the Trinity—the *Imago*, the *Verbum*, and the *Filius*. Aquinas says the reasons Beauty is appropriate to the Son are threefold: that integrity *(integritas)* is like the son "who in himself has the Father's nature [*naturam*] truly and fully"; that harmony *(consonantia)* is "proper to the Son inasmuch as he is the express image of the father" *("inquantum est Imago expressa Patris");* and radiance, or "brightness," "coincides with what is proper to the Son as he is the Word" *(Verbum)*. Stephen, in his appropriation of the procession of imagining and writing a poem and being reborn, has implanted in his soul the possibility that he is a secular version of the *Imago*, the *Verbum*, and the *Filius*. He has appropriated to himself as artist the idea that his making art is also the secular and imaginative creation of the "second person," himself as the artistic "son," the son of "beauty." Hence, the theory and images of his imagination's conceiving, gestating, and reproducing the poem in "the virgin womb of the imagination" and his giving birth to himself as an artist carried as to compel him by the laws of his thinking to imagine his giving birth to himself *as an artist as a son*.

The consequence for his imagination is clear: the artist of beauty is a son and is like his father's nature *(naturam)*, his father's image *(imago)*, and his father's word *(verbum)*. Which father Stephen resembles does not appear to be a problem in *A Portrait*, in which his changes in his affiliation are clearly marked and reinforced by the organization of the novel, from the "animal," "materialist," and worldly father, Simon (in chapter 2), and from the disembodied, "idealist," and unworldly fathers, the Jesuits (in chapter 3), to the "hawklike," artificer father, "angelic," worldly and wordy, Daedalus (in chapter 4). But, of course, which father is a thumping question in *Ulysses,* where Simon still seems rejected and Leopold available—but the more important question is whether Stephen's soul can appropriate to itself the first person, the father? (Most important, I believe, is whether when Stephen assumed the imagination as, for example, a "virgin womb," he appropriated to it the mother? But that is for another essay.) The double point of Stephen as ambiguous sonfather is expressed in his diary's famous last line, "Old father, old artificer": in this appeal, he appears Daedalian in hope but, perhaps, in having taken this phrase from Plato's *Timaeus,* he also appears Icarian in faith. The Icarian potential in this sentence is clear, for when he writes "old father," as Aquinas points out, he means not only a father but a child of that father, which in this case is a son.

Stephen's theories carry *implicitly* and *potentially* and, nevertheless, *certainly* the burden of these ideas that Aquinas considers here and elsewhere in question 39, such as that images of beauty resemble the Imago of the Son, that the Son is consubstantial with the Father, that the Father who is "principle not from a principle" begets the Son who is "a principle from a principle," and so forth and so on. That is to say, it is obvious that question 39 contains in its eight articles (see the list of its articles, given above) many of the questions that plague Stephen in *Ulysses*. For example, article 4 contains several propositions, true and false, that are encysted in Stephen's anxieties in *Ulysses:* "Further, if the statement 'God has begotten' is true, because the Father begets, with as much reason 'God does not beget' is true, because *the Son does not beget."* Why cannot a son father a poem? "Nor is there implied a God begetting and a God not begetting, except if something involving the persons be brought in, e.g., 'The Father is God begetting, and the Son is God not begetting.' " Aquinas's examples are framed within the law of noncontradiction but call for a Platonic solution to allow contradictory identities. Was Stephen trapped by his own actions when he overcame Aquinas's "similitude" of Beauty and the Second Person to construct an identity and to create himself as an artist? These notions of "begetting" and "self-begetting" are familiar from *Ulysses,* but it must be seen they are all given clearly or implied strongly in Stephen's discourse, especially when its terms are traced back to their textual sources in Aquinas.

The critics interested solely in an ironic interpretation of *A Portrait* find these ideas there as if they are completely actualized in Stephen, not there as potentials whose future is still to be developed. Therefore, they ignore Stephen's accomplishments in his Daedalian theories (and

I state without giving here justifying, only preparatory, argument and evidence, he will accomplish in poetic practice in the future). Orthodox blanket denunciations of angelism in Joyce's characters as Icarian bypass the evident intellectual power of Stephen's discourse and the legitimation of his intellectual angelism. Worse, a narrowly defined yet universally applied Icarian interpretation drowns the immediate story in the critics' interpretations; the critics who prefer to interpret the writing of the poem as a "wet dream" or key it to masturbation are appropriating to themselves Mulligan's attitudes and are assuming that his parody in *Ulysses* is correct for *A Portrait,* and they make it more difficult to understand the first surface level of the Villanelle section, how it recapitulates the soul's "slow and dark birth" and how connections between the soul, the style, and the section and the way the entire novel are coordinated.

VERIPATETIC IMAGO

Quaestio: Whether Stephen in his theoretical Daedalian identification of apprehension and aesthetics has inherited from Aquinas the appropriation of "beauty to the son"? For example, Aquinas has now collocated *brightness, Beauty, Son, Imago, Father, Word,* and adds to the *Verbum, "the light and splendour of the mind [lux et splendor intellectus],* in Damscene's description. Augustine alludes to this in the same text, *as complete* Word *[verbum], from whom nothing is wanting, and the Art [Ars], as it were, of the Almighty [Dei],* etc." Perhaps these identifications, correspondences, and appropriations catch him unaware because he is too casual with the intellectual power of Aquinas, who wrote carefully only of similitude, and he makes an error, as when not much earlier, his "slothful" mind substituted *blackness* for *brightness* in his quotation, "*Brightness falls from the air*" (P 234). The clear echo of Aquinas's *brightness* suggests the substitution that "*claritas* falls from the air," and "*quidditas,*" too.

Responsio: The terms in the Villanelle section combining in biology and imagination, body and mind, continues Stephen's Daedalianism, but they also suggest the possibility that exactly at the point where his acts of perception lead to his beginning to create, the point where "radiance is whatness," the quality of his imagination, the creative subject, is transformed into a godlike artist, that of the *verbum,* or *logos,* the *imago,* in the status of *filius,* a son of beauty. Frank Budgen wrote that Joyce said to him, "Some people who read my book, *A Portrait of the Artist* forget that it is called *A Portrait of the Artist as a Young Man*. He underlined with his voice the last four words of the title."[12] Budgen speculates that Joyce was suggesting his distance from the character. But it suggests more certainly that when the novel ends, in approximately 1902, and *Ulysses* begins, on the morning of 16 June 1904, Stephen's creating a poem will be as "an artist as a young man."

And his own poetic incarnation of the *verbum* will be as the suffering son. Cranly tries to tempt him by suggesting that Jesus "was himself a conscious hypocrite, . . . a blackguard? . . . Were you at all shocked by what I said? . . . And why were you shocked, Cranly pressed on in the same tone, if you feel sure that our religion is false and that Jesus was not the son of God?" (*P* 242–43). Stephen's response indicates the direction of his intentions regarding "the son": "—I am not at all sure of it, Stephen said. He is more like a son of God than a son of Mary" (*P* 243). Stephen's distinction separates the Second Person of the Trinity, the "eternal son" (from eternity to eternity), from the "incarnate son" (from eternity to here), and as an expression of his intentions it denies and emphasizes himself as the suffering son of his mother. Implicit in this approach is a tendency toward recalling a Gnostic version of creativity (also from eternity to here), that to create is to fall! Stephen thinks earlier that when he chose his destiny to be as an artist he chose to fall: "The snares of the world were its ways of sin. He would fall. He had not yet fallen but he would fall silently, in an instant . . . and he felt the silent lapse of his soul" (*P* 162). "Her eyes had called to him and his soul had leaped at the call. To live, to err, to fall, to triumph, to recreate life out of life" (*P* 172). Maybe for him, to create art is to become a son and to sin as a son, as we find in an echoing formula in *Finnegans Wake*: "Great sinner, great sonner" (*F* 607.04). *Sonner* carries the obvious *son* and the etymology of Provençal *son* as sound, song, and poet.

The appropriation of the quality of beauty to the person of the artist and the artist as the "second person" of the *filius* is suggested, as I have shown briefly, in the Villanelle section, but then the idea of the "son of Mary" is intensified and developed clearly in the final section, the diary, where, for example, Stephen reflecting on Cranly draws together the image of Cranly's head, in the classroom, and his imagining weakly Cranly's parents, and so forth, with the result that Cranly is seen intentionally as John the Baptist, as the "precursor." This implies, as is well known, Stephen's self-imaging as Christ. Actualized as divine, as the "godlike son," Stephen's soul is now in potential that of the fleshier son of May (Mary) Dedalus. Thus, the next phase in Stephen's spiritual development is homologized with Jesus in the world. Another immediate and important manifestation of this potential is that the diary covers thirty-nine calendar days, the fortieth day, the Daedalian ascension away from Ireland, is written in as Thursday, 16 June 1904. At the end of *A Portrait,* by "the laws of his own thinking," Stephen has reproduced himself as an artist, as the godlike *son* but not as the godlike *father.* Hence, Stephen's obsession in *Ulysses* is with his being the *son* (of God) and perhaps to be atoned with the "spiritual father," even though, as I wrote before, I believe the more serious atonement to be achieved in Stephen's spirit is "as the son of May," with his mother!

Stephen's predicament at the end is that to create art means he must become the *verbum,* the *imago,* and, therefore, the "son," the "godlike son." (It was not enough to repeat Aquinas's use of similitude by speaking of a "god*like* artist.") A clue to his status is in the phrase from *Finnegans Wake* used for this essay's title, the "veripatetic imago" (F 417.32). Aristotle walking back and forth with his students was a Peripatetic who wrote about tragic reversals, the ups and downs of the tragic hero, in peripeteia. Aquinas wrote about the *Imago* and *Verbum.* Perhaps *"imago"* should be divided into "I am the image and magus of images." Stephen walks to-and-fro with Lynch, he unites Aristotelian apprehension and Platonic beauty in Aquinas by going to-and-fro in 1a.39.8. And, withal, Daedalian, he strains to achieve something new and risks hubris and peripeteia. Thus, combining Aristotle and Aquinas, the "veripatetic imago" may be translated as "the very pathetic (-patetic) truth (veri-) of the image *(imago)* of the magus of images is the truly Aristotelian peripatetic suffering *(pathos)* of the Thomistic son of beauty *(imago).*" Or, as Stephen thinks, in *Ulysses,* "Hiesos Kristos, magician of the beautiful, the Logos who suffers in us at every moment" (*U* 152). Some critics read as "a young man" as immature or lacking charity and, therefore, as Aquinas writes, "things that lack something are thereby ugly." That is certainly a potentiality in him. But I believe this situation does not mean that because he is "a young man," he cannot create: he writes a "villanelle" and will write more. He made an error, hence, made a discovery: "—Bosh! Stephen said rudely. A man of genius makes no mistakes. His errors are volitional and are the portals of discovery" (*U* 156).

Until his soul develops even further, which it may or may not, when he writes he must discover a way to create in the person of the son, within the mode of a son's perspective. Why can't a son father (and mother) a poem? I suggest when he does succeed in discovering a way, he will write a book about how his thinking followed its own "laws" of the son and arrived at this particular predicament and spiritual level. He will call this book *A Portrait of the Artist as a Young Man*, with emphasis on the "four last words."

NOTES

1. All references to Joyce's works are included in the text in parenthesis, with the initial and the page number: *Critical Writings*, ed. Ellsworth Mason and Richard Ellmann (New York: Viking Press, 1959) *(CW)*; *Dubliners*, ed. Robert Scholes and A. Walton Litz (New York: Viking Press, 1969) *(D)*; *Finnegans Wake* (New York: Viking Press, 1959) *(F)*; *A Portrait of the Artist as a Young Man*, ed. Chester G. Anderson (New York: Viking Press, 1968) *(P)*; *Stephen Hero*, ed. Theodore Spencer (New York: New Directions, 1944) *(SH)*; *Ulysses*, ed. Hans Walter Gabler (New York: Random House, 1986) *(U)*. References to the text of Thomas Aquinas, *Summa Theologiae*, trans. T. C. O'Brien, ed. Thomas Gilby (New York: McGraw-Hill, Blackfriars Edition, 1976), are given in the text with the conventional code for the *Summa Theologiae*. References to comments by O'Brien are given in the notes.
2. William T. Noon, *Joyce and Aquinas* (New Haven: Yale University Press, 1957).
3. Umberto Eco, *Art and Beauty*, trans. Hugh Bredin (New Haven: Yale University Press, 1986), 24–26.
4. Umberto Eco, *The Aesthetics of Chaosmos: The Middle Ages of James Joyce*, trans. Ellen Esrock, University of Tulsa Press Monograph Series, 18 (Tulsa, Okla., 1982); and Hugh Kenner, *Dublin's Joyce* (Bloomington: Indiana University Press, 1956).
5. Franz Brentano, *On the Several Senses of Being in Aristotle*, trans. Rolf George (Berkeley: University of California Press, 1975).
6. Eco, *Art*, 26.
7. Sidney Feshbach, "A Slow and Dark Birth of the Soul: A Study of the Organization of *A Portrait of the Artist as a Young Man*," *James Joyce Quarterly* 4 (Summer 1967): 289–300.
8. O'Brien, 98, n.*a*.
9. O'Brien, 129, n.*a*.
10. O'Brien, 99.
11. O'Brien, 124, n.*a*.
12. Frank Budgen, *James Joyce and the Making of "Ulysses"* (Bloomington: Indiana University Press, 1960), 60.

12

Davin's Boots

Joyce, Yeats, and Irish History

MARY REYNOLDS

The year 1987 was the eightieth anniversary of Joyce's annus mirabilis. It was in 1907 that he found his identity as a writer: the argument of this essay holds that he found it in his sense of rivalry with Synge, who was Yeats's chosen protégé, and that out of this rivalry came a vision of Irish history that Joyce presents in dramatic form in his fictions.

In 1907, in a great burst of creative energy, Joyce gave a series of lectures on Ireland and also wrote his great novella, "The Dead." He laid out the final plan for revising *A Portrait of the Artist* into a book of only five closely structured chapters; and he told his brother, Stanislaus, that he would write a book about Dublin in which all the action would take place in one single day, and that he would call this book *Ulysses*.[1]

In these three major works of fiction, all apparently conceived in 1907, there is evidence of Joyce's silent competition with Yeats and Synge, specifically in certain passages that may be called rural images. Since Joyce's fiction is always centered on the city of Dublin, anything that can be called "rural" becomes conspicuous. His rural images seem to me to be a subtle and striking mode of contrast; they direct attention to elements of dissimilarity in Joyce's world, his Dublin, his Ireland, as compared with the Irish peasant life that was so effectively celebrated by Yeats and Synge.

Although he was so much younger, Joyce wished to equal these two men and intended to surpass them. He made this revealing statement: "I will become indeed the poet of my race," and he spoke also of "those boundless ambitions which are really the leading forces in my life." But remarks like this were extremely private, made in intimate letters to his wife.² It is unlikely that Yeats and Synge knew in 1907 that they were being directly challenged.

It is a supreme paradox that Ireland's greatest prose writer was not in its literary movement. Joyce's relationship to the Irish Revival was shaped and settled very early, in his college years and just afterward. In *Ulysses* he devotes an entire chapter to the literary revival, placing the principal writers by name in a conversation in the National Library in Dublin. Always aware of his own talent, he assumed that there would be a place for him in the revival. But there was a significant barrier: Joyce had been born into the Catholic tradition of Irish nationalism. Yeats and Synge were born into a different tradition, the dominant tradition, the Protestant Ascendancy with its sense of position as Ireland's ruling establishment.

Yeats was kindly, especially to young writers, but kindly in his own way and on his own terms. Joyce was temperamentally incapable of being anyone's disciple. So there was both an obvious personal basis for rivalry and also a very real historical basis, which has perhaps been overlooked or underestimated. The issue was not religious. Edward Martyn was a devout Catholic; George Moore had been born into a wealthy Catholic family; Padraic Colum and Oliver Gogarty were Catholics. Yeats wanted to bring Catholic writers into the movement—but he saw it as *his* movement.

Joyce's college essays, written before he was twenty-one, mark his differences from Yeats. He already thought of himself as a writer. In high school he went to a performance of Hermann Suderman's *Magda,* and afterward he said to his parents, "The subject of the play is genius breaking out in the home and against the home. You needn't have gone to see it. It's going to happen in your own house."³ The house of Yeats—The Irish Literary Revival—soon received an equivalent challenge.

As a student, Joyce first identified himself with Yeats and his group; then he drew away from them. In his first year of college, in May 1899, Joyce saw the first performance of Yeats's new literary theater. The play was Yeats's *Countess Cathleen*. It brought violent opposition from the Catholic community as a whole, and especially from the students in Joyce's university. But Joyce, then seventeen, applauded vigorously when most of the audience booed—the galleries exploded with catcalls and groans. Joyce also refused conspicuously to sign a petition against the play; he could simply have abstained, but he made a point of gesturing publicly toward identification with Yeats and against the Irish clergy's censorship.⁴

Before his eighteenth birthday Joyce wrote an essay for the College

Literary Society ("Drama and Life"), which still stands as one of his rare statements on aesthetics. He had begun to define his aims and intentions. He argues for realism, and for "commonplace diction." In this essay Joyce takes a position opposed to Yeats's early aestheticism. "Life," says the youthful Joyce, "we must accept as we see it before our eyes, men and women as we meet them in the real world, not as we apprehend them in the world of faery."[5] The arguments were not strikingly novel, but it was a sophisticated critical statement that placed Yeats at cross-purposes with Joyce's argument.

At the beginning of his final year, Joyce openly challenged the leaders of the revival. He attacked the program announced for the new season of Yeats's theater in a short essay, "The Day of the Rabblement." Originally, Yeats had intended to produce European masterworks, such as Ibsen and Hauptmann; now he wanted plays only by Irish authors, even plays in Gaelic. Joyce thought Dublin playgoers should first be educated by exposure to the best examples of European drama; he charged that Yeats and Lady Gregory had given up the "immoral" European writers in order to hold their Catholic audiences. Joyce, the Catholic student writing for the literary magazine of Dublin's new Catholic University, called Yeats's new policy "a surrender to the trolls." He said, "A Nation which never advanced so far as a miracle play affords no literary model to the artist and he must look abroad."

The function of a literary theater in that country at that time was indeed the education of Irish audiences. Irish writers needed a forum and needed encouragement to write. But of course this was just what Yeats and his group were trying to do—precisely what they thought they were doing.

Joyce, knowing his coreligionists better than Yeats, thought otherwise. He attacked the leading writers by name, saying, "It is equally unsafe at present to say of Mr. Yeats that he has or has not genius," and again, "Mr. Martyn and Mr. Moore are not writers of much originality." He also distributed critical praise: Martyn's work suggested Strindberg; Yeats's most recent book, *The Wind Among the Reeds*, was "poetry of the highest order"; and George Moore had "wonderful mimetic ability."[6]

The essay was turned down by the college paper, but Joyce had it privately printed and distributed by hand to the principal writers. George Moore was later quoted as saying that the essay was "preposterously clever," and there is some slight evidence of Yeats's irritation.

The last of these early essays, though less polemical, was a much more significant challenge to Yeats's leadership. This was a paper on

James Clarence Mangan, which Joyce read before the literary society on 15 February 1902; it was published in the college magazine in May.

Mangan, who was the best of the poets in the earlier literary movement—the mid-nineteenth century nationalist movement known as Young Ireland—was not a great original poet, but he had been the most authentically Irish voice writing in English. He alone had captured successfully the cadences of the ancient Gaelic poetry.

The Mangan essay was Joyce's first direct challenge; it was a clear encroachment on Yeats's territory. There is a famous line about Mangan in one of Yeats's poems, and he had also commented on Mangan in an essay. Now the young Joyce took Mangan as his example for a theory of the imagination that could be extended and made the foundation of a new literature. Mangan is not a model, as he was for Yeats, but a cautionary example, a warning. Joyce uses Mangan for a deliberate critique of the revival; he makes Mangan a figure of the romantic artist who has let himself become a prisoner of Irish history. I shall examine the substance of Joyce's critique.

Joyce in this essay develops and explains his view—a highly negative one—of the Celtic sagas. Note that he does this at a time when Yeats, the established poet, is making the Celtic sagas the very center of his work. The heroic tales of Finn and Cuchulain are described by Joyce as "the latest and worst part of a legend upon which the line has never been drawn out and which divides against itself as it moves down the cycles." We recognize these words from *A Portrait of the Artist*,[7] but they appear first in the 1902 essay. Later, in the novel, they are used to describe the character of Davin, "the young peasant [who] worshipped the sorrowful legend of Ireland." I will come back to Davin later.

Why did Joyce object to the Celtic legends? In the 1902 essay he says that the sagas represent a dark and bloody tradition; that Mangan was imprisoned within it; and—here is the crux of the matter—that "he has not known how to change it, as the strong spirit knows." Joyce does not mention Yeats because he does not need to; Yeats's poetry glorified the lives of those pagan heroes, Fergus and Diarmuid and Finn. Yeats's imaginative vision is, by implication, like Mangan's; to them Ireland is "an abject queen upon whom, because of the bloody crimes that she has done and of those as bloody that were done to her, madness is come and death is coming." A vivid indictment: as timely in 1987 as it was in 1921, and as it was foretold by the young Joyce in 1902.

Now, of course, Yeats was not sanguinary; it was his fanatical nationalist opponents, the contemporary Catholic nationalists, who were that. Nor was Joyce accusing Yeats of bloody-mindedness, only of *failing to perceive behind the myth the bloody reality*. It was the wrong-minded vision of history, of Irish history, that Joyce was unhappy about. Mangan, says Joyce, is the last voice of "a narrow and hysterical nationality," the voice of hate. Joyce, on the contrary, asks for an Irish imagination that will make a new beginning, "make an end to sorrow for the love of sorrow and despair and fearful menaces." Joyce in this essay asks for "the miracle of light . . . renewed eternally in the imaginative soul."[8]

It is surprising that this critical essay of Joyce's has never been connected with another of Yeats's plays, *Cathleen ni Houlihan*, which was produced in April that same year. The leading role was played by Maud Gonne, and the play was instantly successful, capturing the Irish mind more than any other single work of the period.

The title is the traditional name for Ireland: Cathleen ni Houlihan is the "poor old woman," calling on her children for help, asking them to die for her. The time is 1798, the year of the great rebellion, with a French invasion force gathering off the coast to help the rebels against the English. A young couple are planning their wedding when an old beggar woman arrives. Asked what her trouble is, she sadly replies, "Strangers in the house," meaning the English, who have taken her four green fields, Ireland's four provinces. The old woman says mysteriously, "Many men have died for me," and eventually the bridegroom disappears to join the insurrection. Another character, asked whether anyone had seen the old woman, says, "No; but I saw a young woman; and she had the walk of a queen."

Yeats's play invokes the mystique of heroic death: the old woman's last words are an incantation, "Their names shall be remembered forever." This play greatly influenced Patrick Pearse, leader of the doomed Easter Rising in 1916. After the execution of Pearse and his companions, Yeats set the seal of martyrdom on their actions in a poem:

> I write it out in a verse—
> MacDonagh and MacBride
> And Connolly and Pearse
> Now and in time to be,
> Wherever green is worn,
> Are changed, changed utterly:
> A terrible beauty is born.[9]

Yeats's immortal phrase—"a terrible beauty is born"—continues even into the present generation as a justification of violent nationalism.

Yeats's play reappears in *Ulysses*, in the Circe chapter, as a hallucination when Stephen Dedalus is knocked down by an English soldier. Cathleen ni Houlihan materializes; but now Joyce's name for her is "Old Gummy Granny." She thrusts a dagger toward Stephen's hand and says: "Remove him, acushla. At 8:35 a.m. you will be in heaven and Ireland will be free. (she prays) O good God, take him!"[10] By the time he wrote *Ulysses,* Joyce could treat as bitter farce the ideas he had stated so seriously in his 1902 essay.

Yeats glamorized the image of Ireland as the poor old woman who would be rejuvenated by the blood of young men willing to die for her. Joyce, with a few comic words, deflates the high moment of Yeats's play: in the bright light of comedy the bridegroom's willingness to die for the dream of Ireland's freedom looks quite different. Joyce thus puts into the form of fiction a critical comment on one of the great plays of the Literary Revival; he has given dramatic form to the critical observation he made in his 1902 essay. He was on Yeats's side in general, but he would not accept Yeats's literary leadership or his view of history. Joyce would be a rival, not a disciple. He knew at a very early age exactly where he was going as a writer.

* * *

How did the story come out?

Joyce's relationship with the Literary Revival did not prosper. After graduation, he fell spectacularly from the high promise of 1902. In about eighteen months he had put himself hopelessly in the wrong, and he left Dublin to make his way in Europe. He left behind a bitter poem that ended, "And though they spurn me from their door / My soul shall spurn them evermore."

Joyce's personal experiences, as well as his ideas, explain the breach with the Revival writers. His college turned him down for the part-time tutoring that would have paid his way in medical school. He had given the authorities plenty of excuses: he had failed to take an honors degree; his teachers, however, never doubted his brilliance. Part of the explanation for this rejection must have been Joyce's unwillingness to attend mass and otherwise keep up a front of membership in his church.

Then, in the summer after graduation, Joyce met Yeats and George Russell and Lady Gregory. Poor and unknown though he was, Joyce nevertheless treated these elders as his equals, freely and arrogantly criticizing what they had written. They were impressed and briefly took him up as a protégé. Joyce then decided to take a medical course in Paris, supporting himself by teaching English and working as a journalist. Yeats and Lady Gregory wrote letters for him, got him book reviewing jobs; everything looked hopeful and auspicious. But at the Sorbonne, once again he could not come up with the cash for the required fees.

In this spring of 1903, he met Synge, who had also been unable to make ends meet in Paris. Synge, eleven years older than Joyce, gave him the manuscript of his one-act tragedy about the fishermen of the Aran Islands, *Riders to the Sea*. Joyce responded with a severe critique of the play but immediately saw that Synge's peasant realism was something new and important, the work of a massive talent, and he wrote his true impressions in a letter to his brother, saying, "Thanks be to God Synge isn't an Aristotelian."[11]

Synge's impressions of Joyce, published only recently, were written to Lady Gregory:

> He seems to be pretty badly off, and is wandering around Paris rather unbrushed and rather indolent, spending his studious moments in the National Library. . . . He talks of coming back to Dublin in the summer to live there on journalism while he does his serious work at his leisure. I cannot think that he will ever be a poet of importance, but his intellect is extraordinarily keen and if he keeps fairly sane he ought to do excellent essay-writing.[12]

Lady Gregory liked proper behavior; no doubt Synge's picture of the unbrushed Joyce had some influence on her subsequent attitude and therefore on Joyce's relations with the Revival. When he returned, Joyce found himself excluded from the Dublin literary parties. On one occasion he came anyway, without an invitation; Lady Gregory did not turn him away.

Joyce did, as he had told Synge he would, go on with his serious writing. But now his circumstances deteriorated. His mother died, and the family she had held together declined to a devastating degree. And in his twenty-first year, 1903, Joyce met Oliver St. John Gogarty, the man who became Buck Mulligan in *Ulysses*.

Padraic Colum says that at this time there were two Joyces, one of them the comic persona that Gogarty had invented—a clownish figure who could never be taken seriously as a writer. Gogarty would have said, "He's too thin-skinned; can't he take a joke?" but perhaps there is more to it than that.

Their association has become legendary. Gogarty was four years older than Joyce; rich and elegant; a poet; and a virtuoso of bawdy limericks. They called him the wittiest man in Ireland. He rapidly developed Joyce as a foil for his witticisms, a buffoon, an inexhaustible source of drama with which to amuse an audience. More seriously, in the first weeks of their acquaintance, Joyce furnished Gogarty with the final line for a poem Gogarty submitted in the prize competition at Trinity College; Gogarty's poem won, with Joyce's line singled out for special commendation.

Joyce was dazzled and flattered. He thought he had found in Gogarty a personality for whom serious poetry was a way of life. If you put the worst face on it, Joyce was happy to have a rich friend. If you put forward the best case, Joyce imagined Gogarty as a friend who shared intellectual interests and his ironical turn of mind, and had an appetite for life that Joyce admired.[13]

But the record now shows that Gogarty had decided to make Joyce over. Gogarty's tastes were brutish, and they became comrades in dissipation. Previously, Joyce had at least been abstemious; he was afraid of following his father's sad example of spendthrift alcoholism. And Joyce had a limited capacity for alcohol, a weakness made worse by inadequate diet; and he never could have rivaled Gogarty's enormous vitality. Gogarty told one of their friends that he would make Joyce drink "to break his spirit," and one day in a group when Joyce quoted Shakespeare's line, "A quart of ale is a dish for a King," Gogarty broke in, saying, "A quart of ale! A quart of milk is more in your line!" Their drunken revels, and Joyce's constant borrowings, were favorite items of gossip. A group of Gogarty's letters, recently published, show in his own contemporary account the kind of tales he was telling about Joyce at Dublin parties.

Gogarty's wit, wealth, and talent gave him full entrée to the literary evenings that were so important in this small city. Joyce was denied these gatherings to which all his friends were invited. He said to Colum, "Doors are being closed on me." George Moore said contemptuously of Joyce's small borrowings, "Why, he's nothing but a beggar!" Joyce's drinking and his talent for being offensive developed mythic proportions under the pressures of 1904.[14]

Nevertheless, he was writing. He even sold some of his work: five poems were published in this year. The first three short stories of *Dubliners* were written and published. He wrote a fictional essay for the new Dublin magazine, *Dana*; this was his very first version of *A Portrait of the Artist*, which was the essay's title. The piece was rejected; Joyce at once began to develop the central idea into a novel, and by midsummer he had written twelve chapters.[15]

Everything came to a head when Joyce met Nora Barnacle, fell in love, and departed Dublin. He left behind a ninety-six-line diatribe in verse, "The Holy Office."[16] In this poem he attacked the Revival directly, accusing it of hypocrisy. He pictured the Establishment writers as a gossipy clique, not a serious literary movement, and condemned the amused satisfaction with which they had watched his fall from grace.

Joyce opens the poem by saying that he will interpret the year's events himself, "lest bards in the attempt should err," the bard being of course his comrade, Gogarty. The Revival, Joyce's poem says, is fraudulent; the writers congratulate each other on their daring radicalism; they "hazard extremes of heterodoxy," but their writings and their lives are ruled by commonsense and prudent compromise. He takes some of Yeats's verse for a parody. Yeats had written:

> Know that I would accounted be
> True brother of a company
> That sang, to sweeten Ireland's wrong . . .

and Joyce changes these lines to attack the "mummers" of Yeats's Irish Literary Theatre in Yeats's own cadences:

> But I must not accounted be
> One of that mumming company . . .

From here he goes on to lampoon Yeats, Russell, Synge, Colum, Gogarty, and the others by name and by unmistakable cruel allusions.

Joyce's point is that they enjoy vicariously the spectacle of drunkenness and fornication for which he has become notorious. "My scarlet leaves them white as wool." The attack is personal, but it is also literary: Joyce exposes the internal tensions of the Revival movement. He is particularly virulent about the dominant strain of mysticism, Theosophy, and occultism so dear to Yeats and Russell. If a Joyce had not existed, he says in effect, one would have had to be invented.

> But all these men of whom I speak
> Make me the sewer of their clique.
> That they may dream their dreamy dreams
> I carry off their filthy streams.

This bitter diatribe shows how, at this time, Joyce had made himself a party of one. The truly remarkable feature of the poem comes at the end, when Joyce invokes his Jesuit training, despite his alienation from the Church, as a defense against his enemies. He says,

> Those souls that hate the strength that mine has
> Steeled in the school of old Aquinas.

In this defiant confrontation Joyce sets up the high intellectual tradition of the angelic doctor against George Russell's mysticism and Yeats's magical practices.

Joyce was marking out his distance from the writers of the Revival when he defied them in such extravagant language. He found his identity for the first time in this defiance. He was preparing, perhaps not yet consciously, to express in his own way the highly complex mixture of cultural elements in his own background—spiritual, economic, and political aspects. In "The Holy Office" he first identified his own background, in contrast to the Ascendancy background of Yeats and Synge, as the true mainstream of Irish national consciousness.

* * *

George Moore said that a literary movement is half a dozen people living in the same city, all of whom cordially hate each other.[17] Joyce's assault on the Revival was no more vituperative than what the writers said of each other. There were even some tensions between Yeats and Synge. It was said in Dublin, "When you want an enemy choose a friend: he knows where to strike." One historian of the movement has said, "How those people managed to get along in a small city remains a mystery. Their friendships were dotted with minefields."[18]

In the next ten years Joyce did some of his best writing; his record is clearly superior to Synge's achievement at the same age. But Joyce could not get published. He was never taken seriously by literary Dublin until *Ulysses* had won the acclaim of French and English reviewers.

A typical Dublin opinion shows in a letter from James Stephens, written as late as 1917 (after the publication of *A Portrait* and *Dubliners*):

> You ask about James Joyce. He is an Irishman, of course. [Stephens lists his books, giving a wrong title for *A Portrait* and calling *Dubliners* "a rather disconnected unpleasant prose work . . . which is anything but representative of Dublin."] I think that, in the handling of words, he is a clever, competent writer, but he is by no means a great writer. . . . I think it was a mistake in technique to dwell so persistently on the gross side of life . . . his life I should say. . . . He is a disappointed, envious man, in my judgment, and a success de scandale [*sic*] is all he can hope for. His two books are exceedingly and unnecessarily unpleasant, and they are thin into the bargain.[19]

Stephens, obviously, had not really read Joyce's two books; he and the other Dublin writers had done no more than glance through them.

The Dublin Establishment should have realized, if they had been able to read without prejudice, that in both his short story "The Dead" and in his novel, Joyce had tacitly acknowledged the power and veracity of Synge's and Yeats's mature work, in which they had made contemporary rural Ireland, the west of Ireland, a living reality in Irish literature. As noted above, Synge's peasant realism is the source of the rural images that Joyce put into *A Portrait of the Artist* and "The Dead," the indispensable capstone to *Dubliners*. "The Dead" has the naturalism and historicity of the other fourteen stories; Joyce shows crisply the frustrated condition of men and women of all ages in Dublin at the turn of the century.

In the final story, Joyce brings into the book the Gaelic Revival, using it to call to the reader's attention an element of Irish life that is necessarily absent from his urban, Dublin-based stories. He creates a redeeming image of "the West," and with this he suggests the mysterious values of Ireland's Gaelic past, its ancient historic glories.

The story describes a Christmas party, with dinner and dancing, in a prosperous, middle-class Catholic home. Gabriel Conroy, the central character, is a young intellectual who has complacently accepted the patronage of the colonial rulers; he has a secure position as a teacher, essayist, and book critic for the *Dublin Daily Express*. Joyce has also embodied the idea of another Ireland, "the West," in Gretta, Gabriel's wife. She is Catholic, Galway-bred, implicitly Celtic. She represents rural Ireland—an Ireland that is physically remote from the English-dominated capital city and also remote from or alien to those qualities of mind that allowed her husband to settle so comfortably into the English colonial tradition.

Thus the story emphasizes the differences between Gretta and the Dubliners among whom she is thrown by her marriage. She is simple-hearted, with a simplicity that controverts the materialistic values and the affectations of her husband. She embodies traditional Irish values that Gabriel and his friends have forgotten in their pursuit of material success. Gabriel prefers not to think of himself as Irish; secretly he despises her Galway background.

She longs to visit the Aran Islands; he prefers a summer pilgrimage eastward, to England and the Continent. But he is not insensitive. When he sees his wife at the party listening intently to an old Galway ballad, "The Lass of Aughrim," he remembers its Gaelic origin and thinks, "The song seemed to be in the old Irish tonality."

The Ireland that Synge portrayed so well, the image of a western land and a rural culture where life is fully and passionately lived, is brought to the reader—but very differently from Synge!—through Gretta's artless revelation of an episode in her youthful life. Michael

Furey, "a boy from the gas works," stood in the rain under her window for love of her and died at seventeen. "He died for me," says Gretta; her words are an echo of the conclusion of Yeats's play, *Cathleen ni Houlihan*.

This story, which Gretta tells at bedtime, ruins Gabriel's evening. Gabriel, alone with his wife, is filled with passionate love for her. But as he is about to take Gretta into his arms, she bursts into tears and reveals that her thoughts are not of him at all. She is thinking of the boy who died for love in Connacht. Gabriel is forced into the shocked realization that he really does not know his wife. Joyce has carefully prepared for this moment, so that Gabriel's flash of understanding broadens into an awareness that he knows nothing of his own country, nothing of his own people.

Of course I have greatly simplified a complex story in order to make this brief summary of its connection with Synge. Joyce is saying poetically that the Irish writer who does not know all of his country is imprisoned in nonidentity, alienated from his tradition. Gabriel Conroy is in trouble because he believes that he, as an intellectual, is superior to the peasant tradition in which the Irish past survives. John Kelleher, Harvard's great Celtic scholar, has said that Gabriel's painful awakening is a retribution for having forgotten his origins.[20]

Five years later, in *A Portrait of the Artist,* Joyce again used the rural peasant consciousness that Synge had first expressed. In the unfinished first draft known as *Stephen Hero,* the Irish peasant is seen only from a train window or in a brief visit to a rural area. But the germ of the conception described above in "The Dead" is present even this early, for young Stephen Dedalus is aware of a deep gulf between himself and the peasant. He says that "they stared very hard . . . as if he were some rare animal." Joyce was cured of this kind of anemic descriptive comment by the example of Synge's great dramatic art.

In the final version of *A Portrait of the Artist* the sense of dissimilarity survives, but now it is more sharply constructed. Joyce makes it a dramatic element of division and nonidentity between educated intellectual and uneducated peasant. Thus it becomes a valid and authentic representation of a fact of Irish life in his day—not so much economic, however, as cultural.

First, the childish Stephen at boarding school has a sharp physical impression of the peasants who knelt at the back of the chapel at mass. Then, at the end of the novel, an older Stephen, finished with college, records in his diary a newspaper story of a peasant, "an old man in a mountain cabin." This is just such a story as Synge might have written, and it comes into the diary as though Stephen had been reading about John Millington Synge's travels in the Gaeltacht.

"14 April," the diary begins. "John Alphonsus Mulrennan has just returned from the west of Ireland." Joyce is describing not the peasant but the experience of encountering the peasant. The diary continues: "Old man had red eyes and short pipe. Old man spoke Irish." Thus far the traveler is speaking; now comes the comment of the intellectual, young Stephen. "I fear him. I fear his redrimmed horny eyes. It is with him I must struggle all through this night till day come, till he or I lie dead, gripping him by the sinewy throat till . . . Till what? Till he yield to me? No. I mean him no harm" (P 251–52).

What is the context, what is the purpose of these brief encounters between urban intellectual and Irish peasant? They are connected with an important episode in the last chapter of *A Portrait*. In this episode the contemporary peasant mind is shown as an aspect of Irish history. Davin is the young peasant student of this episode; he is Stephen's classmate and friend. Davin tells a story that parallels, in form and substance, Synge's play, *In the Shadow of the Glen*. Joyce saw the play performed in 1903.

The young wife in Synge's play, Nora Burke, is a mountain girl who straightforwardly takes the passing stranger into her bed if she feels like it. Nora Burke is the model for Davin's story of a young woman in the Ballyhoura hills whose husband was off in Queenstown and who invited Davin into her cottage for the night. "Come in and stay the night here. You've no call to be frightened. There's no one in it but ourselves." Through Davin, Joyce brings his own version of Synge's peasant realism into his Dublin, into the middle-class city that by 1900 the Catholic Irish had made their own. Joyce involves Stephen in another dramatized confrontation, as he did in "The Dead," between the intellectual mind and the peasant mind.

Stephen's mind, the story tells us, "is eager of speculation and the hidden ways of Irish life." So he sees vividly the woman of Davin's story; she has "the eyes and voice and gesture of a woman without guile." This is the same guileless simplicity that we see in Synge's Nora Burke and also in Joyce's Gretta Conroy. So Stephen, like Gabriel Conroy, has a sudden glimpse of another Ireland than the one he knows, a rural culture where life is fully and passionately lived.

But now Joyce's portrayal of Davin goes beyond Synge; he writes into his novel a different view of the Irish peasant and his place in Irish history. Through Davin, Joyce expresses and also explains the tenacity of the Irish peasant's attachment to his church and to the fervid nationalism of the Gaelic Revival. Davin is a prosperous peasant: Stephen, who is poor and ill-dressed, marvels at Davin's "well-made boots that flanked the wall pair by pair." (Joyce had a thing about shoes.) Stephen has no boots; he wears cheap canvas shoes with broken soles that make him stumble. Davin, however, is exceptionally well shod. What kind of peasant is this? Davin is not Synge's half-pagan peasant; he is William Carleton's peasant of the hedge schools, educated by the church when all other education was denied the Catholics.

Davin's boots remind the reader that by 1900 the peasant had made the soil of Ireland his own; in Daniel Corkery's colorful phrase, he had fought for it against the English rulers with no assets except his bare courage and the knowledge that he was the native.[21] Notice how Joyce's novel proceeds. As Stephen stares at Davin's boots, he remembers that the peasants for centuries had endured "the terror of soul of a starving Irish village in which the curfew was still a nightly fear." ("Irish village" here means Gaelic and Catholic, in contrast to English and Protestant.) This is history. Irish villages were not starving in 1902. From this reminder of history, Stephen realizes that what repels him in his peasant friend (the kind of reaction, that is, that Stephen later puts into his diary) is Davin's slow reluctance of speech and deed—these qualities are actually a survival of the peasant response to the English terror, a dehumanizing effect: "a grossness of intelligence or by a bluntness of feeling or a dull stare of terror in the eyes" (*P* 180).

Here, then, is a true picture of Irish rural life, even more realistic than Synge's but utterly different. It is not a picture that Synge or Yeats, coming from the Protestant Ascendancy, could have or would have produced. It is a picture that James Stephens should have caught and applauded. Stephens wrote his own autobiographical story, "Hunger," as he said, to save his sanity; Stephens was desperately poor, but he was raised in the Protestant Irish tradition. He was taken up by the Literary Revival, given a job, invited to their parties, allowed to write some of the dialogue for George Moore's stories. James Stephens's comment on *Dubliners* and *A Portrait* is a perfect mirror of thoughtless and automatically negative contemporary prejudgment of Joyce and his writing.

Joyce had always followed Synge's career with rapt interest—envy, too—in the Irish newspapers. "Synge is a storm center," he wrote home to his brother, "but I have done nothing." In 1907 the unprecedented riots at the Abbey Theatre over Synge's *Playboy of the Western World* turned Joyce's energies toward writing something that would directly rival Synge.

"This whole affair has upset me," Joyce told his brother. "I feel like a man in a house who hears a row in the street and voices he knows shouting but can't get out to see what the hell is going on. It has put me off the story I was 'going to write,' to wit, 'The Dead.'" Joyce finished this story only a little later, in the summer of that same year, 1907.[22]

Joyce, as we now know from his letters, hoped to return to Dublin. Synge died in 1909. When Joyce visited Dublin that year he brought with him the revised manuscript of *Dubliners* that now included "The Dead." His letters to Nora suggest that he hoped and expected to be recognized as Synge's successor. A fateful contract for the book was signed with a Dublin firm, and when that contract was breached in 1912 Joyce's break with the Revival became final.[23] He never set foot in Dublin again.

Joyce certainly did not associate Yeats with the *Dubliners* debacle. But the rupture was so complete that when Yeats invited him to become a member of the new Irish Academy of Letters in 1932—twenty years later—Joyce courteously declined. Nevertheless, all the histories of the Irish Renaissance do include Joyce's work, as they must. Yeats and Synge are secure reputations, even towering reputations, but Joyce's vision of Irish history has prevailed. In writing "The Dead," Joyce opened the way for the first time—as he did again in *A Portrait* and, more massively, in *Ulysses*—for future poets and novelists to express a world of Irish experience that was necessarily foreign to Yeats and Synge.

What was this world of Joyce's? What was singular in his experience of Irish history? Yeats all his life opposed his great art to what he called "the filthy modern tide." He celebrated the aristocrat and the peasant, making the Protestant Ascendancy more aristocratic and more responsible than it was historically, with his wonderful lines about "hard-riding country gentlemen," and "the indomitable Irishry." Joyce, quite to the contrary, as one critic puts it, "knows the filthy modern tide and immerses himself in it to do his work."[24]

Joyce belonged to and accepted the flood tide of Irish national life that came to power through Daniel O'Connell. This side of Irish reality has been called "the tribe of Dan"—all those ordinary middle-class Irish townsmen, only one generation from the traditional rural peasant culture. They are eloquent but also conniving, witty but often as small-minded and mean-spirited as their peasant forebears. Joyce expresses all this life with urbanity and wit and ironical affection. In his sane and joyful comedy Joyce becomes, as the poet Thomas Kinsella says, "The first major voice to speak for Irish reality since the death of the Irish language."

By now, eighty years later, Joyce at last is acknowledged in his native land. Whether they actually read his books is still a doubtful question. It is understood, of course, that his books must be salacious; clichés set in motion in Gogarty's day still circulate. But in 1977 the

Jesuits of University College Dublin set over the main entrance to Joyce's college, where he wrote his first statements of artistic principle, a bronze plaque with their three most illustrious names: John Henry Cardinal Newman; Gerard Manley Hopkins; and James Augustine Joyce. And the timeless universe of permanent literature now includes Joyce's achievement; the Irish experience has finally been seen by his countrymen and by the world in his nicely polished mirror.

NOTES

1. Richard Ellmann, *James Joyce* (New York: Oxford University Press, 1982), 264–65. Hereafter cited as *JJ* 2.
2. *Selected Letters of James Joyce*, ed. Richard Ellmann (New York: Viking, 1975), 169 (5 September 1909); 174 (27 October 1909). Hereafter cited as *Selected Letters*.
The *Selected Letters* restored many missing portions of letters that had been partially printed in *Letters of James Joyce*, vols. 2 and 3, ed. Richard Ellmann (New York: Viking, 1966), hereafter cited as *Letters*.
3. *JJ* 2, 54.
4. Ibid., 64–67.
5. *Critical Writings of James Joyce*, ed. Ellsworth Mason and Richard Ellmann (New York: Viking Compass Books, 1964), 45.
6. Ibid., 71.
7. *A Portrait of the Artist as a Young Man*, ed. Chester G. Anderson (New York: Viking Press, 1968), 181.
8. *Critical Writings*, 81–82, 82–83.
9. W. B. Yeats, "Easter 1916," in *Collected Poems* (New York: Macmillan, 1951), 177.
10. James Joyce, *Ulysses* (1934; reprint, New York: Random House, Modern Library, 1961), 584; and *Ulysses: A Critical and Synoptic Edition*, prep. Hans Walter Gabler, with Wolfhard Steppe and Claus Melchior, 3 vols. (New York: Garland Press, 1984), 2:1317. Hereafter cited as *U* and *U-G*, respectively.
11. *Letters* 2: from Lady Gregory, 23 November 1902, 15–16; to Lady Gregory, 1 December 1902, 18, and 21 December 1902, 24; from Synge, 8 March 1903, 34; to Stanislaus Joyce, 9 March 1903, 35.
12. For Synge's letter to Lady Gregory, see *JJ* 2, 125n.
13. *JJ* 2, 172–75.
14. Mary and Padraic Colum, *Our Friend James Joyce* (New York: Doubleday, 1958), 36, 39–40, 68–70; Stanislaus Joyce, *My Brother's Keeper*, ed. Richard Ellmann (New York: Viking, 1958), 174–76, 241–43, 245–46; Oliver St. John Gogarty, *Many Lines to Thee; Letters to G. K. A. Bell, 1904–1907*, ed. James F. Carens (Dublin: Dolmen Press, 1971). Cited in *JJ* 2, 169, 762.
15. *JJ* 2, 165.
16. *The Portable James Joyce*, ed. Harry Levin (New York: Viking Press, 1947), 657–660.
17. George Moore, *Vale*, vol. 3 of *Hail and Farewell* (New York: Heinemann, 1914), 165.
18. Herbert A. Kenny, *Literary Dublin: A History* (Dublin: Gill and Macmillan,

1974), 222. See also Richard Fallis, *The Irish Renaissance* (Syracuse, N.Y.: Syracuse University Press, 1977); and Peter Costello, *The Heart Grown Brutal* (Dublin: Gill and Macmillan, 1977).

19. *Letters of James Stephens,* ed. Richard J. Finneran (New York: Macmillan, 1974), 209. When Joyce first met Stephens, Joyce told him "that my knowledge of Irish life was non-Catholic and so non-existent." *James, Seumas and Jacques: Unpublished Writings of James Stephens,* ed. Lloyd Frankenberg (New York: Macmillan, 1967), 149. See also Ellmann, *JJ* 2, 591–94, 619.

20. John Kelleher, "Irish History and Mythology in James Joyce's 'The Dead,'" *Review of Politics* 27 (1965): 416.

21. Daniel Corkery, *Synge and Anglo-Irish Literature* (1931; New York: Russell & Russell, 1965), 211, 236.

22. *Selected Letters,* 148, 150 (to Stanislaus, 11 February and 16 February 1907); *Letters* 2, 211, 215.

23. Ellmann, *JJ* 2, 310–11, 313–15, 322–24, 328–32, 334–38.

24. Seamus Deane, "The Literary Myths of the Revival: A Case for their Abandonment," in *Myth and Reality in Irish Literature,* ed. Joseph Ronsley (Waterloo, Ont.: Wilfred Laurier University Press, 1977), 317–29; and "The Joycean Triumph: *Ulysses* Fifty Years After," *Encounter* 39 (November 1972): 42–52.

Contributors

BERNARD BENSTOCK teaches at the University of Miami, where he edits the *James Joyce Literary Supplement*. He has written four books on Joyce, the latest being *Narrative Con/Texts in "Ulysses,"* and has edited or coedited nine others, most recently *James Joyce: The Augmented Ninth* and *Critical Essays on Joyce's "Ulysses."*

SHARI BENSTOCK teaches at the University of Miami. She has written widely on critical theory and on the works of James Joyce and other modernist authors in a number of journals and in her *Women of the Left Bank*. She serves on the editorial board of *Joyce Studies*.

ZACK BOWEN teaches and serves as chair of the English Department at the University of Miami. His books include *Padraic Colum, Musical Allusions in the Works of James Joyce, Mary Lavin,* and *"Ulysses" as a Comic Novel*. He coedited (with James Carens) *A Companion to Joyce Studies*, edited the *Irish Renaissance Annual*, and is general editor of G. K. Hall's Critical Essays on British Literature Series.

SUSAN D. BRIENZA studies law at Stanford University, with special interests in the Constitution and in medical ethics. She has published a book, *Samuel Beckett's New Worlds: Style in Metafiction* and several articles on Beckett's drama, including one on Sam Beckett's influence on Sam Shepard. She has also written on Pynchon, Pinter, and Doctorow, but her strongest scholarly passion is for James Joyce.

VINCENT J. CHENG teaches at the University of Southern California and is author of *Shakespeare and Joyce: A Study of "Finnegans Wake," "Le Cid": A Translation in Rhymed Couplets*, and numerous articles on Joyce and on modern literature. He is currently completing a book about Ford Madox Ford.

RICHARD CORBALLIS teaches at the University of Canterbury, Christchurch, New Zealand. He has published a study of Tom Stoppard's plays entitled *Stoppard: The Mystery and the Clockwork* and has also written extensively on Irish and Commonwealth theater and on Shakespeare and other Elizabethans.

JANET EGLESON DUNLEAVY teaches at the University of Wisconsin–Milwaukee. She has written widely on Irish subjects. Her books include *George Moore: The Artist's Vision, the Storyteller's Art* and, with G. W. Dunleavy, *The O'Conor Papers* and a biography of Douglas Hyde. She has edited *George Moore in Perspective* and (forthcoming) *Classics of Joyce Criticism*.

SIDNEY FESHBACH teaches at the City College of New York. He is president of the James Joyce Society and has published essays on Hermann Broch, Marcel Duchamp, Empedocles, A. M. Klein, and Wallace Stevens, as well as on James Joyce. The essay "Veripatetic Imago" is part of a book in progress on the work of Joyce up to 1916.

MELVIN J. FRIEDMAN teaches at the University of Wisconsin–Milwaukee. He is the author or editor of some fifteen books. His latest title is *Pound/The Little Review: The Letters of Ezra Pound to Margaret Anderson*. He serves on the editorial boards of *Journal of Modern Literature, Contemporary Literature, Studies in the Novel, Studies in American Fiction, Journal of Beckett Studies, International Fiction Review, Fer de Lance, Yiddish, Journal of Popular Culture, Journal of American Culture, Arete: The Journal of Sport Literature*.

MICHAEL PATRICK GILLESPIE teaches at Marquette University and has written widely on authors from the modern period. His most recent book, *Reading the Book of Himself: Narrative Strategies in the Works of James Joyce*, appeared in 1989.

DANIEL P. GUNN teaches at the University of Maine at Farmington. He has recently published essays on Austen, Pope, and the Talking Heads. Currently, he is working on a book about ideology and moral rhetoric in six English novels.

SUZETTE A. HENKE teaches at the State University of New York at Binghamton. She is the author of *Joyce's Moraculous Sindbook: A Study of "Ulysses"* and of *James Joyce and the Politics of Desire* and coeditor of *Women in Joyce*. Her publications in the field of modern literature include essays on Virginia Woolf, Samuel Beckett, Anaïs Nin, Dorothy Richardson, Doris Lessing, W. B. Yeats, and E. M. Forster. She is presently working on a study of "women's life-writing" in the twentieth century.

Contributors

PATRICK A. MCCARTHY teaches at the University of Miami. He is the author of *The Riddles of "Finnegans Wake," Olaf Stapledon,* and *"Ulysses": Portals of Discovery.* He has also edited *Critical Essays on Samuel Beckett* and coedited *The Legacy of Olaf Stapledon: Critical Essays and an Unpublished Manuscript.* At present he is working on a study of Malcolm Lowry.

MARY REYNOLDS has taught at Yale University as visiting lecturer in the College Seminar program. She has published widely on Joyce in numerous journals and is author of *Joyce and Dante: the Shaping Imagination.* She serves on the editorial boards of *James Joyce Quarterly* and *Joyce Studies.*

FRITZ SENN heads the Zürich James Joyce Foundation and has taught at various universities in the United States and Switzerland. He helped found *A Wake Newslitter* and serves on numerous editorial boards, including *European Joyce Studies.* He has authored many articles, some of which are collected in *Nichts gegen Joyce: Joyce Versus Nothing* and in *Joyce's Dislocutions: Essays on Reading as Translation.*

Index

Adams, Robert M., 59, 78 n.3
Aeneid, The. See Virgil
"Aeolus," 25, 44, 61, 62–63, 91, 92, 150, 156 n.3, 160, 176
ALP, 91, 101, 102, 103, 104, 105, 107, 108, 110, 112, 113, 114, 116, 121 n.14, 122 n.15, 122 n.16, 125, 173
Alter, Robert, 45 n.3
Amory, Mark, 161, 169 n.14
Anagrams, 33, 77, 111
Anderson, Chester G., 193 n.1, 217 n.1, 233 n.7
Androgyny: in *Ulysses,* 46–58, 184
"Anna Livia Plurabelle," 102, 103, 104–6, 113, 119 n.4, 125, 128, 132, 134, 135, 136, 173
Apostrophes, 95–124
Appassionata Sonata. *See* Beethoven, Ludwig van
Aquinas, Saint Thomas, 142, 195–217; *Summa Theologiae,* 195–217
Arabian Nights, 77–78. *See also* Sinbad
"Araby," 174
Aristotle, 75, 196, 197, 200, 201, 202, 203, 205, 208, 209–210, 224
Armand, Inessa, 170 n.31
Arrah-na-Pogue. See Boucicault, Dion
Art and Beauty in the Middle Ages. See Eco, Umberto
At Swim-Two-Birds. See O'Brien, Flann
Atherton, James S., 30 n.12
Attridge, Derek, 58 n.4, 120 n.6, 123 n.19
Aubert, Jacques, 120 n.6
Augustine, Saint, 18, 197, 199, 200, 214; *Confessions,* 18

Bakhtin, Mikhail, 52
Bats, 125–37
Baudelaire, Charles, 28, 104, 105; "Le Cygne," 104; "Moesta et Errabunda," 105
Bauerle, Ruth, 79 n.13
Beckett, Samuel, 162, 165, 168, 169 n.15, 170 n.23; *The Unnamable,* 165
Beethoven, Ludwig van, 167; *Appassionata* Sonata, 167
Beja, Morris, 137
Benstock, Bernard, 11, 30 n.15, 113, 121 n.11, 122 n.15, 123 n.20, 235
Benstock, Shari, 11, 121 n.11, 122 n.15, 235
Berman, Edward, 169 n.22
Bishop, John, 30 n.12, 92, 94 n.12, 120 n.7
Blake, William, 73, 135
Bloom, Harold, 85
Bloom, Leopold, 15–32, 33–45, 46–58, 60, 61, 62, 65, 66, 68, 69, 70, 72, 73, 74, 75, 76, 77, 80, 81, 83, 84, 86, 114, 127, 130, 131, 132, 133, 135, 143, 144, 145, 146, 148, 150–51, 152–53, 154, 155, 156, 165, 167, 172, 173, 178–79, 181, 182, 184, 188, 189, 191, 192, 201, 213
Bloom, Milly, 16, 23, 31 n.22, 48
Bloom, Molly, 16, 17, 19–20, 21, 22, 30 n.7, 31 n.25, 40, 48, 49, 50, 54, 55, 57, 58 n.8, 69, 78, 93, 114, 121 n.11, 133, 144, 151, 152, 153, 154, 155, 156, 165, 174, 189
"Book of Kells," 103, 107, 110, 114, 139, 185
Borach, Georges, 160
Boucicault, Dion, 114; *Arrah-na-Pogue,* 114
Boyle, Patrick, 45 n.12
Boyle, Robert, 10, 81, 93 n.1
Bowen, Zack, 11, 22, 31 n.19, 31 n.22, 195, 235

239

Bowers, Fredson, 45 n.8
Bredin, Hugh, 217 n.3
Brentano, Franz, 196, 217 n.5
Brienza, Susan, 82, 94 n.3, 94 n.7, 235
Brook, Peter, 162
Brooks, Cleanth, 168
Brown, Richard, 128, 136
Bruno, Giordano, 197, 198, 202, 210
Budgen, Frank, 194 n.17, 214–15, 217 n.12
Burlesque, 60, 71
Butler, H. E., 193 n.10

"Cad, The," 90–91, 106–7, 112
"Calypso," 16, 20, 21, 23–24, 25, 31 n.22, 31 n.25, 37, 38, 39, 40, 42, 61, 67–69, 71, 74, 143–44, 150, 156 n.3, 178–79
Carens, James F., 233 n.14
Carson, Johnny, 81
Cathleen ni Houlihan. *See* Yeats, W. B.
Catholicism, 219, 226, 228
Cervantes, Miguel de, 68; *Don Quixote*, 63, 68
Chamber Music, 126–27, 129, 131, 136, 136 n.1
Cheng, Vincent, 85, 86, 94 n.8, 125, 126, 136, 235
"Circe," 19, 24, 28, 29, 31 n.25, 34–35, 36, 37, 38, 41, 44, 45 n.5, 45 n.12, 49–57, 58 n.3, 58 n.8, 72–73, 130, 131, 133, 135, 144, 145–47, 148, 151, 152, 156, 156 n.3, 183–84, 222–23
Cixous, Hélène, 56, 58 n.7
Claritas, 200, 203, 206–8, 209, 214
Cohn, Ruby, 169 n.15
Colum, Mary, 233 n.14
Colum, Padraic, 219, 224, 226, 233 n.14
Comedy, 53, 59–78, 85, 168, 173, 223, 224, 232
Confessions. *See* Augustine, Saint
Conrad, Joseph, 89
Consonantia, 200, 203, 205–6, 207, 212
Corballis, Richard, 11, 169 n.4, 235–36
Corkery, Daniel, 231, 234 n.21
Costello, Peter, 234 n.18
"Counterparts," 174
Countess Cathleen, The. *See* Yeats, W. B.
Crosby, Bing, 159
Culler, Jonathan, 11, 95, 96, 104, 105, 118, 119 n.2, 119 n.3, 121 n.13, 121–22 n.14, 124 n.23
Cyclic structure: of *Finnegans Wake*, 97, 98
"Cyclops," 27, 30 n.7, 30 n.15, 36, 39, 42, 61, 67–69, 71, 74, 150, 156 n.3, 176, 179–80, 181, 188

Daedalus, 190–91, 192–93, 197, 205, 208, 209, 213, 214, 216
Dante, 191; *Inferno*, 191
Darantière, 39
Davis, Robert Con, 58 n.8
"Day of the Rabblement, The," 220
de Courtivron, Isabelle, 58 n.7
de Groen, Alma, 158; *Going Home*, 158
de Man, Paul, 105, 121 n.14
De Valera, Eamon, 122 n.17
"Dead, The," 173, 174, 192, 218, 228, 229, 230, 231–32
Deane, Seamus, 234 n.24
Dedalus, Stephen, 16, 17, 19, 22, 23, 24–25, 26, 27, 28, 31 n.18, 36, 43, 45 n.12, 48, 55–56, 57, 58 n.8, 60, 61, 63, 65, 73, 74, 75, 76, 80, 82, 83, 85, 89, 92, 126, 127, 128, 129, 130, 131, 132, 133, 134, 136, 138, 139, 140, 141, 142–43, 147–48, 149, 150, 152, 153, 155, 156, 164, 165, 169 n.21, 172, 174–75, 177, 178, 179, 189, 193 n.12, 195–217, 222–23, 229–31
Defence of Poesy. *See* Sir Philip Sidney
Defoe, Daniel, 18; *Moll Flanders*, 16, 17, 22; *Robinson Crusoe*, 18
del Greco Lobner, Corinna, 126, 136
Deming, Robert H., 30 n.1, 30 n.2
Derrida, Jacques, 99–100, 101, 111, 119 n.1, 120 n.8, 120 n.9, 120 n.10, 121 n.11, 122–23 n.18, 123 n.19, 123 n.21, 124 n.22
Devlin, Kimberly, 94 n.2
Dickens, Charles, 88
Dictionary of Slang and Unconventional English. *See* Partridge, Eric
Dirty Linen. *See* Stoppard, Tom
Dogg's Our Pet. *See* Stoppard, Tom
Don Quixote. *See* Cervantes, Miguel de
Dreams: and dreaming, 98, 99, 101, 102, 156
Dreyfus, Alfred, 122 n.17
Dubliners, 16–17, 69, 173–74, 189,

192, 208, 218, 225, 227, 228, 229, 230, 231, 232; "Araby," 174; "Counterparts," 174; "The Dead," 173, 174, 192, 218, 228, 229, 230, 231–32; "Eveline," 174; "A Mother," 174; "A Painful Case," 174; "The Sisters," 174

E, 102, 107, 108, 109, 110, 112, 114
Easter Rising of 1916, 222
Eco, Umberto, 196, 217 n.3, 217 n.4, 217 n.6; *Art and Beauty in the Middle Ages*, 196
Eglinton, John, 22, 30–31 n.18
Eliot, T. S., 15, 30 n.1, 71
Ellmann, Richard, 30 n.8, 31 n.22, 33–34, 44, 44 n.1, 45 n.13, 45 n.15, 158, 159, 160, 161, 165, 169 n.8, 169 n.11, 169 n.17, 170 n.24, 217 n.1, 233 n.1, 233 n.2, 233 n.5, 233 n.6, 233 n.14, 234 n.19, 234 n.23
"Enoch Arden." *See* Tennyson, Alfred Lord
Enter a Free Man. See Stoppard, Tom
Epic, 85, 92, 208
Epstein, E., 45 n.4
Esrock, Ellen, 217 n.4
Etymological Dictionary. See Skeat, Walter William
"Eumaeus," 22, 27, 31 n.25, 33, 62, 73–75, 80–93, 94 n.3, 127, 133, 156 n.3, 173, 179, 189
"Eveline," 174
Every Good Boy Deserves Favour. See Stoppard, Tom
Exiles, 55, 160, 192

Fallis, Richard, 234 n.18
Felman, Shoshana, 49, 58 n.3
Ferrer, Daniel, 49, 58 n.4, 120 n.6, 123 n.19
Feshbach, Sidney, 217 n.7, 236
Ficino, Marcilo, 197
Finnegan, Tim, 80, 84, 95, 96, 97, 108, 118
Finnegans Wake, 19, 29, 30 n.9, 30 n.12, 76, 80–93, 95–124, 125, 126, 127, 128, 132, 133–35, 136, 136 n.1, 139–40, 162, 171, 172–73, 176, 185–88, 190, 192, 193 n.9, 215, 216; chapter I.1, 89, 98, 101, 104, 107, 108–9, 110, 111, 116, 187; chapter I.2, 104, 106–7, 108, 110, 112, 114; chapter I.3, 104, 108, 113; chapter I.4, 90–91, 98, 101, 102, 104, 109, 113; chapter I.5, 86, 103, 104, 107, 110, 113, 114, 116, 122 n.17, 139, 185; chapter I.6, 29, 83, 91, 92, 101, 104, 112, 113, 114, 123 n.19, 123 n.20, 126, 134–35, 139, 140; chapter I.7, 80–93, 104, 109, 122 n.17, 126, 134, 135, 139–40; chapter I.8, 102, 103, 104–6, 113, 119 n.4, 125, 128, 132, 134, 135, 136; chapter II.1, 102, 104, 111–12, 120 n.7, 123 n.19, 123 n.20, 140; chapter II.2, 30 n.12, 86, 90, 91, 92, 93, 100, 101, 103, 109, 112, 113, 114, 116, 123 n.20, 134, 186; chapter II.3, 104, 122 n.17, 123 n.20, 134; chapter II.4, 114, 122 n.17; chapter III.1, 104, 115–16, 216; chapter III.2, 84, 99, 104, 112, 113, 114, 134, 185; chapter III.3, 90, 98, 101, 104, 108, 113, 114, 120 n.7, 122 n.17; chapter III.4, 30 n.12, 92, 102; chapter IV, 90, 92, 102, 104, 110, 114, 122 n.17, 186, 190, 193 n.9, 215. *See also* ALP; "Anna Livia Plurabelle"; "Book of Kells"; "The Cad"; "Glugg and Chuff"; HCE; Issy; "The Letter"; "The Mookse and the Gripes"; "Nuvoletta"; "The Prankquean"; "The Riddles Chapter"; Shaun; "Shaun the Post"; Shem; "Shem the Penman"; Sigla
"Finnegan's Wake" (ballad), 96, 97
Finneran, Richard J., 234 n.19
Flaubert, Gustave, 44
Foucault, Michel, 58 n.3
France, Anatole, 38
Frank, Joseph, 15, 30 n.3
Frankenberg, Lloyd, 234 n.19
French, Marilyn, 16, 30 n.4, 59, 75, 78 n.1, 78 n.6, 79 n.11
Freud, Sigmund, 46, 52, 57 n.1, 83, 185
Friedman, Melvin J., 236

Gabler, Hans Walter, 30 n.6, 45 n.14, 94 n.3, 193 n.2, 217 n.1, 233 n.10
Gallop, Jane, 57 n.1
Garnett, Edward, 173, 193 n.6
George, Rolf, 217 n.5
Gilbert, Stuart, 30 n.8, 37, 190, 193–94 n.13, 194 n.16

242 Index

Gilby, Thomas, 217 n.1
Gillespie, Michael Patrick, 94 n.6, 236
"Glugg and Chuff," 140
Gogarty, Oliver St. John, 219, 224–25, 226, 232, 233 n.14
Going Home. See de Groen, Alma
Goldberg, S. L., 172–73, 193 n.3, 193 n.4, 193 n.5, 193 n.10
Gordon, Giles, 169 n.18
Gordon, John, 82, 93, 94 n.3, 94 n.4, 94 n.5, 94 n.13, 94 n.14, 133, 136
Gorki, Maxim, 167, 170 n.30
Graduate, The, 75
Greene, Graham, 163, 169 n.19
Gregory, Lady, 220, 223, 224, 233 n.11, 233 n.12
Groden, Michael, 59, 78 n.4, 184, 194 n.19, 194 n.20
Gunn, Daniel P., 236

"Hades," 152, 156 n.3
Hamlet. See Shakespeare, William
Hancock, Leslie, 130, 136
Harmon, Maurice, 137
Harris, Frank, 51
Hart, Clive, 45 n.5, 133, 136, 137
Hartman, Geoffrey, 67, 78 n.5
Harty, John, 169 n.21
Hauptmann, Gerhart, 220
Hayman, David, 34, 45 n.2, 45 n.5, 137
Hayman, Ronald, 169 n.12, 169 n.13, 170 n.25, 170 n.27, 170 n.28, 170 n.29
HCE, 80, 81, 86, 89, 90, 91, 92, 99, 100, 101, 102, 103, 106, 107, 108, 109, 110, 111–12, 113, 115, 120 n.10, 122 n.15, 122 n.16
Heap, Jane, 149, 156 n.9
Henke, Suzette A., 137, 236
Herring, Phillip, 137
Homer, 29, 51, 56, 83, 85, 86, 88, 178, 184, 193–94 n.13; *The Odyssey,* 76, 85, 164, 191, 194 n.23
Hopkins, Gerard Manley, 233
Hubris, 173
Hughes, Ted, 162, 169 n.16
Humor, 71; and wit, 59–60, 61
Hurley, Robert, 58 n.3

Ibsen, Henrik, 220
Importance of Being Earnest, The. See Oscar Wilde

Inferno. See Dante
Integritas, 200, 203–5, 207, 212
Irish Fest Players, 10
Irish Literary Revival, 219, 220, 223–27, 231, 232
Irish Literary Theatre (Yeats), 225
Irony, 71, 73
Isaacs, Bernard, 170 n.31
Iser, Wolfgang, 17, 30 n.9
Issy, 29, 100, 101, 105, 113, 115, 122 n.16, 123 n.20
"Ithaca," 16, 19, 25, 26, 29, 31 n.18, 33, 34–35, 36, 38–39, 41, 42, 43, 44, 45 n.12, 45 n.14, 61, 62, 75–78, 84, 133, 150, 153, 156, 156 n.3, 160, 164, 181–82, 190

Jackson, Holbrook, 15, 24, 30 n.2, 31 n.23
Janusko, Donna, 10
Johnson, Barbara, 95, 105, 121 n.11, 121 n.12
Jones, Stephen, 169 n.19
Joyce, James: as character in *Travesties,* 157–70. Works: *see under* individual titles
Joyce, Nora, 219, 225, 232
Joyce, Stanislaus, 233 n.14, 234 n.22
Jumpers. See Stoppard, Tom
Jung, Carl, 185

Kant, Immanuel, 206, 208
Kelleher, John, 234 n.20
Kenner, Hugh, 17, 18, 20, 30 n.9, 30 n.10, 30 n.13, 34, 36–37, 45 n.2, 45 n.5, 80, 196
Kenny, Herbert A., 233–34 n.18
Kinsella, Thomas, 232
Kristeva, Julia, 58 n.6
Krupskaya, N. K., 170 n.31

Lacan, Jacques, 58 n.8
Latini, Brunetto, 126, 137
Lawrence, Karen, 45 n.3, 59, 68, 71, 75, 77, 78 n.2, 78 n.7, 79 n.8, 79 n.10, 79 n.12
"Le Cygne." *See* Baudelaire, Charles
Leavey, John P., Jr., 121 n.11
Lenin, Vladimir Ilyich Ulyanov, 158, 166–69, 170; as character in *Travesties,* 157–70

Index

"Lestrygonians," 17, 20, 25, 27, 37, 43, 48–49, 144, 146, 147, 150, 156 n.3
"Letter, The," *(Finnegans Wake)*, 86, 104, 116, 122 n.17
Letters of James Joyce, 93
Lévi-Strauss, Claude, 122 n.18
Levin, Harry, 233 n.16
Linati, Carlo, 37
Little Review, The, 149
Litz, A. Walton, 193 n.7, 217 n.1
Lord Malquist and Mr. Moon. See Stoppard, Tom
"Lotus Eaters," 18, 22, 27, 31 n.21, 36, 47, 143, 151, 152, 156 n.3
Lowry, Malcolm, 19; *Under the Volcano*, 19

MacCabe, Colin, 26, 31 n.26, 32 n.32, 45 n.3
McCarthy, Patrick A., 11, 30 n.16, 32 n.30, 86, 94 n.10, 125–26, 128, 130, 131, 137, 237
MacCool, Finn, 96
McHugh, Roland, 122 n.16
Maddox, James, 80, 82, 83, 94 n.3
Magda. See Sudermann, Hermann
Mangan, James Clarence, 221, 222
Marcus, Steven, 58 n.3
Marivaux, Pierre, 193 n.11
Marks, Elaine, 58 n.7
Martyn, Edward, 219, 220
Mason, Ellsworth, 217 n.1, 233 n.5, 233 n.6, 233 n.8
Melchior, Claus, 233 n.10
Metamorphoses. See Ovid
Metempsychosis, 20, 21, 22–23, 29, 82, 100, 132
Mimesis, 52, 71
Mink, Louis O., 30 n.9
Modernism, 157–70
"Moesta et Errabunda." See Baudelaire, Charles
Moll Flanders. See Defoe, Daniel
Montrelay, Michele, 57 n.1
Monty Python, 66
"Mookse and the Gripes, The," 112, 123 n.19, 134–35
Moore, George, 219, 220, 225, 227, 231, 233 n.17
Moore-Robinson, Miriam, 163
Moseley, Virginia, 45 n.9, 45 n.11
"Mother, A," 174

Murphy, D. B., 80–93; as Sinbad, 84; as Buffalo Bill, 87
Music, 61, 63–67, 73, 78, 96, 97, 114, 157, 182

Nabokov, Vladimir, 45 n.8, 74
Narrative patterns, 59–78, 174
"Nausicaa," 23, 36, 39, 42, 47, 48, 69–71, 125, 127, 128, 130, 131, 132, 133, 134, 135, 152, 153–54, 155, 156 n.3, 159, 181, 188
"Nestor," 149, 156 n.3, 190
New Yorker, 152
Newman, John Henry Cardinal, 233
Newman, Robert D., 32 n.30
Night and Day. See Stoppard, Tom
No Man's Land. See Pinter, Harold
Noon, William, 195–96, 217 n.2
Norris, David, 137
Nutting, Myron, 44
"Nuvoletta," 112, 134–35

O, 102, 103, 104, 105, 106, 107, 108, 109, 110, 112, 119 n.4, 121–22 n.14, 187
O'Brien, Flann, 163; *At Swim-Two-Birds*, 163
O'Brien, T. C., 217 n.1, 217 n.8, 217 n.9, 217 n.10, 217 n.11
O'Connell, Daniel, 232
"Ode to the West Wind." See Shelley, Percy Bysshe
Odyssey, The. See Homer
Oedipus, 76
Olfactory perception, 138–56
Ong, Walter, 26, 28, 31 n.28, 31 n.29, 32 n.31
Othello. See Shakespeare, William
Ovid, 23, 180; *Metamorphoses*, 180
"Oxen of the Sun," 60, 61, 71–72, 74, 75, 76, 156 n.3, 159, 191
Oxford English Dictionary, 82, 119 n.5, 126, 137
Owens, Craig, 169 n.6

"Painful Case, A," 164
Parnell, Charles Stewart, 109, 110, 122 n.17, 173
Parody, 60, 64, 65, 67, 68, 69, 71, 72, 73, 76, 178, 179, 183
Partridge, Eric, 131, 137; *Dictionary of*

Slang and Unconventional English, 131
Pater, Walter, 197; *The Renaissance,* 197
Pearse, Patrick, 222
"Penelope," 16, 30 n.7, 44, 78, 149, 151, 155–56, 156 n.3, 188
Perfume. See Süsskind, Patrick
Petrarch, 18
Phenomenology, 196
Pico della Mirandola, Giovanni, 197, 198, 202
Pigott, Richard, 109, 110
Pinter, Harold, 158; *No Man's Land,* 158, 168
Plato, 142, 197, 200, 201, 202, 203, 204, 205, 208, 209–10, 213; *Timaeus,* 213
Pomes Penyeach, 127
Portrait of the Artist as a Young Man, A, 24, 25, 26, 27, 28, 125, 126, 127, 128, 129–30, 131, 133, 135–36, 136 n.1, 138, 139, 140, 142–43, 147–48, 149, 171, 174–75, 177, 189, 193 n.12, 195–217, 218, 221, 225, 227, 229–30, 231, 232
Postmodernism, 157–70
Pound, Ezra, 22, 182–83
Power, Mary, 21, 22, 30 n.14, 30 n.17
"Prankquean, The," 123 n.20
Professional Foul. See Stoppard, Tom
"Proteus," 16, 45 n.14, 140, 142, 150, 153, 156 n.3, 164, 169 n.21
Provections, 171–94

Quidditas, 206, 207–8, 209–10, 211, 214
Quintillian, 95, 119 n.2, 193 n.10

Rabaté, Jean-Michel, 58 n.8, 131, 137
Rabelais, François, 38, 140
Rader, Ralph, 82, 94 n.3
Raleigh, John Henry, 82, 94 n.3
Rand, Richard, 121 n.11
Read, Forrest, 194 n.15
Reade, Amye, 21–22; *Ruby. A Novel. Founded on the Life of a Circus Girl,* 21–22
Reading strategies, 15–29, 55, 61–62, 69, 70, 71, 95–124
Real Thing, The. See Stoppard, Tom
Renaissance, The. See Pater, Walter
Reynolds, Mary, 237

Richards, Grant, 16
"Riddles Chapter, The," *(Finnegans Wake),* 29, 83, 91, 92, 101, 104, 112, 113, 114, 123 n.19, 123 n.20, 126, 134–34, 139, 140
Riquelme, John Paul, 44 n.1, 45 n.3, 94 n.9, 94 n.11
Robinson, Crusoe. See Defoe, Daniel
Rogers, Margaret, 11
Romeo and Juliet. See Shakespeare, William
Rosenbach manuscript, 39
Rosencrantz and Guildenstern Are Dead. See Stoppard, Tom
Ruby. A Novel. Founded on the Life of a Circus Girl. See Reade, Amye
Ruby: The Pride of the Ring, 20, 21–22
Russell, Diarmuid, 30 n.18
Russell, George, 223, 226, 227

Sadomasochism, 21, 47, 52, 56, 57
Sammells, Neil, 169 n.20
Satire, 60, 63
Saussure, Ferdinand de, 122 n.18
Schlossman, Beryle, 58 n.5
Schmitz, Ettore, 165, 168
Scholes, Robert, 193 n.7, 217 n.1
Scott, Bonnie Kime, 32 n.30, 127, 137
Scott, Sir Walter, 88
"Scylla and Charybdis," 19, 22, 37, 55, 56, 126, 156, 156 n.3, 162, 164, 199, 204, 216
Secular humanism, 202
Senn, Fritz, 11, 28, 32 n.32, 33–34, 37, 39, 44 n.1, 45 n.4, 45 n.6, 45 n.7, 45 n.9, 45 n.10, 45 n.11, 45 n.12, 80, 130, 131, 137, 237
Shakespeare, William, 16, 19, 24, 55, 56, 83, 86, 87, 88, 89, 92, 110, 124 n.22, 169 n.21, 178, 225; *Hamlet,* 19, 55, 86, 178; *Othello,* 173; *Romeo and Juliet,* 117, 124 n.22
Shandyism, 75
Shaun, 83, 89, 90, 93, 99, 100, 101, 112, 114, 115–16, 120 n.10, 122 n.16, 135; as Justias, 83, 90
"Shaun the Post," 99, 115–16
Shelley, Percy Bysshe, 106; "Ode to the West Wind," 106
Shem, 80–93, 99, 100, 101, 110, 112, 115, 116, 120 n.10, 122 n.16, 126,

127, 134, 135, 139–40; as Glugg, 140; as Jerry, 83
"Shem the Penman," 80–93, 94n.3, 99, 109, 122n.17, 126, 134, 135, 139–40
Shepard, Sam, 157, 158, 169n.2, 169n.3; *The Tooth of Crime*, 157, 169
Sidney, Sir Philip, 18, 30n.11; *Defense of Poesy*, 18
Sigla, 107–116, 122n.16
Sinbad, 84
"Sirens," 24, 34, 36, 37, 38, 48, 61, 63–67, 70–71, 129, 156n.3, 172, 180–81, 182–83
"Sisters, The," 174
Skeat, Walter William, 126, 137; *Etymological Dictionary*, 126
Smith, John B., 129, 137
Soens, Lewis, 30n.11
Sollers, Philippe, 119n.4
Spencer, Theodore, 217n.1
Spivak, Gayatri Chakravorty, 122–23n.18
Staley, Thomas F., 93n.1
Steiner, George, 26, 31n.27
Steiner, Wendy, 57n.2
Stephen Hero, 126, 127, 128, 131, 133, 135, 136n.1, 171, 173, 209, 229
Stephens, James, 227, 231, 234n.19
Steppe, Wolfhard, 233n.10
Stoker, Bram, 137
Stoppard, Jose, 166
Stoppard, Tom, 157–70; *Dirty Linen*, 159; *Dogg's Our Pet*, 165, *Enter a Free Man*, 166; *Every Good Boy Deserves Favour*, 163; *Jumpers*, 163, 166; *Lord Malquist and Mr. Moon*, 163; *Night and Day*, 166; *Professional Foul*, 163, 166; *The Real Thing*, 163, 166; *Rosencrantz and Guildenstern Are Dead*, 166; *Travesties*, 157–70
Strindberg, August, 220
Sudermann, Hermann, 219; *Magda*, 219
Sullivan, John, 173
Summa Theologiae. *See* Aquinas, Saint Thomas
Süsskind, Patrick, 141, 142, 145, 148, 149, 156n.4, 156n.5, 156n.6, 156n.7, 156n.8; *Perfume*, 141, 142, 145, 148, 152
Sweets of Sin, 18, 24, 40, 43, 151
Swift, Jonathan, 169n.21
Swinburne, Algernon Charles, 169n.21, 178
Synge, J. M., 218, 219, 224, 226, 227, 228, 229, 230–31, 232, 233n.11, 233n.12; *In the Shadow of the Glen*, 230; *Playboy of the Western World*, 231; *Riders to the Sea*, 224

"Telemachus," 17, 29, 60, 141, 142, 148, 149–50, 156n.3, 160, 164, 177, 178, 179
Tennyson, Alfred Lord, 18–19; "Enoch Arden," 18–19
Thackeray, William Makepeace, 88
Thomas, Brook, 16, 30n.5, 45n.3
Thornton, Weldon, 32n.30
Tindall, William York, 125–26, 127, 129, 137
Tooth of Crime, The. *See* Shepard, Sam
Tragedy, 68, 76, 85
Travesties. *See* Stoppard, Tom
Tristan, 122n.16
Tynan, Kenneth, 168, 170n.32

Ulysses, 15–32, 33–45, 46–58, 59–79, 80–93, 114, 121n.11, 125–36, 136n.1, 140–56, 157, 158, 159, 160, 162, 164, 165, 166, 169n.21, 172–73, 174, 176, 177, 178–79, 180–84, 188, 189, 190, 191, 194n.23, 197, 199, 200, 201, 204, 205, 206, 209, 212, 213–14, 215, 216, 218, 219, 222–23, 224, 227, 228, 232. *See also* individual chapter titles
Under the Volcano. *See* Lowry, Malcolm
Unkeless, Elaine, 125–26, 131, 137
Unnamable, The. *See* Beckett, Samuel
Updike, John, 152, 156n.10

Valéry, Paul, 152
van Caspel, Paul, 31n.22, 34, 45n.2
Vico, Giambattista, 90
Virgil, 18, 175–76; *The Aeneid*, 18, 75, 175–76

Wallis, Brian, 169n.6
Walzl, Florence, 10
"Wandering Rocks," 18, 27, 38, 39, 43, 151, 156n.3

Warhol, Andy, 74
Weaver, Harriet Shaw, 22, 93, 122 n.16, 194 n.16
Wells, H. G., 24, 31 n.24
Whittaker, Stephen, 137
Wilcox, L. I., 169 n.1
Wilde, Oscar, 161, 162, 163; *The Importance of Being Earnest*, 161, 162, 164
Wind Among the Reeds, The. See Yeats, W. B.
Wit: and humor, 59–60, 61
Wood, Peter, 160
Woods, John E., 156 n.4, 156 n.5, 156 n.6, 156 n.7, 156 n.8

Woolf, Leonard, 79 n.9
Woolf, Virginia, 79 n.9, 112
Work in Progress, 93, 173, 185

Yeats, W. B., 218, 219, 220, 221, 222, 223, 226, 227, 228, 229, 231, 232, 233 n.9; *Cathleen ni Houlihan*, 222–23, 229; *The Countess Cathleen*, 219; Irish Literary Theatre, 226; *The Wind Among the Reeds*, 220

Zola, Emile, 47